Designing Career
Development Systems

Zandy B. Leibowitz
Caela Farren
Beverly L. Kaye

Designing Career
Development Systems

Jossey-Bass Publishers

San Francisco • Oxford • 1991

DESIGNING CAREER DEVELOPMENT SYSTEMS
by Zandy B. Leibowitz, Caela Farren, Beverly L. Kaye

Copyright © 1986 by: Jossey-Bass Inc., Publishers
350 Sansome Street
San Francisco, California 94104

Jossey-Bass Limited
Headington Hill Hall
London OX3 0BW

Zandy B. Leibowitz
Caela Farren
Beverly L. Kaye

Library of Congress Cataloging-in-Publication Data

Leibowitz, Zandy B. (date)
   Designing career development systems.

   (The Jossey-Bass management series) (The Jossey-Bass
social and behavioral science series)
   Bibliography: p. 305
   Includes index.
   1. Career development. I. Farren, Caela. II. Kaye,
Beverly L. III. Title. IV. Series. V. Series: Jossey-
Bass social and behavioral science series.
HF5549.5.C35L45   1986   658.3'124   86-45623
ISBN 1-55542-024-9 (alk. paper)

Manufactured in the United States of America

The paper in this book meets the guidelines for
permanence and durability of the Committee on
Production Guidelines for Book Longevity of the
Council on Library Resources.

JACKET DESIGN BY WILLI BAUM

FIRST EDITION

HB Printing 10 9 8 7 6 5 4

Code 8638

A joint publication in
The Jossey-Bass Management Series
and
The Jossey-Bass
Social and Behavioral Science Series

Consulting Editors
Human Resources

Leonard Nadler
Zeace Nadler
College Park, Maryland

Contents

To our clients,
Our best career developers

Preface

Most working adults make three to five career transitions in their lifetimes. Such changes are prompted by corporate mergers, changes in labor-management relations, shifts in technology, the trend toward later retirement, the increasing concern for the quality of work life, and a host of other factors. The complexity and rapidity of changes in the world of work and in the lives of workers mean that organizations, managers, and employees are faced with the challenge of facilitating career transitions in a constantly shifting environment.

In our efforts to help organizations meet this challenge, we have seen the inadequacy of addressing the issue of career development in one- and two-day workshops. People who attended these events may have been spurred to devise exciting career plans—but when the workshops were over and they were back on their jobs, they would frequently feel frustrated and disillusioned. We found that many workshop participants received no support from their managers or that they had no information by which to judge the feasibility of their ideas. Organizations were providing no continuing structures to help employees make realistic plans and turn those plans into realities.

Over the past five years, we have also seen the focus shift from career planning programs for individual employees to the broader area of career development programs within organizations. Some of the approaches devised to provide employees with organizational support and structure have met the challenge of complex change, but others have not.

Within this shifting arena, we began to design programs that would meet the needs of frustrated employees as well as address organizational concerns. We became convinced that as human resource professionals we needed not only a more diverse set of skills and competencies but also a model or framework for managing career change. We found the skills we needed in such different disciplines as counseling, psychology, personnel, and organization behavior. The framework we began to develop and use successfully came from three discipline areas: career planning, organization development, and personnel and training (that is, performance appraisal, job posting, training and development).

Throughout this process of distillation and synthesis, we encountered a dearth of resources. Most books in the career development field helped individual employees plan their careers, though others focused on personnel and training practices and still others addressed organization development. No one book integrated aspects of all three areas. Neither did any one book cross the boundaries of counseling, psychology, personnel, and organizational behavior to provide the combination of skills and approaches we believed were needed to create effective career development systems. Out of necessity, we devised our own tools.

This book is designed to make the techniques and models we have used and refined available to other human resource professionals who are designing and implementing career development systems in their organizations. The framework we use is constructed to accommodate human needs and organizational factors. We recognize that putting a career development program in place is instituting a change in the organization, and thus the book also addresses the steps and principles for accomplishing change effectively.

Among those who will find this book useful are human resources directors and executives, employee development specialists, human resource consultants, trainers, and career consultants. The book should also be useful to students of management, counseling, career development, industrial or organizational psychology, organizational behavior, and human resource development who want to familiarize themselves with the state of the art in career development approaches.

Overview of the Contents

We have organized this book around four major steps. The first three ensure that the elements essential for creating change—needs, vision, and an action plan—are in place; the fourth assures that the change will stay in place.

The first chapter sets the stage by reviewing the basic concepts underlying the model. Part One then focuses on defining specific needs and identifying key target groups, assessing human resource structures already in place in the organization, and investigating organizational culture and norms. Part Two describes ways of establishing a vision of change based on sound theory, choosing employee interventions, exploring ways to involve managers, and linking career development and human resource structures. A number of systems models are presented. Part Three focuses on the formulation of a practical action plan. Among the topics considered are ensuring top management's support, forming advisory groups, setting up a pilot program, and developing a staff. Part Four examines the problem of maintaining changes once they are achieved. Chapters in this section outline institutionalizing career development, publicizing accomplishments, and evaluating the results of the career development effort. The final chapter looks ahead to future trends that will affect career and human resource development.

Acknowledgments

Many people contributed to the completion of this book. Any endeavor of this sort requires the support, understanding, and time of those who are close. In this case, our families provided all. We would like to thank them: Barry, Haley, and Alex Leibowitz (who had the audacity to be born while the book was being written); Barry Levitt, who taught us to appreciate engineers; and Meaghan Farren-Smith, who taught us not to take ourselves so seriously.

Others who helped us included Octavia Seawell and Shelly Krantz, who willingly and ably collected the initial interview data; Sandy Harding, who typed relentlessly; Lucy Blanton, who miraculously helped us blend our writing styles to achieve an integrated voice; Charlie Seashore, who encouraged us in hard times; Katherine Reynolds, who assisted with editing; and Jeff Stoner, who proofread and painstakingly reviewed references. We also thank all of the organizations and clients whom we have learned from and worked with. Their work and involvement with us were essential to the writing of this book. Finally, we would like to thank those many colleagues whose work has influenced our own and has challenged our thinking. We are especially grateful to Edgar H. Schein, Douglas T. Hall, and, in particular, Richard Beckhard, whose model we have lovingly adapted for the book.

We would also like to thank the Jossey-Bass editors and staff for their support and encouragement, and Leonard and Zeace Nadler for their helpful comments.

August 1986   Zandy B. Leibowitz
                                                 College Park, Maryland

                                                 Caela Farren
                                                 Falls Church, Virginia

                                                 Beverly L. Kaye
                                                 Sherman Oaks, California

The Authors

Zandy B. Leibowitz is a counseling psychologist in the Counseling and Personnel Services Department at the University of Maryland. She received her Ph.D. degree (1974) from the University of Maryland. She directs the Career Development Center at the National Aeronautics and Space Administration's Goddard Space Flight Center, which has served as a model for numerous organizations. She has written extensively on the topics of human resources and adult and career development. She is the coeditor of a recent book, *Adult Career Development: Concepts, Issues, and Practices* (1986). A recognized authority in designing career development systems, Leibowitz is a member of the American Society for Training and Development's Career Development Professional Practice Area Executive Committee.

Caela Farren is a management and human resource development consultant with more than fifteen years' experience in private, public, and educational settings in the United States and Canada. She received her Ph.D. degree (1972) from Case Western University in Cleveland in organizational behavior and has studied at the Gestalt Institute of Cleveland. She has consulted in the implementation of human resource development systems in large organizations and the development of management strategies that foster collaboration and improve the quality of work life. Farren is a member of the Organization Development Network and the American Society for Training and Development.

Beverly L. Kaye is an organization consultant with a specialty in the area of career development. She received her doctorate (1976) from the University of California at Los Angeles, specializing in change management. For the past ten years, she has designed and implemented career development systems in *Fortune* 500 companies across the United States and recently in Australia. Her systems approach is the subject of the film *Career Development, A Plan for All Seasons* (1977), and the book *A Guide for the Career Development Practitioner: Up Is Not the Only Way* (1985). In 1980, she received the American Society for Training and Development's Career Development National Professional Award for her contribution to the field.

Designing Career
Development Systems

Introduction

Organizational Benefits of Career Development Systems

> "We're losing our most promising engineers to competitors. The turnover ratios are increasing dramatically. What can we do?"
>
> "Five of our top eight exeuctives are retiring in the next three years. How can we prepare for this?"
>
> "We're bringing in the best people from college campuses, training them—and they're gone in three years. Why?"

Problems like these provide the impetus for designing career development systems. Effective responses demand organization-wide interaction, because discrete parts of an organization cannot resolve such problems. Cooperative interaction is needed that involves benefits and compensation specialists, employees, executives, human resource professionals, midlevel managers, specialists in the quality of work life, recruiters, and others. When business organizations are viewed as fluid, constantly changing, and developing, mechanisms can be set up to facilitate the interdepartmental effort needed to support changes and developments that can, for example, slow down the exodus of capable people. A well-designed career development system at the center—or vortex—of change can provide the best solution.

Several demographic, technological, social, and economic concerns contribute to today's necessary focus on careers.

• *A shift in the age distribution of the working population:* In 1975, the average age of the work force was twenty-eight; in 1990, the average is projected to be over forty. For the first time, the average age for workers now exceeds thirty-two. This means that, today, the baby boomers are beginning to compete for limited opportunities, particularly in middle management positions. Career development programs help these employees look at options other than moving up.

• *A slowing of the early retirement trend:* The baby boom workers are also beginning to compete "for promotions and advancement not only with themselves but with their fathers and uncles, who are deferring retirement," according to J. Rosow, president of the Work in America Institute (quoted in the *Washington Post,* July 26, 1982, p. A-8). Career development programs help both younger and older employees plan their careers in concert with the real needs of an organization.

• *A shift in values:* "New-value" workers search for self-fulfillment in their work, rather than simply working for pay (Yankelovich, 1981). "Metaindustrial" workers want freedom of choice and control over their lives, and they tend to live for the present (Harris and Harris, 1983). There is a dramatic shift from such traditional concepts as equating work with pay, and such values as organizational loyalty, dependence on the organization for security and stability, and deferred gratification. No longer do employees assume cradle-to-grave careers in a single organization or accept the implicit psychological contract that if they are loyal and competent the organization will take care of them. Instead, today's employees are pressing organizations for approaches and programs to help them get the most out of their careers.

• *New technology:* Today's rapid advances in technology are unprecedented in human history (Butler, 1982). Career development programs help employees assess their technical skills and select appropriate activities to update them.

• *A need for high-touch work relationships to offset high-tech work environments:* The movement of robots and computers into organizations needs to be offset by the organization's movement into programs such as career development, according to Naisbitt (1982). Career development can send the message that organizations care about their employees.

- *A shift in the organizational pyramid:* Naisbitt (1982) also predicts that the hierarchical system, which was designed to manage and keep track of people, will no longer be needed in the future. This means employees will need assistance in redefining career aspirations beyond promotions.

Terms, Definitions, Concepts

As we focus on careers and career development systems, we enter the field of human resources. Throughout this book, the term *human resources* is used to refer to the overall field, which includes such areas as human resource management, human resource development, and organizational development. (Table 1 shows this interrelationship.) In some organizations, career development is included under human resources; in others, it is a separate unit.

Table 1. Interrelationships in Field of Human Resources.

Human Resource Development	Human Resource Management	Organizational Development
Training	Recruitment	Job enrichment
Education	Selection	Job enlargement
Development	Placement	Organizational change
	Appraisal	
	Compensation	
	Work-force planning	

Source: Adapted from Nadler, 1980.

Human resource management includes many of the traditional personnel functions, such as recruitment, selection, appraisal, and compensation of employees. A key function here, in relation to career development, is human resource planning—the process by which an organization determines career characteristics of its employees and balances them against future work-force needs. As a result of human resource planning, organizations are able to determine internal availability for certain key positions and skill areas.

Human resource development includes training, education, and development of employees. In training, employees acquire the skills needed to perform their present jobs. In education and development, they prepare for future jobs or for growth in general within the organization.

Organizational development includes enriching and enlarging the scope of jobs and building teams and strategies to increase the productivity of work groups. Large-scale change projects, such as helping an organization adapt to a merger or acquisition, may also fall into this area.

The term *career planning* refers to a process by which individuals determine their skills, interests, and values; consider which options "fit" them; and set goals and establish plans for achieving their goals. Career planning activities are usually conducted in workshops, through vocational counseling, or by using workbooks or career resource centers.

The key concept of this book is the *career development system*: an organized, formalized, planned effort to achieve a balance between the individual's career needs and the organization's work-force requirements. It integrates activities of the employees and managers with the policies and procedures of the organization. It is an ongoing program linked with the organization's human resource structures rather than a one-time event. It also serves to refine and develop present human resource activities.

Career development systems must be integrated with other human resource structures. For example, because layoffs in one part of a company affect the people who are leaving and (just as important) those who are remaining, a career development system works with the outplacement programs to address the needs of the leavers, the survivors, and the managers and colleagues of both. Similarly, when a promising engineer joins a prestigious company in hope of exciting, challenging work with plenty of intellectual support, the career development system helps the orientation program build strong partnerships among the new engineer, his or her manager, colleagues, other technical experts in the system, and the project team, to help assure that the engineer's expectations are met.

In many technical organizations, excellent independent contributors are tapped for management roles. In such cases, the career development system devises programs to help these new supervisors develop their skills, values, and interests and understand what makes effective managers; the system also tries to provide support to both the new supervisor and his or her work group in making the transition.

As such examples suggest, a change in one area resounds throughout the organization. The effectiveness of a career development system lies in its consideration of the interaction, interdependence, and integration of all the elements within an organization.

A career development system must have clearly defined responsibilities to the employees, the managers, and the organization; offer them a variety of development options; and form the link between current performance and future development, which includes the notion of best "fit" or "match."

Individual employees are responsible for initiating their own career planning and assessing their current job satisfaction. It is up to them to identify their skills, values, and interests; discuss their expectations with their managers; and seek out information about career options, in order to set goals and establish career plans. Managers are a critical link in the career development of their employees. Although they are not expected to be career development experts, they need to provide vital support for employee career planning by encouraging employees to take responsibility for their careers, supporting them in doing a realistic personal assessment, providing clear and honest feedback about current performance and its implications for future development, communicating the formal and informal politics of the organization culture, providing exposure for employees, and linking them to appropriate resources and people. The organization is responsible for providing key information on organizational mission, policies, and future directions as well as on current options and possibilities; for providing tools and support for employee self-assessment, training, education, and development; and for reinforcing managers' roles in career development.

A career development system must include a variety of options, more than simply the option to move up. There is not enough room for everybody to move up in an organization—and some people may not want to. In an effective career development system, employees and managers also look to job enrichment and lateral moves, and such multiple options help dispel management concerns about employee frustration and lack of reality in career planning.

A career development system provides an interface between current performance and future development. Employees and managers consider factors related to improving and maintaining their performance in current jobs, possible steps to pursue, and the relationship between current job functions and future options, while striving for a best fit, or best match, between their skills and the organization's requirements.

Organizations and Career Development Systems

Increasing numbers of organizations are looking at career development as a response to key organizational issues. Service organizations, such as banks, implement programs to help lessen the traditionally high turnover among their employees. Insurance companies institute career development to help structure discussions between new bosses and employees after a merger. High-tech organizations look to career development to strengthen the coaching skills of technical managers, to help pinpoint when the skills of their technical workers need updating, and to retain valuable employees. Marketing organizations install career development programs to help their employees find new challenges and to assess their fit with their current jobs.

Large manufacturing organizations also are involved in career development. In a recent study by Gutteridge and Otte (1983), twenty-three of the forty organizations in their survey had between 5,000 and 50,000 employees; eleven of these were characterized as general industrial manufacturing firms.

What benefits have these organizations realized from their

career development programs and/or systems? As Table 2 indicates, the benefits range from better utilization of employee skills to increased abilities of employees and managers to manage their own careers realistically.

Table 2. Benefits of a Career Development System.

Managers/ Supervisors	Employees	Organization
Increased skill in managing own careers	Helpful assistance with career decisions and changes	Better use of employee skills
Greater retention of valued employees	Enrichment of present job and increased job satisfaction	Increased loyalty
Better communication between manager and employee	Better communication between employee and manager	Dissemination of information at all organizational levels
More realistic staff and development planning	More realistic goals and expectations	Better communication within organization as a whole
Productive performance appraisal discussions	Better feedback on performance	Greater retention of valued employees
Increased understanding of the organization	Current information about the organization and future trends	Expanded public image as a people-developing organization
Enhanced reputation as a people developer	Greater sense of personal responsibility for managing career	Increased effectiveness of personnel systems and procedures
Employee motivation for accepting new responsibilities		Clarification of organization goals
Build talent inventory for special projects		
Clarification of fit between organizational and individual goals		

What about risks? Organizations considering involvement in career development often fear that such an effort will raise employee expectations and frustrations and that, as a result, employees—particularly the good ones—will leave. The contrary is true, however; most organizations involved in career development find that employees are more apt to stay because they feel they do not have to leave to utilize their skills and talents.

Organizations also often feel that they risk losing the money and effort put into organizing their career information. They may not have good job descriptions on which to base a career development program, and preparing them can be a paralyzing (and stopgap) task. But a career development system can be started without current competency-based job descriptions and up-to-date career ladders. (Chapter Seven suggests possible options for gathering the needed career information.)

Organizations also fear that their employees and managers may not want to be involved in career development programs. But pilot efforts create enthusiasm and support among employees, and career development does not have to be mandatory. In addition, if managers are provided training and rewarded for their work with employees, they are much more likely to want to be involved.

Organizations may also see a risk in timing. For example, an organization may have gone through so many recent changes and upheavals that it feels the timing for career development is not right. Indeed, the timing may not be right; organizations do need time to adapt. Nevertheless, other organizations may view the timing as optimal because the integrative approach of career development will help them deal more successfully with future changes and upheavals.

An organization that decides to become involved in career development will find a systematic plan more effective than, for example, simply providing workbooks or workshops to employees. As already noted, a career development system is more than a one-time event; it encompasses other human resource structures and involves managers, employees, and the organization in a variety of ways. A system of career development gives an organization such advantages as these:

- An opportunity to reinforce such human resource structures as job posting, tuition assistance, and orientation and to integrate them into a cohesive program.
- An approach to identifying employees' career goals and abili-

ties in order to match employees with job requirements and to plan for succession.

- A chance to coach line managers and employees in taking responsibility for their work life and careers by providing mechanisms that promote self-exploration and ongoing conversations between managers and employees.
- An opportunity for different parts of the organization to work together and to strengthen the informal networks that are necessary for increased productivity and effectiveness.
- An opportunity to shift from the traditional perception of personnel as crisis oriented to that of responsiveness to such issues as loss of key employees.

An organization needs also to note possible disadvantages or risks associated with a systems approach to career development.

- An integrated or systems approach necessitates that human resource professionals be willing to accept input from line managers and employees. Some human resource people may have to shift their views of line managers as experts in understanding their needs.
- More time and money are required to create unique approaches and to complete in-depth analysis than are required for an off-the-shelf solution. Organizations used to "quick" solutions may need to be convinced of the greater payoff of this approach.
- Traditional human resource professionals may have to shift from training roles to consultative roles.
- Because a systems approach necessitates a clear understanding of organization culture and contacts with key people, content expertise alone will not suffice.

Creating Change

Designing and implementing a career development system means introducing change into an organization. In order for a system to be effective, something must be different after the effort. But creating change is difficult. Organizations, like individuals, are creatures of habit and like to do things the way they always have. They prefer a steady state or an equilibrium. They are by nature resistant to change.

How, then, can we create a change through a career development system? One effective way is to use a model described by Beckhard and Harris (1977). In this model, three key elements must be in place before an effective change can be brought about: There must be a *need,* problem, or opportunity for change; there must be a clear *vision* or picture of how the change would affect the organization; and there must be a set of first steps, an *action plan.* Beckhard and Harris describe the relationship among these three elements and the cost of change. Any change in an organization, they say, cannot be greater than the level of need or dissatisfaction, the vision of what the organization would look like in the future, and the action plan. This relationship is displayed in a formula:

$$\text{CHANGE} \quad \rhd \quad \text{NEED} \times \text{VISION} \times \text{FIRST STEP}$$

If one of these three elements or conditions—needs, vision, or action plan—is missing, the organization will not have enough driving force to offset the energy and cost involved in making such a change. Therefore, if we want to achieve change through a career development system, we must make sure that all three elements are in place. In order to find out how to ensure that these three essential elements are in place and to determine which strategies organizations use, we interviewed human resource professionals in approximately fifty organizations. These companies ranged from high-tech computer to research and development to manufacturers to service organizations. As in the Gutteridge and Otte (1983) study, most organizations we contacted had between 5,000 and 50,000 employees and the majority were on either the East or West coast.

We used a questionnaire and then conducted telephone interviews. The questions focused on current career development activities, the populations involved, and the purpose of the program. We also asked how long the organization had been involved in career development, what organizational needs were being met through career development, what human resource structures had been incorporated, how effectiveness was evaluated, what had contributed most to the program's success, what the organization would do differently if it could start over again, and what steps it planned to take next.

This book is based on the twelve principles for creating change through effective career development systems that emerged from our interviews. The principles relate to the three essential elements for change in the Beckhard and Harris model (needs, vision, action plan) and to a fourth element: results, or maintenance of change. These principles, grouped by elements, are as follows:

- *Needs: Defining the present system*
        Address specific needs and target groups
        Assess current human resource structures
        Investigate organization culture
- *Vision: Determining new directions and possibilities*
        Build from a conceptual base or model
        Design multiple interventions for employees and the
            organization
        Involve managers
- *Action plan: Deciding on practical first steps*
        Assure top management support
        Codesign and manage project with an advisory group
        Create a pilot and establish a budget and staffing plan
- *Results: Maintaining the change*
        Create long-term, formalized approaches
        Publicize the program
        Evaluate and redesign

This book is organized into four major parts to correspond with the four elements in the preceding list. Chapters within each part focus on the pertinent principles. Each part has an introduction that includes a list of questions to be considered in order to assure that the essential element under discussion is in place.

PART ONE

Assessing Needs and Current Systems

Part One describes three tasks for diagnosing what needs currently exist in an organization. The tasks include identifying specific needs and target groups, assessing current human resource structures for possible linkages, and determining what cultural characteristics the system must accommodate.

To achieve this step, the following questions need to be answered:

- What are the most critical problems to be addressed? Which people and groups exemplify these problems? What strategies are suggested by the needs of these people and groups?
- What human resource systems already exist? From which of these systems can career development programs grow? What is the organization culture like? How ready is it for career development?

The first chapter in Part One (Chapter One) provides an overview of needs assessment considerations and techniques and discusses the needs of target groups. Chapter Two presents a framework to use in determining the effectiveness of current human resource structures and their potential links to career development programs. Chapter Three discusses the importance of fitting any program into the organization's culture and includes a model for assessing the organization's cultural readiness for career development, as well as an approach to creating change based on paradoxical thinking.

Chapter One

Identifying Organizational Needs and Target Groups

"If it's good for XYZ organization, then it must be good for us—let's implement the same program," says a training director who just attended a conference on career development programs.

"Let's call these folks and see if we can do the same thing," suggests a chief executive officer who has read a management journal article about another firm's career development system.

"It's just another human resource fad," shrugs a top management executive when told that career development increases productivity and improves employee morale and satisfaction.

The problem in all these statements is that the solution is being promoted before the problem has been identified—and career development for its own sake simply does not work. There must be a direct link back to a specific need, or problem, and target group within the organization in order to justify expending the time, money, and resources.

To help create this link, the first task in defining the present system, this chapter discusses strategies and techniques for collecting needs assessment data, the relationship of organizational needs to specific target groups and to individuals within

15

those groups, and the relationship between needs assessment and evaluation.

Needs Assessments: Why?

Suppose that an employee is given a mandate by his boss to initiate something in career development? The boss has been given this responsibility by *her* boss and will be held accountable for it in her performance appraisal plan. Collecting data from the organization will take time, and a program must be put in place quickly. Why should the employee bother to do a needs assessment?

The answer is that only such an assessment—identifying needs, problems, and opportunities in an organization—will provide the leverage required to bring about any changes. As already noted, one characteristic of an organization is that it tries to maintain a steady state. Enough sources of dissatisfaction or opportunity need to be identified within the organization to assure the energy necessary to make changes. Needs assessment data that document such problems or opportunities provide a vital and basic tool for challenging the status quo.

A needs assessment also provides the information required to customize a career development program. Needs and opportunities differ widely across organizations. Some organizations are declining and stabilizing; others are growing quickly. Their problems are different. Slow- or no-growth organizations are often characterized by few options and employees who feel stuck or on plateaus. Fast-growth organizations wrestle with the problems of retaining experienced employees, integrating those newly hired, and bridging the gap between technical and managerial skills.

A needs assessment, when conducted among a wide constituency, can ensure that the important problems and needs that surface are broad enough to warrant extensive intervention. Further, well-documented key concerns can provide a benchmark against which to measure the success of a career development system and, if the needs assessment is constructed as a pre-post assessment, will also provide long-term data on the merits and results of the intervention. Finally, because a needs assessment involves key people and departments of an organization from the beginning of a career development effort, those key people are more likely to be behind the recommendations in the design and implementation phases of the effort.

This needs assessment phase, the planning and data collection phase, is traditionally viewed as a linear process, often involving only a limited group until time for full implementation. Doyle and Strauss (1980) instead envision the planning and data collection phase of any project as an accordion (see Figure 1), an ongoing process with a constituency widening to

Figure 1. Alternative Planning Models.

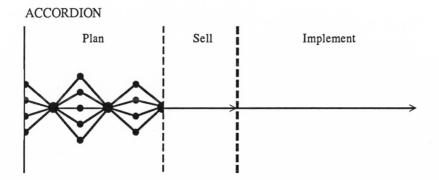

include multiple groups and multiple levels rather than a one-time, one-group step. Because the planning and needs assessment phase not only searches out needs already in the organization but also is a political step in building agreement and readiness to address the problem, this accordion approach is often more effective than the traditional linear planning model.

For example, when the process is envisioned as an accordion, others can be brought into the data collection in each phase of a project. As planning occurs, short-term, visible programs can be carried out. While the initial needs assessment of the organization is being completed, panel discussions on career opportunities or career planning workshops can provide both visibility and additional data. By combining such approaches, one can collect data for designing a long-term system and, at the same time, meet the short-term needs of the boss in the example at the beginning of this section.

Strategies and Techniques
for Designing a Needs Assessment

Needs assessment approaches can range from extensive computer-scored surveys to informal focus groups. The best approach for a particular organization depends on certain key factors. For example, the scope of the assessment (the number of people to be involved, the range of methods to be used) should relate directly to the potential scope of the program. Whether the program can spend $10,000 or $100,000, the needs assessment should be in proportion to the total budget and resources.

Look at Existing Data. Begin by looking at existing data; don't reinvent the wheel. Look, for example, at attitude or climate surveys. (These are often put aside because the organization is afraid to address—or does not know how to address—the many problems or issues that surface.) Questions in these surveys often deal with career issues, and a quick scan will reveal whether they provide relevant data. Some indicators of the climate in an organization that can reveal potential problems as well as potential target groups include ratings on such statements as "I have frequent performance discussions with my supervisor," "I feel rewarded for developing my people," "I have specific career plans and goals," or "Frank discussions about career potential are encouraged." Further, an annual climate survey can provide an effective pre–post assessment. Personnel records, equal employment opportunity (EEO) records, and exit interviews will supply data on attrition, growth areas, and length of service. Such data often reveal central problems and specific target groups and may be further refined before an organization decides to do a broader needs assessment.

Ask Questions. Human resource professionals and those from line organizations who have expressed interest or identified concerns that career development might be able to address are other valuable, readily available data sources. Ask these people to identify possible organizational needs, opportunities, and problems by using the needs questionnaire in Exhibit 1. Ask them also to identify target groups (that is, those groups that represent the problems) on the needs questionnaire. These target groups can be a specific level of employee (first-line managers, entry-level employees, clerical employees at the top of their grade), a specific job category (electrical engineers, customer service representatives, reservation agents), or a specific functional unit, division, or geographical region (store managers in the eastern region, electrical engineers in the quality control division, data processing specialists at headquarters).

The goal is to achieve a consensus on which problems and issues are most pressing—and important enough for the organization to commit resources for dealing with them. Choosing and identifying a discrete target group as well as specific problems gives focus, direction, and manageability to a career development program. Blanket programs rarely produce visible, long-term results; programs with discrete purposes have a higher chance of resolving problems.

If agreement is reached on specific problems and target groups, these areas can serve as a focal point for a more extensive needs assessment. Note, however, that the issues or problems identified on the needs questionnaire form include those that are perceptual or attitudinal (items 1–8) as well as those based on data (items 9–22). Follow-up strategies may need to differ for different categories of identified needs and target groups. For example, if most of the problems identified are perceptual, an effective strategy will be to sample a large number

Exhibit 1. Needs Questionnaire.

Career development efforts can be prompted by a variety of needs or problems. To help identify needs and priorities, check those needs/problems in the left-hand column that are present in your organization.

For each need that you check, indicate in the right-hand column the group(s) most affected by the need/problem, most in need of being the target of a career development effort.

NEEDS/PROBLEMS	TARGET GROUPS
Perceptual	
1. ☐ Employees feel stuck/lack career mobility	
2. ☐ Unclear career paths	
3. ☐ Little information on career opportunities	
4. ☐ Managers feel inadequate in coaching their employees about career plans	
5. ☐ Limited promotional possibilities	
6. ☐ Employees unaware of how to manage their careers	
7. ☐ Lack of support/reward for technical excellence	
8. ☐ Inadequate communication of organization mission and goals to employees	
Data Based	
9. ☐ Shortage of promotable employees	

Exhibit 1. Needs Questionnaire, Cont'd.

NEEDS/PROBLEMS	TARGET GROUPS
10. ☐ Numerous employees fixed on vocational plateaus	
11. ☐ Little planning for succession	
12. ☐ Rapid turnover of nonexempt employees	
13. ☐ Slow growth or shrinking organization	
14. ☐ Loss of promising employees	
15. ☐ Rapid expansion or decentralization of the organization	
16. ☐ Shrinking middle management cadre	
17. ☐ Need to adapt to rapidly changing technology	
18. ☐ Blending talent due to merger/acquisition	
19. ☐ New employees leave soon after starting their jobs	
20. ☐ Lack of "bench strength" in managerial ranks	
21. ☐ Lack of compliance with EEO standards	
22. ☐ Changing role of clerical/support staff	

of people to achieve consensus. But if the problems are data based, the best next step may be to locate additional data in order to confirm or disconfirm them.

More extensive needs assessments allow initial perceptions to be checked out with a wider sample of the organization. They will also broaden the data base and garner additional support.

But some key questions need to be considered before a more elaborate needs assessment is designed—questions that help pinpoint the *kinds* of data needed, the *source* of data, and possible *methods* for collecting the additional data.

To what extent are needs already known?

How and by whom are the data to be used?

To what degree are key members of the organization committed to career development?

Do these key members prefer one method over another?

Are hard or soft data needed?

What resources are available to collect and analyze the data?

How much time is available before a program needs to be implemented?

Do the data collected need to be confidential or anonymous?

What degree of reliability or validity is required of the data?

Is high or low employee participation preferred?

Is there a preferred or familiar technique?

Table 3 details the pros and cons of various needs assessment techniques. (Specific examples of needs assessment items and methods are provided in Resource A.) Whatever method is selected, simplicity and brevity, as well as high involvement of the people who will ultimately be affected and their managers, are crucial.

Use Multiple Methods. Another consideration in selecting methods from Table 3, and reviewing examples in Resource

Table 3. Needs Assessment Techniques.

Method	Pros	Cons
Questionnaires Can be open-ended or forced choice	Reach a large group of people in short amount of time Relatively inexpensive to administer Can be scored and quantified if forced choice Guard anonymity and confidentiality High reliability and validity	Limit free expression if forced choice Time needed to develop instrument Doesn't allow opportunity to probe or clarify needs Often has a low return rate Hard to analyze if open-ended
One-on-One Interviews Can be formal or informal, structured or unstructured Can be used to sample a large group Can be conducted on the phone or in person	Allow for free expression Provide ideas for possible solutions Give a sense of *what* the real problems and needs are	Time consuming Hard to analyze data Take a skilled interviewer May put employees "on the spot"
Group Interviews Can be formal or informal Can sample from a representative group of employees Can use group problem-solving techniques such as brainstorming	Allow for a synthesis of different viewpoints Can combine filling out a questionnaire with group discussion Get people to start discussing Build support for effort	Time consuming May be difficult to integrate different points of view
Records/Reports/Related Surveys Can include organizational charts and data, such as attrition figures, length of service, and age profiles of employees Can include existing data collection techniques, such as climate/attitude surveys or communication audits	Can be accessed easily Inexpensive Of concern to and understood by management Can be used as checks and clues with other methods	May not reflect current situation Provide limited perspective of concerns and needs

A, is that a combination of methods is probably the most effective. Steadham (1980, p. 59) gives the following advice for designing an organizational needs assessment:

- *Methods potpourri, or never use one when two will do.* There is strength in using a blend of data collection techniques.
- *Energy conservation.* Do not use so much time and energy that you have nothing left when it comes to designing and implementing your program.
- *Freedom to respond.* Design surveys and interview questions so that respondents have some freedom to respond.

One reason for the effectiveness of combining assessment methods is that behaviors, attitudes, and practices all need to be explored: What do people do? How do they feel? How do they perceive organizational policies and practices? A multiphased approach, using written surveys followed up by small focus groups to clarify or extend the data, often is most effective (see the examples in Resource A). In the small focus groups, however, questions and discussion need to be structured in such a way that people are provided with parameters while they give their input, because people who are asked directly what their needs are usually cannot answer. In addition, specific enough data have to be elicited from the group so that the information can be used to design the next steps.

An advisory group can also be used to augment data collection and promote involvement. A well-chosen group, with members representing different groups and levels in the organization, is in an excellent position to identify problems and assess needs. The group can respond to data already collected and report on their implications: It will have a feel for what needs to be done, what will—and will not—work. Such a group can distribute questionnaires and surveys, or its members can be trained to conduct sensing sessions or focus interview groups themselves. Involving an advisory group at this stage helps build commitment as well as wider acceptance of the career development effort. (Chapter Ten discusses in detail issues in forming advisory groups and using them during the course of a career development effort.)

Narrow Down. When existing data and data from needs questionnaire forms and other methods of needs assessment are all in hand, multiple needs for career development efforts may be evident. It is time to narrow the focus: Select what seem to be the top three issues using the matrix in Exhibit 2 and, by noting "Yes" or "No," indicate whether the statements in the left-hand column apply. Which of the three top needs/problems has the highest total yeses? Does the advisory group support and confirm the priority that emerges from the matrix? When agreement is made, it is, in most cases, time to focus on a key target group for career development. For example, the priority need/problem may be employees fixed at plateaus. Who are these plateaued employees? Midlevel professional workers? Clerical workers? A particular group needs to be firmly designated as the key target group.

Key Target Groups

It is not safe to assume that what works well for one group will work well for another. Different target groups have unique needs and problems that must be identified; the more specific the identification, the more likely the program design is to achieve powerful results. One reason is that, without actual experience with a particular group, incorrect assumptions may be made and thinking can be based on stereotypes; biases must be checked out or confirmed. Another reason is more subtle but equally important: the need to build involvement and commitment in the group for which the program will be designed. Plans made in a vacuum are more apt to build resentment and resistance when they are implemented. Work in which there is collaboration from the beginning builds support and ownership.

The needs of key target groups can be identified in the

Exhibit 2. Matrix to Determine Needs to Be Addressed.

A program designed to meet this need	Problem/Need 1:	Problem/Need 2:	Problem/Need 3:
Will address a felt need			
Can produce observable/visible results			
Does not appear too threatening			
Will have readily available advocates/champions in key management positions			
Can focus on a finite, identifiable target group			
Is in line with top management's interests			
Can be linked to existing human resource structures			
Can be built from personal energy and interest of human resource staff			
Total Yeses			

Source: Leibowitz, Farren, and Kaye, 1983.

same way that needs or organizations are identified, but the most effective way to clarify or extend the data already obtained in the organizational needs assessment appears to be interviews of small focus groups among the targeted employees. In these interviews, a set of questions is used to probe the concerns and issues of the target group, such as plateaued employees, technical employees, new employees, or managers. One effective way is to use a transitions model, in which transitions are defined as events (a job promotion, a job loss) or nonevents (a static job) that result in changes in the individual's expectations or relationships (Leibowitz and Schlossberg, 1982).

A career transition can be seen as "the period during which an individual adjusts to a different setting and/or work role. A transition period is associated with any major job or role change, whether the individual is in the early, middle, or late stage of his or her career" (Lewis, 1982, p. 73). A transition is also a period of vulnerability. Individuals going through transitions may not be sure of the guidelines, informal rules, or accepted ways to behave in their new status.

Thus, data collection in group interviews can be facilitated by a set of questions designed to uncover the issues and concerns that the specific group of employees may face during transition periods—for example, a promotion, a new job, or the realization they are plateaued.

The transition model can also be used in designing programs to help employees successfully manage their career transitions. Lewis (1982) suggests that key elements of such programs include helping employees to appreciate "typical" transition experiences (such as feeling overwhelmed and surprised), define the "ideal" transition, consider potential problems and resources, clearly understand tasks to be mastered (such as establishing a role identity), and set priorities. To assist employees with these tasks, programs and strategies need to form clear links with the unique needs of each career transition.

Employees in upward-mobility programs, managers, minorities, new employees, plateaued employees, preretirement employees, technical employees, and women are among the target groups for organizational career development programs. The following sections of this chapter provide overviews of the needs, problems, and issues of four of these groups: new employees, technical employees, plateaued employees, and managers.

New Employees. New employees are receiving increasing attention. "More and more companies are recognizing that this period of adjustment is a prime determinant of the employees' future job success and satisfaction" (Pearson, 1982, p. 286). If new employees are to move successfully into an organization, they have to understand the organization's expectations of the job, clarify their own career goals and needs, and develop interpersonal relationships with co-workers and supervisors. Among the specific tasks that new employees must confront are the following:

- *Mastering the basics of the job:* New employees need to have clear information on the skills and tasks required in the job. Most important, they need to understand supervisor expectations for their performance and the standards by which they will be measured.
- *Creating a current frame of reference:* They need to understand the organization's culture. How are things done in the organization? What is permitted? What is appropriate? What are the existing rituals and norms? What informal language is used?
- *Mapping key players:* New employees need to understand who fits where; that is, the names, roles, and functions of important people in terms of the formal, informal, and social methods of the organization.
- *Creating an identity in the organization:* Early impressions are critical and tend to stick. New employees need to understand that the way they behave initially will cause other members of the organization to perceive them in a certain way. They need to decide how they want others to perceive them—as conformists, challengers, plodders—and how to act accordingly.
- *Establishing a work role:* New employees need to clarify their roles and how they relate to the overall objective and mission of the work groups and organization.
- *Establishing relationships with co-workers and supervisors:* They need to build social networks inside and outside their immediate work area.
- *Managing the conflicts with nonwork life:* New employees need to negotiate their multiple roles successfully.

- *Managing internal conflict:* New employees must reconcile personal values and perceived discrepancies between the expectations and realities of their jobs.

These key issues to be addressed in working with new employees are given further emphasis by a recent survey of seventy-six new employees at the National Aeronautics and Space Administration's (NASA) Goddard Space Flight Center. The employees indicated that they wanted knowledge of the overall mission of the center and where different employees fit within that mission; interaction and exposure outside their work area and with directorate-level managers; challenging work assignments; assistance in formulating career plans; information on career paths and options; and clear expectations, directions, and feedback from their supervisors.

Chapter Five describes a general framework for viewing and designing interventions to meet the needs of new employees and other target groups. To help define the present system, consider briefly what sorts of specific interventions will help new employees confront their necessary tasks. Among these interventions are the following:

- *Realistic job previews:* These are a critical element of the recruitment process, as Hall (1976) and others point out. Training recruiters to provide more realistic, less idealized descriptions of first jobs lessens the possibility of a clash between high expectations of new employees and the reality of the job's frustrations.

- *Broadened orientation programs:* Effective orientation programs need to address the new employee as a total person, emphasizing not only the rules and regulations of the organization and basics of the job but also such issues as negotiating work and nonwork roles. For example, at Corning Glass Works, orientation is designed as a process rather than a program. It extends over a period of fifteen to eighteen months, involves both employees and supervisors in ongoing assignments and discussions, and includes seminars as well as guided self-learning (McGarrell, 1983).

Orientation programs also need to stress appreciation of

the issues involved in the transition to a new job. For example, at NASA's Goddard Space Flight Center, the orientation program introduces new employees to the stages they may experience: being overwhelmed, being surprised, taking leave from the old job, having to establish a new frame of reference, needing to link expectations to the new organization's informal systems.

• *Ongoing supervisor feedback:* Crucial to the future success of new employees is continuing, ongoing feedback from their first supervisor (as the new employees themselves indicate). To make sure that new employees receive the right combination of independence and direction and that their supervisors supply what Hall (1976) calls a sense of "supportive autonomy," many organizations today are providing supervisors with training and support in how best to establish job expectations, give assignments, monitor work, and supply the essential ongoing feedback.

• *Challenging first job assignments:* The desire of new employees for meaningful and challenging work often conflicts with the organization's accommodation of low productivity in the first year on the job. One way to solve this problem, Hall (1976) suggests, is to reanalyze critical jobs in order to provide the challenge. Another possible intervention, he says, is to eliminate job rotation programs. When the first job is a permanent one, "this generates job success rather than a succession of jobs" (p. 75).

• *Career development programs:* New employees want to see the future. They need a picture of the opportunities available to them. In many organizations, career development programs provide the means for new employees to identify their own strengths and gain information on options and opportunities from such sources as seminars and colloquiums with representatives from different parts of the organization.

Technical Employees. Many organizations are faced with the challenge to motivate, retain, and enhance the productivity of their technical employees: engineers, scientists, and data processing professionals. Comments such as the following provide insights into these employees:

- "The thing that keeps me excited is continually being involved in new projects that use my skills."
- "I always thought that I wanted to stay the best in my field of laser technology, but it looks like the only way to move is into a management role. I'm not sure I want to do that."
- "I feel like I've been passed over and there's no place to go. The organization has written me off. They seem to think a fifty-year-old engineer can't produce anymore, and I'm beginning to feel the same way about myself."
- "I have this guy working for me who just doesn't seem to make it anymore. He used to be one of my best performers, but now he's retired on the job. What can I do?"

Bailyn (1980) describes technical employees working in the scientific, engineering, or computer fields as having an early inclination toward scientific, mechanical, or quantitative rather than aesthetic interests; a desire to deal with things rather than people; a high need for achievement; a concern with order and stability; less flexible behavior patterns than those in the humanities; and a convergent rather than divergent cognitive style. Among career problems that emerge with this particular target group are pressure for such employees to move into management in order to improve their status, power, and income; high attrition of the most talented of these employees as they move on to what they see as more challenging and varied tasks; a need to create a reward system that supports technical excellence instead of penalizing it; and rapid obsolesence of technical skills. This target group also often demonstrates an increasing lack of organization loyalty. For example, in a recent survey by the Institute of Electrical and Electronics Engineers (reported in the June 1984 issue of their journal), 60 percent of 4,000 employees surveyed said that engineers are less loyal to their employers than they were.

Specific interventions to consider (as noted, a general framework appears in Chapter Five) to help technical employees stay motivated and productive include the following:

- *Dual career ladders:* Technical employees need advancement opportunities that are equal to an advance into management; dual-career ladders are one answer. Goodyear, for example, has two equitable and challenging ladders with equal compensation packages (Sacco and Knopka, 1983). At Atlantic Richfield (ARCO), technical employees are allowed to stay in, and advance in, the research area by qualifying for four technical levels: adviser, senior adviser, executive adviser, and distinguished adviser. When employees are selected to be advisers under this program, they "are expected to propose projects, identify areas of technical opportunities, solve problems, share their expertise throughout ARCO, and help junior staff employees" (Buckles, Siebert, and Hosek, 1984, p. 29).

• *Programs assessing the move into management:* Rewarding technical employees by moving them into management may cause mismatches of skills, values, and motivations that are costly for both organizations and employees. The profiles of successful managers and technical employees, as Bayton and Chapman (1977) point out, are often quite different; for example, managers are motivated primarily by the desire to exercise authority, whereas technical employees primarily want to do new and different tasks. Some organizations have programs that give technical employees an opportunity to explore these differences before they decide on a move. For example, the Next Step Management seminar at NASA's Goddard Space Flight Center allows technical employees considering moves to management to assess their own profiles against those of successful managers and then to plan their next career steps, either while remaining in a technical role or continuing to consider management (Leibowitz and Schlossberg, 1982).

• *Updating technical expertise:* Technical obsolescence— "the lack of current technical knowledge and skills that are necessary for effective performance of job assignments" (Farr and others, 1980, p. 1)—is as bad for organizations as it is for technical employees. Organizations are increasing efforts to keep technical employee skills and knowledge up to date.

• *Programs based on career stages:* Needs for technical employees change over the career cycle. According to Raelin (1985), engineers progress through three stages: finding a niche, digging in, and entrenched. In some organizations, effective programs for technical employees are based on these stages. For example, in the finding-a-niche (or early career) stage, employees want to find work that provides variety and challenge. Interventions to meet the needs of these beginning employees include assigning them to high-payoff, high-visibility projects. Digging-in (or middle career) employees look for a strong sense of professionalism, and successful interventions include assigning them to small work groups with friendly associates. The entrenched (or late career) group of employees has lowered aspirations and professional commitment. An effective intervention to promote their continued involvement is to enlist them as mentors to younger employees.

Plateaued Employees. Stoner and his associates (1980, p. 1) define career plateaus as "the point in a career where the likelihood of additional hierarchical positions is very low." Many organizations today have considerable numbers of employees who fall into this category. One reason for this phenomenon is the collision of the baby boom population with the 1970s slowdown of the economy. A second reason is that later retirement has caused bottlenecks in many organizations. Another is that some organizations have reduced the ranks of their midlevel managers. The result is a group of employees who have no place to move in their organizations.

Most of these plateaued employees are described by their organizations as effective performers and solid citizens. The challenge to management is to continue to motivate these employees so that their performance remains high and so that they do not drift into the ranks of poor performers.

The needs of this group are made clear in a list of the factors associated with effectively performing plateaued managers (Carnazza and others, 1981):

They have opportunities to demonstrate their capabilities.
Their job duties are clear.
They perceive their jobs as important to the organization.
Their jobs are challenging.
Their jobs are interesting and enjoyable.

They receive feedback about their performance.
They have opportunities to set goals.

Among the specific interventions to consider in order to keep plateaued employees performing effectively are those Abdelnour and Hall (1980) found most frequently used in their survey of twenty-eight organizations: task forces, project teams, university executive programs, and lateral moves. (A general framework for interventions is found in Chapter Five.)

One of the best ways to maintain interest and continued involvement of plateaued employees is to redesign and enrich their jobs. Based on concepts developed by Hackman and Oldham (1980), many organizations have changed the jobs of plateaued employees by combining tasks (putting together existing, fragmented tasks to create new work groupings), forming natural work units (tying work to geographical boundaries or customer account units), establishing direct relationships between employees and clients, vertically loading the job (increasing the employee's authority, decision-making power, and control), and opening and increasing feedback channels between employees and the work itself.

Other successful interventions for plateaued employees include more flexible work hours, job rotation, greater specificity in managerial career ladders, career counseling, performance feedback, self-awareness programs, improved rewards systems, and increased recognition for good performance.

Managers. Among the problems relating to this target group are a shrinking middle management cadre, a lack of bench strength (that is, replacement pools) in the managerial ranks, little planning for succession, and the inadequacy some managers feel in coaching and developing their employees.

An important consideration for manager interventions is that managers must be engaged not only in their own career development but also in that of their employees. In fact, their involvement in employee career development is essential. Chapter Six is devoted entirely to interventions for managers, particularly those aimed at getting managers involved in employee career development. (A general framework for interventions is provided in Chapter Five.)

Needs Assessment: A Critical First Step in Evaluation

Needs assessment data link a career development program, the organization's specific needs or problems, and key target groups. Needs assessment data also provide an important link for evaluating a career development program. In identifying specific problems and target groups (and establishing their relationships to the organization's present system), the needs assessment establishes benchmarks against which the effectiveness of a career development effort can be evaluated. (This is particularly true, as noted earlier, when the needs assessment is constructed as a pre-post assessment.) For example, if the specific problem is attrition of computer specialists, the evaluation of a program designed and implemented to address that specific problem should be able to demonstrate a reduction in attrition.

Measures of success are therefore implicit in the key problems and target groups selected through the needs assessment process. In addition, measures of success for each of the key players that the program will affect—employees, managers, and the organization or top management—can also be considered. For example, success of a program for plateaued midlevel employees might be measured in additional job responsibilities. Success of the program for top management might be measured in redistribution of the organization's skill mix; that is, the realignment of employee skills with new areas of growth in the organization. Identifying such indicators of success at the beginning of a program helps assure that the program responds to the real needs of all key players. (See Chapter Fourteen for a full discussion of these indicators and other evaluation issues.)

A Final Word

Identifying needs, problems, and opportunities at both the organizational level and with particular target groups is an important first step in the design and evaluation of an effective career development system. Involving a wide variety of people in the needs assessment process increases their support and commitment. Reporting back to those who participate in the assessment on its findings and possible solutions further increases participation—and assures employees of the organization's responsiveness to their concerns. Both wide involvement and reporting back guarantee credibility for a career development program.

Finally, it is important to remember that, once a needs assessment process is started, the expectations of all those involved start to build. To avoid employee cynicism and suspicion, the organization must make a commitment to take some kind of action based on the data collected.

Chapter Two

Evaluating Existing Human Resource Structures

"Our organization's reaction to career development was . . . 'It's just the human resource fad of this year.' "

"It seems that we put a lot of time, money, and energy into a new system like performance appraisal, but once it's up and running we forget it."

Such laments are all too common. A great deal of effort is put into new human resource efforts, but little energy is put into coordinating these efforts so that they reinforce one another. For this reason, career development programs must be integrated into the existing human resource structure; that is, the policies, procedures, practices, or formal systems within the normal organizational umbrella of human resources.

This chapter examines the problem of determining the effectiveness of the human resource structures already in place, the second task in defining the present system. Such assessment could provide a base from which to strengthen the current programs and practices and integrate them into a career development system—and so avoid the kinds of laments just noted. The use of existing human resource structures also helps preclude the need to reinvent the wheel, as did the use of existing data to begin the needs assessment process.

In addition, integrating the existing human resource structures into the career development system reinforces both structures, increases their effectiveness, adds to the economy of effort and time in putting a system in place, and builds on the commitment and investment that are already part of organizational activities. By starting with familiar concepts (rather than struggling for acceptance of new ones) and making use of the organization's "track record," the career development system keeps missed opportunities to a minimum, establishing further commitment, lessens resistance, and harnesses the energy of people already involved in activities essential to career development.

Unfortunately, the notion of mutual reinforcement is not evident in many career development programs. As Moore (1979, p. 14) notes, "There is rarely any connection between career planning and development for individual employees and corporate human resources planning and management aimed at organizational staffing needs. In essence, career planning programs are not viewed from a systems perspective and, as a result, have not been fully integrated into the organization." In addition, "many career planning activities or techniques have taken place in isolation in classroom settings. They are unrelated to actual job needs or experience."

• *For example:* A major department of a large, nationwide organization decides to initiate its career development program by helping employees develop profiles of their skills and experiences. Workshops are held and self-assessment forms completed. At a wrap-up session, one wise participant brings along a set of past performance appraisal forms and job descriptions, saying, "I finished my entire profile before I realized that it was all here in a nutshell." Nobody had thought to include the organization's performance appraisal system or job descriptions in the career development program's design. If these had been included, there would have been greater economy of effort, the process might have started at a different point, and the employees might have had better information related to their job futures.

• *For example:* Executive secretary Sally Morales has identified report and proposal writing as an area of keen interest to her and shows some skill in the area during a career development goal-setting exercise. In recent years, several large departments have posted jobs in their information and editorial branches. Sally embarks on a series of workshops and seminars to polish her skills and increase her promotability. Imagine Sally's dismay and surprise when the organization's newsletter mentions that all information and editorial offices are being centralized, with reductions in the number of people doing such work. The news item points out that forecasting efforts indicated a trend toward procuring larger but fewer contracts, thus decreasing the need for proposals and reports. Nobody involved in the career goal-setting exercise had thought to establish links with the organization's ongoing forecasting program.

• *For example:* Jerry Saunders, a computer operator for eight years in a government agency, is sure that his true calling is in the area of programming. As he looks at routes out of data retrieval and into programming, he notes little opportunity for the training and job openings that he would need. At last, he moves to a large corporation, which needs his present skills and will train and place him in programming, and the government agency loses a real asset. In fact, the agency had a job rotation program and over 100 first-level programmer positions scattered throughout its various divisions. A career development program, linked to human resource activities such as career paths and forecasting, might have alerted Jerry to these possibilities and enabled the agency to retain a valuable employee.

These examples are unfortunately more typical than hypothetical. They happen when there is no career development system or when there is no linkage between the career development and human resource systems.

Properly planned and positioned career development programs can form a communications network for all human resource activities—a network that is badly needed in most organizations. A career development system acts as a clearinghouse for collecting and sharing information that can increase the effectiveness of human resource decisions, for letting the left hand know what the right is doing. A career development system coordinates and better utilizes a variety of seemingly separate human resource practices. And, as Figure 2 illustrates, career development is reinforced by its close integration with human resource practices. Human resource practices, in turn, are

Figure 2. Human Resource/Career Development Interaction.

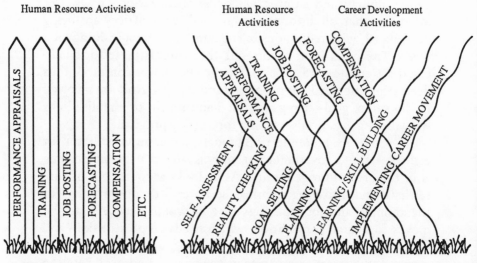

Human Resource Activities

The Human Resource Picket Fence

Human Resource Activities   Career Development Activities

The Human Resource/Career Development Chain Link Fence

reinforced by the coordinating effects of career development. Job posting, for example, is no longer a separate picket but a strong link in a network providing easily accessible information to employees and managers for setting goals and considering options.

Taking Stock

Assessment of an organization's human resource structures to determine how they might strengthen and be strengthened by career development programs often seems an overwhelming task. Human resource activities may appear to go all over the map, and human resource departments or divisions can be organized in many different ways. One way to cut through this confusion is to think of human resource structures in categories that reflect the way they link to career development. Figure 3 illustrates how human resource structures relate to some of the essential aspects of the career development process. For

Figure 3. Two-Way Support: Career Development/Human Resources.

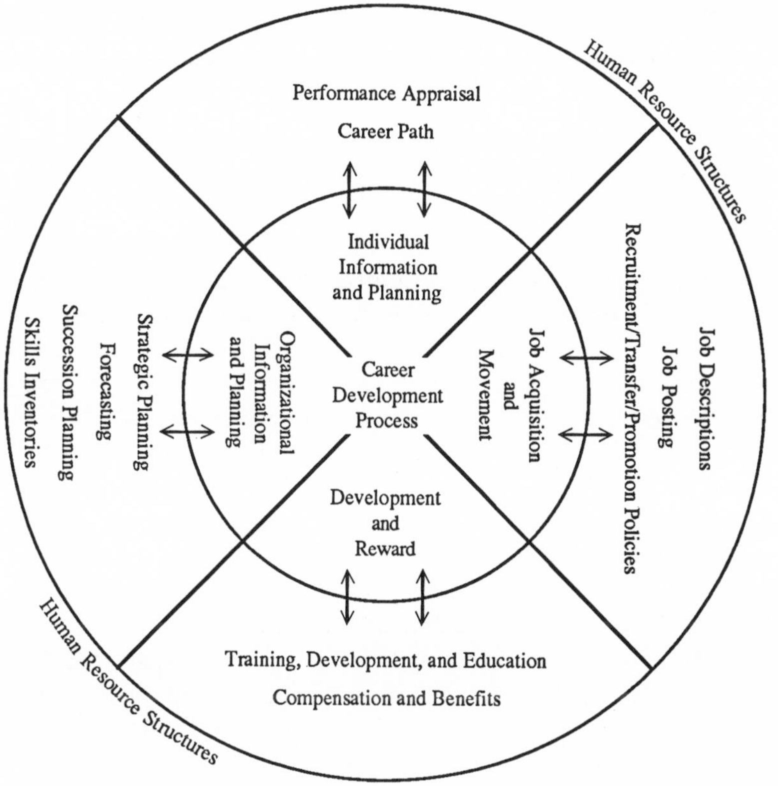

example, in order for employees to judge the "reality" of their career goals, they need organizational information—information that such key human resource structures as strategic planning, forecasting, succession planning, and skills inventories can provide.

Figure 3 also illustrates that organizations sponsor many human resource efforts, which could form natural links to career development programs. To develop and formalize a career development system, an organization usually does not need to start from scratch but merely to position what is already there. Myriad career development activities and supportive processes are already under way, though they may be characterized as human resource practices and may be taking place separately from one another.

Questions for Assessing Human Resource Structures

The questions included in this section form the base from which to assess the effectiveness of various human resource structures already present in an organization. The questions are representative of key structures that exist in many organizations rather than of all possible structures. As we ask these questions, we need to be thinking of how the human resource structures being investigated, even those only slightly implemented, might be linked to key career development needs and target groups (which were identified in the task in the preceding chapter). We also need to keep in mind the picture of two-way support in Figure 3.

- *Performance appraisal:*
    Do employees view performance appraisals as an opportunity to learn about their skills and competencies and to test their self-perceptions against reality?
    Are managers skilled in giving candid performance feedback and engaging employees in discussions of skills and abilities?
    Are performance appraisals used as an occasion to discuss future plans and opportunities?
- *Career paths:*
    Are career path data readily available to managers and employees?
    Are managers able to explain career path data to employees?
    Is career path information up to date?
- *Job descriptions:*
    Are job descriptions accurate and up to date?

Are job descriptions written to include not only duties but also competencies and behaviors required in the job?

Are job descriptions readily available to employees who want to examine them?

- *Job posting:*

  Do all employees have an adequate opportunity to know about vacancies before they are filled?

  Is posting of jobs resisted by managers, who may want more latitude in which to make their own selections?

  Can potential applicants get enough information about posted jobs to learn how the jobs fit with their past experience, abilities, and career goals?

- *Recruitment, transfer, and promotion policies:*

  Are current policies in these areas understood by managers and employees and viewed as thorough and fair?

  Do employees understand policies about recruiting from within versus from outside?

  Are appropriate systems available for transferring employees into positions that fit their qualifications?

- *Training and development:*

  Is training and development equally available to all employees who show a need and desire?

  Are training needs regularly assessed in order to update what is offered by or through the organization?

  Are supervisors and managers able to counsel employees on training opportunities, including on-the-job training, and willing to support their efforts to receive adequate training?

- *Compensation practices and benefits:*

  Do employees understand the compensation and benefits systems and consider them fair and equitable?

  Do compensation policies support career movement other than simple advancement?

  Can reward systems be structured to recognize managers who actively support the career development of their employees?

- *Strategic planning:*

  Where in the organization is the strategic planning function located? Is it a function of the central staff or of each department?

  Is strategic planning information specific and up to date?

  What information is currently disseminated to employees about the organization's future plans?

- *Forecasting:*

  Is there a formal system for forecasting future human resource needs throughout the organization?

  Is the forecasting system kept up to date and accurate both in the short and long term?

- *Planning for succession:*

  Are there plans for succession into key positions?

  Is there openness about succession plans, so that employees can react to them and incorporate them into individual career planning?

  Do recruitment and selection activities reflect succession planning?

- *Skills inventories:*

  Is there a system in place that provides for storage, updating, and retrieval of information about employee skills, experience, and training?

  Is information updated in skill inventories in a timely and consistent manner?

  Do managers use the inventories or do they bypass them when they fill staffing needs?

A Final Word

This chapter addresses the issue of integrating human resource structures with career development by asking key questions to assess the effectiveness of current structures. (Identifying which of these effective structures can best be harnessed to respond to various career development needs or target groups will be covered in Chapter Seven, as organizational interventions are fully discussed.) Note that, as data on existing human resource structures are collected, a data base is being built that can be utilized throughout all stages of career development system design and implementation. In fact, very often we may be able to identify gaps or problems that can be addressed even before the career development effort is finalized and under way.

Chapter Three

Adapting Career Development to the Organizational Culture

"Our organization is very conservative; it would never buy anything touchy-feely."

"You never put more than two reporting levels in a room in our organization—you just don't."

"This is a marketing organization; the medium is the message, and materials for a program must look glitzy."

These statements reflect the importance of organization cultures—cultures that according to some contemporary theorists "are perhaps the most complex and subtle, yet most pervasive influence on organization effectiveness" (Tichy, 1982, p. 62). But culture is like air: Its shared beliefs and values are often so taken for granted, and so far from most people's awareness, that their power and influence easily escape the attention of those most concerned (Sathe, 1983).

Investigating the organization's culture is the third (and final) task in defining the present system. The key characteristics of the culture must be discovered, so that these characteristics can be incorporated into any career development program. It is also important to discover which norms and practices are sacrosanct. This means searching for the culture, distinguishing its elements, pinpointing "the way we do things around

46

here," and unveiling the patterns that mean business as usual (Hickman and Silva, 1984). Those who do this must be detectives, anthropologists, and sleuths. Only through such an investigation of an organization's culture will we be able to identify the career development programs that have the best chance of success—because they are tailored to fit the organization's patterns.

This chapter first suggests ways to decipher an organization's culture and to find out whether that culture incorporates the six important characteristics that relate directly to building an effective career development system. Another section describes an approach to change that respects the existing culture while challenging its patterns, an approach based on paradoxical thinking. A final section provides illustrations of career development activities specifically tailored to fit different organizations.

An organization's culture is a system of shared values (what is important) and beliefs (how things work) that relate to an organization's people, structures, and control systems to produce norms (the way we do things here) (Uttal, 1983). Culture, according to a Procter and Gamble executive, is "a great deal of consistency around here in how certain things are done and this is critical to sustained success—you know the game you're in—you know whether you're playing soccer or football" (Pascale, 1984, p. 34). Culture gives employees a sense of what counts in their organization. It proscribes certain activities in policies and procedures manuals and reinforces other activities through education, mentors, and war stories about the past.

Culture in an organization, according to Schein (1983, p. 14), is "the *pattern* of basic assumptions that a given group has invented, discovered, or developed in learning to cope with its problems of external adaptation and internal integration—a pattern of assumptions that has worked well enough to be taught to new employees." These assumptions determine the norms, the business-as-usual patterns, of behavior, policy, office layout, and dress. They are what characterize the major differences between a Delta and a Pan Am, a Digital and an IBM. Sometimes the assumptions combine to form a single pervasive culture; at other times multiple cultures may be present. For example, the culture of a scientific division in an engineering organization comprised mostly of physicists will be different from the culture in the organization at large.

In deciphering organization culture, in getting at what makes the company unique, we need to consider four elements: thought (the basic assumptions about the world, the way the organization works); action (the consistent pattern of behaviors in meetings, the flow and form of communications, customer relationships, rewards, practices, procedures), speech (what is talked about and remembered, including mission statements, written policies, advertising slogans, war stories, allegories, metaphors), and artifacts (what is seen, including dress, architecture, office decor, facilities).

Four major data sources help us gain the sense of an organization and how it is maintained:

- *People:* Talk to individuals and groups, particularly target groups, and ask them a series of structured questions.
- *Written documents:* Read the available literature, including annual reports, mission and objectives statements, business plans, newsletters, newspapers, letters from the president, policy manuals, reports, personnel statistics.
- *Human resource structures:* Examine the structures already in place, including performance appraisal systems, job postings, training and development programs, plans for succession, and compensation packages.
- *Informal systems:* Observe and note the general landscape, including work flow and communication patterns.

Questions to ask people in exploring organization culture include the following:

Are the mission and objectives of the organization clearly articulated? What are they?
Do employees and managers have a sense of "what counts" in the organization?
What are the underlying norms in the organization?

What are the main characteristics of people who "make it" in the organization?

What are the main messages from the top about what is important?

For what are people rewarded?

How do you know what is important around here?

For what are people criticized?

Written documents to investigate for clues to organization culture and norms include annual reports and messages from the chief executive officer (note what stands out, what commitments are expressed), mission statements and business plans, newspaper coverage and in-house newsletters (note what gets covered, what image emerges). Among the human resource structures that can shed light on organization values are orientation programs, budget and business planning processes, and compensation and benefits practices (note whether rewards are given for competition or collaboration, team efforts or individual accomplishments). Observe informal systems to glean information on the organization's customs, such as how people communicate with one another, what titles are used, what work rituals exist, who goes to lunch with whom, and how people dress.

Clearly, addressing specific needs and key target groups and assessing human resource structures necessitated beginning an investigation of the organization culture. Information about culture both augments the data already collected and looks at them in a different way.

Ascertaining Cultural Readiness

An organization with a culture ready for a career development system is exemplified in these six statements:

1. Business plans and forecasts are publicized.
2. People have easy access to job information.
3. Networks foster innovation, high performance, and exploration of career options.

4. Enrichment, development, and mobility are valued.
5. Employees and managers are mutually supportive.
6. People fit the organization culture.

Exploring the aspect of culture each of these statements represents—using people, written documents, human resource structures, and informal systems as data sources—can focus an investigation of the organization's culture and, at the same time, reveal or confirm needs/problems and key target groups for a career development program.

Business Plans and Forecasts Are Publicized. In organizations that publicize their business plans and forecasts, people are rarely surprised about new ventures, growth areas, declining areas, new technologies, industry trends, or future human resource needs. The organization's mission and key business objectives are communicated broadly, frequently, and fully. Information on future plans is readily available, top managers are willing to answer questions from employees and other managers about those future plans; when information is not shared—due, for example, to competitive markets—employees are told why.

Questions to ask of people to find out if and how business plans and forecasts are made available include

How do you get information about where the organization is going?

Are you encouraged to study where the industry is going and plan accordingly?

Do you know what's going to happen ahead of time or after the fact?

What are the future plans for your department? The organization?

What kinds of discussions do you have about your career potential? With whom?

Other useful steps include investigating the availability within the organization of written documents containing forecasts, business plans, and objectives, as well as professional papers on future trends and industry projections; finding out if organization plans are made available through forecasts, open succession planning systems, and management systems that relate future aspirations to organization plans; and examining informal communication channels (to see if people have a sense of purpose and control in their work lives) and artifacts such as bulletin boards in cafeteria and reception areas (to see if they display slogans, themes, and pictures related to future plans and directions).

People Have Easy Access to Job Information. In organizations where people have easy access to job information, people see opportunities and feel empowered to take charge of their careers. They know what jobs are emerging in the future and what the options are now. Information is provided periodically to all employees, at all levels and locations. The organization is not secretive or restrictive; there is no belief that looking at other options is a negative reflection on the current job; and there is no stigma attached to interviewing for a new job or reading job posting boards.

Questions to ask to find out if people have easy access to job information include

> Are jobs posted? What levels? Where?
> Are position descriptions readily available? Are they current and specific?
> Is informational interviewing accepted?
> Is it easy to learn about positions in other parts of the organization?
> Does your manager encourage searching out other information?
> Do you know how to find out about positions in other parts of the company?
> Is your manager willing to connect you with people from other functional areas?

Also investigate such written documents as annual reports that describe the functional areas in key business units, newsletters that describe departments or units and give a flavor for the kind of positions existing there, and promotional materials for selection and hiring. The more details such information contains and the more it indicates the flavor for the uniqueness of different functional units, the more helpful it can be for internal employees.

Another step is to find out if the human resource organization supports easy access to organization job information. These can include job posting systems, position descriptions, career days, personnel representatives in each functional area, resource centers containing all the information in an organized way, organization directories, and career counselors. (Organizations with numbers of these systems in place and frequently used probably have a culture that values the belief that "people have a right to job information.") In addition, examine informal systems by observing where jobs are posted, who receives the posting (bosses only?), what feedback is given in interviews, whether position descriptions fit and aptly describe the job.

Networks Foster Innovation, High Performance, and Exploration of Career Options. Career options and innovative opportunities are related to the strength of personal networks and allies, as is the ease of moving from one part of the company to another. "The frequency with which peers in other areas cooperate readily, in the highly innovative companies [which have effective networks], contrasts sharply with the absence of horizontal cooperation in segmentalist organizations [with no networks]" (Kanter, 1983, p. 162). It is not surprising, then, that in open cultures peers are helpful, giving information and support regarding career inquiries.

Questions to ask in uncovering the state of networks include

What are the opportunities for networks, horizontal and vertical, inside and outside the organization?

What kinds of formal groups and social groups exist? What informal groups? What cross-functional work teams?

Is mentoring encouraged?

Do people work together or compete? Whom do you interact with? Where? Do you sense racist or sexist attitudes? Is the organization fighting any discrimination suits? Can you move easily from one area of the organization to another to get information?

Do you have a sense of the business overall or just of your department? How many people outside of your immediate department do you know? Call by first name? Have easy access to?

Questions relating to this characteristic will provide important data for program design. For example, answers will reveal whether groups should be heterogeneous or homogeneous; whether programs can mix people of different grade levels; and whether the necessary networks are already part of the culture or will have to be fostered.

Written documents may not be as rich a data source for revealing the quality of networks. Annual reports frequently emphasize work groups and teams rather than individuals, and organization newspapers generally highlight community events and cross geographical and functional unit boundaries.

Human resource organizations that promote lateral moves and short-term job assignments indicate the presence of networks that foster innovation, high performance, and exploration of career options. So, too, do orientation training programs that introduce employees to the whole company, not merely their own units; tours of the various facilities and meetings with other divisions and departments; job rotation programs, cross training, and transfer policies that encourage rather than discourage lateral transfers; and incentive and bonus systems that reward teamwork rather than only individual effort.

Informal network systems can be discovered by observing whether people mix or form cliques in the cafeteria, what the floor and elevator patterns are, whether landscaping is open or closed, whether conference and meeting rooms are set up to foster group problem solving and communication, and whether people have easy access to others or are expected to use definite chains of command.

Enrichment, Development, and Mobility Are Valued. Vital companies have vital people who do not feel demoralized, bored, stagnant, or underutilized. Innovative companies do not bemoan the poor morale of their people. Instead, they reward new ideas, inventions, more efficient use of time, money, and resources. Innovative managers believe that things are always changing and that employees need to be changing, too, to keep abreast.

Questions that help ascertain whether enrichment, development, and mobility are valued include

> Do planning for succession and human resource planning happen regularly and with some vigor?
> Are development efforts planned and budgeted for a year or more?
> Does this organization value follow-up and evaluation?
> Are the results of various tracking systems reported?
> How long do programs stay around?
> Are options related to demonstrated objectives of employees?
> Who is responsible for assessing outcomes of training events?
> Is on-the-job training fostered and rewarded?

To discover norms relating to the ease of moving in all directions (lateral, down, up, and out), questions such as the following are helpful:

> How much internal mobility is there?
> What is the direction? Up? Lateral? Down?
> What is the feeling about downward mobility? Lateral mobility? Do people pay a price?
> Is there a reward for moving or a punishment?

Written documents that indicate a belief in development include written performance improvement and career development plans, as well as statistics on turnover, rate of movement, and number of outside versus inside hires. Also indicative are newsletters that recognize novel career moves or breaking out of stuck positions and needs assessments that give direction to managers regarding deficiencies in employee skills and knowledge.

Formal personnel systems that indicate a belief in ongoing development, enrichment, and mobility include tuition aid programs that reward learning and preparation for a new job rather than a present one; open succession planning and manpower forecasting systems that foster hiring from within and publicizing future positions and requisite competencies; performance appraisal systems that emphasize results and reward performance rather than mediocrity; and assessment centers that foster critical self-evaluation and the importance of reality checking and getting feedback on perceived competencies.

Informal network systems to look for here include buddy systems and informal mentoring.

Employees and Managers Are Mutually Supportive. Trust is as essential to relationships as to organizations. In his study of the qualities of leadership, Bennis (1984) noted that the main determinant of trust is reliability or consistency. His research indicated that people prefer to follow individuals they can count on, despite opposing views, rather than individuals who shift their positions frequently. Trust also comes from mutuality, two-way communication, and candid feedback. People who know where they stand with each other and with their work do not have to waste energy worrying and wondering; their energy can go into results and invention.

Questions that can demonstrate the commitment to mutual support between managers and employees and unveil whether there is trust include

> Do managers support, coach, and encourage employees?
> Do managers get the support they need to do that: money, recognition, training?
> Do people feel alone or supported and working together?
> Are careers talked about? With whom? How frequently?
> Are managers rewarded for developing their people? How?
> Do managers feel responsible for developing people?

Do managers hold on to or easily let go of their employees?

Do managers seek feedback and input from their employees?

Is candor valued and rewarded?

The written documents most indicative of the quality of
manager and employee trust and support are performance appraisal forms and performance improvement and career development plans. From the specifics and details noted in such
documents—from the checked boxes, ranked traits, and grandi-
ose, vague plans—emerges the quality of the discussions. Frequent, honest, inquiring coaching between managers and employees is immediately apparent.

Personnel systems that reinforce mutual support include
two-way performance appraisal systems; career and performance
improvement programs; rewards and compensations systems
that foster people development and reward performance; career
resource centers that educate managers and employees in feedback skills and job enrichment and redesign techniques; and
management programs that foster skills in working with people.

People Fit the Organization Culture. When employees
and organization fit, productivity increases, employees are satisfied, and there are effective recruitment and staffing procedures
at all levels. When the style, skills, interests, values, and personalities of individuals are in sync with their jobs and the organization culture, performance problems or burnout and stress symp-
toms are rare. Suzzman (1983) found that indicators of poor fit
between people and organizations all go together: inadequate
recruitment and selection procedures, employee dissatisfaction,
employee-manager conflict, low productivity, and short employee tenure.

Questions to assess whether there is a fit between individuals and organization include

Does employee style (for example, analytical, snazzy, personal, outgoing, quiet) fit the style of the organization?

Are employee skills valued by the organization?

Are employee interests and ideas reinforced by the organization?

Are employee prime values encouraged and recognized by the organization?

Are employee values aligned with the mission and goals of the organization?

Assuring Cultural Change

Successful change efforts must respect the existing culture of an organization at the same time that they challenge its cultural patterns. One way to assure success in this difficult process comes from Watzlawick, Weakland, and Fisch's (1974) long-term therapeutic work with schizophrenics, in which the notion of paradox is basic to successfully changing the behaviors of these individuals. In their approach, they acknowledge and accept the behavioral patterns of each patient; at the same time, they slowly work to change one behavior. This technique of accepting while, paradoxically, seeking change can be valuable not only in gaining insights into organization culture but also in selecting effective strategies to meet the specific needs and target groups of a career development program and in selecting strategies that assure a cultural change.

The five distinct steps described in this section, based on the paradox of accepting patterns as they are while simultaneously seeking to change those patterns, will help us develop "uncharacteristic" strategies and assure that a career development system can create lasting change, instead of simply fighting the latest fire.

Pick a Problem That Has Been Around. Nothing is new under the sun. If there is a pressing organization problem, it has probably been around for quite a while, and people have already attempted to resolve it. It has probably also been reidentified as a high-priority problem as specific needs and key target groups were addressed. Some problems an organization may have already tried to solve are

Technical specialists not ready for management
Women and minority employees not moving up
Managers feeling inadequate in coaching employees
Employees feeling stuck or at dead ends
Employees' jobs becoming obsolete

List All Prior Attempts at Solution. The purpose of listing prior attempts at solution is to further understand the cultural patterns of the organization. This analysis can be made
through an advisory group or through a series of interviews. If
an advisory group is used, subgroups of four or five can work on
different pressing problems. When prior attempts are listed, tre-
mendous similarities are sure to appear, which will indicate that
cultural patterns are emerging. The list needs to be as long, as
specific, and as descriptive as possible. Out of one such analysis
came this list of prior attempts at solving the problem of wom-
en and minority employees not moving up:

Black/white awareness seminars
Male/female awareness seminars
Quotas
Passing the buck
Badmouthing management
Complaining and grumbling
Giving the problem to personnel to fix
Hiring external consultants
Writing proposals
Shooting down proposals
Sabotaging external consultants
Promoting incompetent women and minority people
Training women and minority people on how to succeed
Showing how consultant recommendations could never
    work
Complaining that there are no competent women and mi-
    nority people
Putting the responsibility on the consultant
Running one-shot training workshops
Providing little time, money, or reinforcement

Such lists can go on and on, and people are usually amazed at how many solutions already have been tried and have failed. If, however, advisory group members or interviewees seem to be running out of steam or are unable to see what has already occurred, ask them to create a sabotage list; that is, a list of everything that could be done to ensure that the problem stays around. A burst of energy and enthusiasm is sure to result as people discover that lists of attempts at solutions and sabotage lists are basically the same.

Determine What Prior Attempts Have in Common. In attempting to determine the cultural patterns and the patterns of business as usual that the list of prior attempts demonstrates, people sometimes need help, particularly since this analysis needs to be very specific. Exhibit 3 contains a checklist of typical patterns of business as usual. Advisory group members or interviewees can read, check, and discuss these to get started. The list is not exhaustive; other patterns may emerge that are not included.

Exhibit 3. Patterns of Business as Usual.

____ Top down	____ Bottom up
____ Teams	____ Layered approach
____ One-way	____ Two-way
____ Written	____ Verbal
____ Trendy	____ Conservative
____ Individual	____ Group
____ Management oriented	____ Employee oriented
____ Invisible	____ Visible
____ Long-term	____ Short-term
____ Planned	____ Reactive
____ Stable	____ Always changing
____ Leaders	____ Followers
____ Problem oriented	____ Solution oriented
____ "Pilots" experimental	____ "The answer"
____ Manager centered	____ Employee centered
____ Informal	____ Formal
____ Project oriented	____ Classroom oriented
____ People centered	____ System centered
____ Consultant/human resource driven	____ Advisory group/line driven
____ Training solutions	____ Line solutions

Based on the prior attempts to solve the problem of women and minorities not moving up, the following characteristic patterns emerged in one organization:

Chain of command approved from on high
Training-oriented solutions
Short-term (two- or three-day workshops)
One-shot (no ongoing support)
Centered on women and minority employees
Detached from line managers and top managers
Consultant driven
Few links to work life
Awareness oriented versus skill oriented
Glitzy and professional

As is often the case, similar cultural patterns were evident in the analyses of other problems facing this organization.

Discover What Norms and Patterns Are Sacrosanct. Paradoxical thinking and strategy formation now enter the picture. To get any change, some patterns and norms need to be altered; at the same time, in order to reduce anxiety, the culture must be maintained and norms must be respected. This means it is critical to tie in those people deeply familiar with the organization. Only "insiders" know what can be changed and what must remain intact.

In the sample problem (women and minority employees not moving up), in light of norms and patterns deemed sacrosanct, the advisory group recommended following these strategies:

Adhere to chain of command
Have a polished, professional package
Retain outside "experts"
Do not raise expectations
Have some training solutions
Have an outside consultant or expert involved

These strategies, closely tied in to the characteristic organization culture patterns already noted, assured that the resulting career development program would present a sufficiently low threat to get it tested and in place.

Create New, Uncharacteristic Strategies. At this point, one or more new, uncharacteristic strategies, which are going to be the ones that produce real change, need to be added to the traditional strategies; that is, those that conform to the organization's culture patterns. By incorporating the few uncharacteristic strategies into the many traditional strategies, we are able to achieve change in a nonthreatening manner.

For example, the following uncharacteristic strategies (for that organization culture) were suggested by the advisory group working on the problem:

Involve white men
Assure six-month program with several components
Tie in high-level managers as mentors and sponsors
Develop skills *and* awareness
Involve the immediate supervisors
Document and circulate profiles of participants

When these culturally uncharacteristic recommendations were accepted, the goal of the program—that women and minority employees would be ready for management positions—was assured.

Importance of Investigating Organization Culture:
Illustrations

The cases in this section illustrate the importance of analyzing organization culture. These examples highlight the need to respect and harness the existing culture while assuring change through a few uncharacteristic strategies.

Case 1. The primary problem in Massachusetts Mutual Insurance was plateaued employees in

a vertical culture. A data processing career exploration program was invented to give "stuck" employees the opportunity to explore a new career
option. Participation was voluntary, but brief program testing was required in order to qualify for
the pilot. Selected people attended a data processing familiarization process for three hours twice a
week for eleven weeks. Career counselors helped
participants explore whether data processing was a
potential new career option for them. If the individual and counselor decided it was a viable option,
the company paid tuition for computer training.
Counselors also helped set up informational interviews for employees already in data processing to
search out more information about job requirements and opportunities.

This program fostered safe exploration, employee retention, and retraining. There was definite "insurance" of success
at each step of the way—true to existing cultural norms. The uncharacteristic strategies of fostering lateral career exploration
and informational interviewing were carefully monitored to in-
sure success.

> *Case 2.* A leading software company in a
> volatile, quickly changing market fosters an entre-
> preneurial spirit among its employees. They are
> admonished to seize or create their own opportu-
> nities; career management is up to them. The com-
> pany has developed a career planning seminar that
> is open to all employees and focused on self-assess-
> ment and planning. Managers are not involved. Em-
> ployees "make it happen" and the seminar is well
> received.

Like the culture, the program is fast moving, employee
driven, quickly responsive, open to all, and needs no manage-

ment sanction for participation. The uncharacteristic strategy is to give employees help in self-assessment and planning although, after that, it is up to them.

Case 3. National Semiconductor's training director described her organization as "fast moving" and "management driven." Although discussions were going on, managers were "raising unrealistic expectations and sometimes making promises they couldn't keep." To meet the need for a positive model of career coaching, with tips on positive things for managers to do, National Semiconductor developed a nineteen-minute videotape that was supported by a one-day, fast-moving, skills-building workshop for managers and by tools structured to support managers in their coaching.

The design of the program took into account cultural norms, such as a fast pace, importance of the manager role, and video orientation. For example, the focus was on managers. Their role as career coaches was reinforced and supported with positive role models and structured tools. One uncharacteristic strategy was to slow the fast pace and lengthen the short time frame for manager involvement by the addition of a seminar. The other strategy was the positive focus on "what works" (rather than on "don'ts") for career coaching.

In each of these three cases, an organization moved one step in the direction of lasting change. Each case also demonstrates the importance of investigating the organization's culture to assure success for a career development program.

The programs described in these cases are parts of career development systems. They are ongoing, evolving, and developing year by year. New components are added, one at a time, and management advisory groups are working continuously to make sure that new programs respect the organization's culture.

A Final Word

The attention, ongoing learning and discussion, and continuing evolution seen in the three cases just presented are based
solidly on in-depth analyses of specific needs and key target
groups, human resource structures, and organization culture, as
described in the three chapters of Part One. By defining the
present system and by focusing on real needs, structures, and
cultures, we have taken the first major step on the way to successful and effective career development programs—and on the
way to a career development system (an organized, formalized,
ongoing effort that integrates multiple components and activities and involves employees, management, and the policies and
procedures of the organization) that can assure lasting cultural
change.

PART TWO

Creating a Vision and Plan

With specific problems and key target groups identified, human resource structures assessed, and organization culture investigated, the needs element for the career development program, the first of the three essential elements for creating change, is firmly in place. Now the focus turns to the second element: vision. Vision means determining new directions and possibilities—gaining a realistic picture of what the organization, its employees, and its managers will look like in five years if the specific needs already identified are truly addressed. Vision also means building a model—a blueprint or road map for achieving the vision—that will link present needs to future possibilities by detailing each of the strategies or interventions to be used.

To achieve this step, the following questions need to be answered:

> What are the elements of a vision for a career development system? What theories will help achieve the vision?
> What are the possible interventions for employees?
> What interventions will get and keep managers involved?
> What interventions will help link human resources structures to career development programs?
> How can these structures and/or interventions be incorporated into a model?

The first chapter in Part Two describes how a vision can be created and provides an overview of theories applicable to

65

career development systems on which a vision can be based. The next three chapters explore strategies for career development efforts. The final chapter in Part Two describes four successfully used systems models and provides effective combinations of interventions.

Chapter Four

Applying Theory to Practice in Career Development Planning

> "A vision represents people's ideals and aspirations."

> "A good theory is like a compass, pointing us in appropriate directions, suggesting landmarks for measuring progress."

What will the organization look like after meeting the specific needs identified in defining its present system? The first task in determining new directions and possibilities is to create a vision, a picture of the ideal future, to use as a guide in selecting and designing the most effective combination of interventions and the best framework and models for utilizing those strategies.

Look ahead, dream, speculate, imagine what the organization could be if the specific needs and key target groups identified in Part One were met, keeping in mind that the vision must be based on appropriate concepts and theories, which will be described in this chapter. That is, the vision must be realistic, so that it provides a strong link between the present situation and future possibilities, between the needs (defined in Chapters One, Two, and Three) and the interventions (discussed in Chapters Five, Six, and Seven). For example, if the problem is a 35 percent rate of attrition among employees who have been with the organization less than two years, because they feel that they receive neither challenging work assignments nor useful information on possible next moves and options, a realistic vision is

the reduction of that attrition rate to 10 percent. The difference between the current state of affairs and the vision of the
future is the basis for selecting effective interventions. These
might include providing more realistic job previews, training
managers in structuring job expectations for new employees,
providing new employees an opportunity to learn about potential options from representatives of other divisions and departments within the organization. Table 4 gives examples of realistic visions to meet three problems and lists possible interventions
for turning the visions into reality. Also included in the table
are the reasons for a gap between the needs and the visions that
lead to best interventions.

One way to help assure that the visions are realistic is to
use an advisory group and its knowledge of the organization.
For example, in one organization the need/problem was the
lack of movement into management, and the threat of a class
action suit, by women and minority employees. The vice president of human resources had received a number of proposals
and plans, none of which he felt would work. The solution
came through an advisory group whose members brought their
own internal expertise to bear in deciding which proposals and
components of proposals would and would not work. This process of choosing, as opposed to proving, was based on data
collected and analyzed in a needs assessment and facilitated by
examining four very different model programs, each of which
fostered upward mobility of promising women and minority
people in different ways, producing different results. After
examining each proposal, advisory group members listed likes
and dislikes and asked challenging clarification questions. Then
they used that input to design a composite model—and even
rough in an action plan—inventively, collaboratively, and en-
thusiastically. As a result, the vision, as well as the means for
accomplishing it, was grounded in reality. (Chapter Ten discusses in detail issues in forming advisory groups and how to
use them while building a career development system.)

Thus, creating a vision links needs with interventions, the
problems with the most effective solutions to accomplish the
ideal. But before discussing a variety of possible interventions

Table 4. Using Visions to Link Needs and Solutions.

Current Situation (Need/Problem)	Vision	Reason for Gap Between Problem and Vision	Possible Interventions
• Rarely have employees realistically assessed their career aspirations (only 25 percent say their career aspirations are well defined)	• Employees have realistically assessed career aspirations	• No organization tools are available for employees to assess career aspirations	• A series of career planning workbooks
• Almost 27 percent of employees have not participated in career discussions with their managers	• Employees have an opportunity to discuss development and opportunities candidly with managers	• Employees view managers as lacking in candor, information, and real ability and/or interest to assist them	• A training program for managers in career coaching skills • A career resource center providing company career information
• Pools of qualified employees are not adequate to meet forecasted job openings or future needs	• Pools of qualified employees meet forecasted job openings/needs	• Departments generally have no system for developing pools of qualified employees to meet forecasted job openings/needs	• Succession planning program

Source: AT&T General Departments.

(in Chapters Five, Six, and Seven) we must consider the foundations for visions. That is, we must consider the various theories that can apply to career development systems, theories that provide the sound footings needed to ensure the best choice of strategies and models. It is essential that visions be built on conceptual bases, on appropriate theories and concepts that can be drawn from as the best interventions are selected for meeting the needs of key target groups.

Why Theory?

Career development is an applied field with a rich background in such disciplines as counseling psychology, industrial psychology, and sociology. The most successful career development programs are most often based on one or more theories grounded in those disciplines. Building from such theories provides a sense of direction, a rationale for approaches, and indicators upon which to measure results, as well as credibility, particularly in scientific or technical organizations, because most theories have been tested and validated in a number of settings. Such theories also provide a set of clues or hypotheses by which to better understand individual differences and complex organizational phenomena and, as a result, create the most effective approaches to career development.

Which theories are best to use as a foundation? No one theory will work for all settings, for all purposes, or for all professions. They range on a continuum from individually based perspectives to organizational conceptualizations. They represent many different viewpoints.

In choosing a theory on which to base a career development program, we need to consider the following issues:

The specific problem and key target group
Familiarity and/or comfort with the theory
Usefulness of the theory, as it relates to the specific problem, design of interventions, and evaluation
Probable acceptance of the theory in the organization

In addition, keep in mind that a combination of theories may be preferred, for different theories may be more relevant to different aspects of career development. Further, theories should be seen as guidelines, not gods. Their purpose is to add direction, not control.

Four types of theories, all of which have served as the basis for career development activities, are discussed in this chapter: adult development, career choice and development, learning, and organization. The adult development theories represent age-stage concepts (Levinson), a variable events perspective (Neugarten), and the uniqueness of female adult development (Gilligan). The career choice and development theorists focus on choice factors (Holland) and stages (Super and Dalton, Thompson, and Price). Learning theory emphasizes learning styles (Kolb and Plovnick), and organization theory looks at the interface between individuals and organizations (Schein). For each theory, a link will be made to actual practice and program implications.

Adult Development Theory

Adult development theories and models focus on the issues faced by adults through the course of their lives. The idea that adulthood is a period of predictability and stability is put to rest: A career choice made at age eighteen is sure to be revised many times over throughout one's life.

Levinson: Age-Linked Developmental Periods. Levinson, a prominent adult development theorist, explains adult behavior as moving through a set of discrete stages, usually related to chronological age. His conclusions, originally derived from an empirical study involving intensive interviews over a number of years with forty men, chiefly white-collar workers (1978), have been augmented by research on women's lives (1986). One of Levinson's key concepts is that young people have a dream about who they will become as adults, that mentors help them realize a life structure for implementing these dreams, and that in midlife they begin to question whether life really meets their dreams.

Levinson (1986) describes an alternating series of age-linked structure-building and structure-changing (or transitional) periods, which he suggests are experienced by both women and men in all cultures and classes throughout history (see Figure 4).

Figure 4. Levinson's Developmental Periods.

Early Adult Transition	Age Thirty Transition	Midlife Transition	Age Fifty Transition	Late Adult Transition
Entering the Adult World	Settling Down	Entering Middle Adulthood	Culminating Middle Adulthood	Late Adulthood

The major stages are early, middle, and late adulthood with significant cross-era transitions between those stages. The developmental periods are as follows (1986, pp. 7–8):

- *Early adult transition* (age seventeen to twenty-two): A "developmental bridge between preadulthood and early adulthood."
- *Entering the adult world* (age twenty-two to twenty-eight): "The time for building and maintaining an initial mode of adult living."
- *Age thirty transition* (age twenty-eight to thirty-three): "An opportunity to reappraise and modify" the initial mode of adult living and "to create the basis for the next life structure."
- *Settling down* (age thirty-three to forty): Youthful aspirations are realized as this major stage of early adulthood is completed.
- *Midlife transition* (age forty to forty-five): "Another of the great cross-era shifts, serving to terminate early adulthood and to initiate middle adulthood."
- *Entering middle adulthood* (age forty-five to fifty): As in the entering-the-adult-world period, this is a time for building the initial basis for a new era.

- *Age fifty transition* (age fifty to fifty-five): "A mid-era opportunity for modifying and perhaps improving" the initial basis.
- *Culminating middle adulthood* (age fifty-five to sixty): "The framework in which we conclude this era."
- *Late adult transition* (age sixty to sixty-five): "A boundary period between middle and late adulthood, separating and linking the two eras."
- *Late adulthood* (age sixty-five to seventy): Again a time for improving the initial basis of a new era.

In the structure-building periods, the task is to make life structures and better one's life within them. In transition (structure-changing) periods—in which, Levinson notes, people spend almost half their lives—the tasks are "to reappraise the existing structures, to explore possibilities for change in the self and the world," and, as the transition comes to an end, to "start making crucial choices, giving them meaning and commitment, and building a life structure around them" (1986, p. 7).

Levinson's developmental perspective, emphasizing alternating age-linked structure-building and transitional periods with identifiable tasks and issues, implies that different programs are needed for adults in early, middle, and late adulthood and that programs aimed at those in transition may be most effective.

In a creative application of Levinson's work, Geddie and Strickland (1984) developed a model to help employees deal with the challenge of each of Levinson's age-linked periods.

In developing their model, they point to the central task of each age-linked transition period: to question and reappraise the existing life structure. In order to accomplish this, in order to get ready to move on to the next stage, one must accomplish certain key goals. Geddie and Strickland believe that, in any transition period, an individual's motivation for learning and goal completion increases. They also believe that a set of obstacles—that is, feelings, perceptions, existing habits, or skill deficiencies—may keep an individual from realizing his or her goals. A perception obstacle might be, for example, the employee's view of reality; an existing habit obstacle, his or her job performance. This means that specific interventions must be available that will help remove the obstacles of the transition period and allow each individual to achieve his or her goals.

In order to apply this concept, Geddie and Strickland designed five transition charts, one for each transition period, which designate the goals, obstacles, and interventions. Table 5 is the chart for the "great cross-era shift" of the age forty to forty-five midlife transition. Each transition chart can be translated into a worksheet to demonstrate a clear link between the goals and tasks of a particular period and the kinds of approaches used.

Neugarten: Variability. In contrast to Levinson's age-linked periods for transitions and structure building, Neugarten (1976) emphasizes individual variability rather than predictability. For example, twenty-year-olds, she says, are more similar to one another than fifty-five-year-olds. She sees the influence of three different kinds of time—historical (calendar) time, social time (age norms and expectations), and life time (chronological age)—all of which interact to produce each individual's different experience. Lives are lived in a historical context; as this context changes (people now live longer; more young people are in graduate school, delaying their entry into careers; more women work full time), ideas of age-appropriate behavior and events (the social clock that prescribes ages to take jobs, change careers, marry, retire) also change. Although there is little to relate our life time to specific behaviors, Neugarten says that nevertheless most people find unexpected off-time life events, such as having to retire at age fifty (perhaps because of a heart attack) or having to change careers at age sixty (perhaps because of being fired), traumatic; in contrast, on-time events, such as retirement at age sixty-five or changing careers at age thirty, are met with equanimity.

A major implication of Neugarten's theory is that this variability of individuals, affected by historical, social, and life time (and events), makes categorization impossible. Therefore, it is necessary to use multiple approaches and strategies in, for example, designing a program to work with plateaued em-

Table 5. Midlife Transition (Age Forty to Forty-Five).

Sample Goals	Sample Obstacles	Sample Interventions

1. Reassess the appropriateness of career track in terms of
   Success
   Satisfaction/fulfillment
   Accomplishments
   Values and priorities
2. Set realistic long-range goals
3. Develop a list of important lessons learned from the first half of life
4. Assess personal performance style
5. Identify important obstacles to personal fulfillment and develop a plan to overcome them
	1. Feelings:
	   Ambivalence
	   Panic/hopelessness
	   Importance/insignificance
	   Dependency/resignation
	2. Perceptions:
	   It's too late to change direction
	   Personal worth depends upon performance
	   Personal values must be subordinated to organizational goals
	   Life is work—that's all
	3. Performance:
	   Making decisions without considering consequences
	   Ignoring personal values in planning and scheduling
	   Reverting to adolescent behavior and reducing credibility
	   Failing to identify lessons learned from experience
		1. Individual/group counseling to promote
		   Accurate identification of personal priorities/values
		   Identification of significant lesson from life experience
		   Assessment of progress toward personal and career goals
		   Development of long-range goals
		2. Training session topics:
		   Managing change creatively
		   Building support systems
		   Assessing personal fulfillment
		   Maintaining personal identity in the company
		   Developing an effective performance style
		3. Supervision goals:
		   Recognize stress/conflict
		   Assess performance in relation to capabilities
		   Reinforce mature decision making

Source: Reprinted with permission from the June 1984 issue of *Training, the Magazine of Human Resources Development.* Copyright 1984, Lakewood Publications Inc., Minneapolis, Minn. (612) 333-0471. All rights reserved.

ployees, even if they are all the same age. Offering a variety of approaches (such as individual counseling, support groups, workshops, or short-term work experiences in other functional areas) ensures that individual differences will be accommodated. Neugarten's work also reinforces the essential nature of needs assessment. Collecting data helps define the variability as well as the universality of needs among members of key target groups.

Gilligan: Sex Differences. Gilligan's (1982) work on the development of women, based on extensive interviews with men and women from ages six to sixty, focuses on differences in perceptions and behaviors based on psychosocial development. She sees women replacing "the bias of men toward separation with a representation of the interdependence of self and other, both in love and work" (p. 170). Thus, she says, the voice of women speaks to attachment and reflects an ethic of care, whereas the voice of men speaks of individual achievement and reflects an ethic of justice. The ethic of care "rests on the premise of nonviolence—that no one should be hurt," while the ethic of justice "proceeds from the premise of equality—that everyone should be treated the same" (p. 174).

The stages of moral development during a woman's life, Gilligan says, move from an initial concern with survival, or selfishness, to a concern with responsibility and relationships, with not hurting others. A key issue for many women, then, is reconciling the need to care for themselves with the need to care for others. Men, on the other hand, must reconcile an emphasis on fairness, rights, and logic with the need to take care of others. Gilligan asserts that, since maturity is different for men and women, this difference needs to be built into adult development models.

Hotelling and Forrest (1985) suggest that Gilligan's research can be used to understand two of the extreme behavior patterns that working women sometimes exhibit: the superwoman attempting to uphold extremely high standards both at work and home and the male model striving to excel at work only. The superwoman role often results in guilt, overload, and physical strain; the male model role, in isolation and lack of communication with others.

Career development programs focused on women need to help them create an in-between role—one that balances the responsibility for care and the need not to hurt others with the prevalent models of logic and individual achievement.

Equally, men need to be offered help in balancing their needs for power and strength with care and responsiveness to others. Profiles of competencies and success in organizations must recognize and balance these so-called male and female behaviors. Programs need to be based on a model of androgyny—whose major theoretical components, according to Kaplan (1976), are situational appropriateness, flexibility, effectiveness, and integration.

Adult Development Theory: Summary Implications. Adult development theory provides a useful, but sometimes contradictory, perspective on adult concerns over the life span.

- Theories that focus on age-linked developmental periods emphasize predictability and inevitability and suggest that different approaches are needed for different age groups. They also suggest the possibility of presenting groups of adults with models and maps for their own development.
- Variability theories emphasize uniqueness and call for multiple strategies and approaches.
- Theories that emphasize sex differences tell us that women face different challenges in their careers than men and need specialized interventions, such as mentor programs, assertiveness training, or seminars in balancing home-life issues.

Career Choice and Development Theory

Theories of career choice and development address questions of direct importance to career development programs—namely, How do we make effective career choices? What helps people continue to develop and keep on track in their careers? This section provides an overview of some of the important theories in this area.

Holland: Congruence. Holland's theory of vocational development deals with the factors influencing career choice and is based on the concept of congruence; that is, the fit between the individual and the environment. Holland (1973) sees vocational interests as an expression of personality and tells us that "people search for environments that will let them exercise their skills and abilities, express their attitudes and problems and roles" (p. 14). He classifies personality types (as defined by particular preferences, interests, and competencies) and environments (including groups of occupations) as follows (pp. 14–18):

- *Realistic:* Involves the "explicit, ordered, or systematic manipulation of objects, tools, machines, and animals." Occupations include architectural draftsman, structural steel worker, computer specialist, and secretary.
- *Investigative:* Involves "the observation and symbolic, systematic, creative investigation of physical, biological, or cultural phenomena." Occupations include economist, physicist, medical technologist, surgeon, and aeronautical engineer.
- *Artistic:* Involves "ambiguous, free, unsystematized activities and competencies to create arts, forms, or products." Occupations include writer, designer, and architect.
- *Social:* Involves "the manipulation of others to conform, train, develop, cure, or enlighten." Occupations include counselor, teacher, and social worker.
- *Enterprising:* Involves "the manipulation of others to attain organizational or self-interest goal." Sample occupations include banker, lawyer, salesperson, and manager.
- *Conventional:* Involves "the explicit, ordered, systematic manipulation of data, such as keeping records, filing materials, reproducing materials, organizing written and numerical data according to a prescribed plan, operating business and data processing machines." A sample occupation is accountant.

Employees can determine their personality type or orientation by completing the Self-Directed Search, a relatively simple instrument designed to assess occupational and other interests. This personal orientation can then be matched with the specific occupations listed for each environment in the Occupation Finder.

Holland's scheme provides an explicit measure of the congruence between a person and a job, and hence of the degree of job satisfaction or dissatisfaction that an individual may experience. For example, a person with a realistic orientation who chooses a career in engineering or computer science should be relatively satisfied with that choice, since both of those occupations are classified as realistic; but a career in law (enterprising) or chemistry (investigative) will bring that same person dissatisfaction and career conflict.

Why are some people's personality codes congruent with their career choices, while others find themselves in incongruent occupations? Several answers are possible to the question of what brings about this mismatching between personality type and job environment.

One is that people may lack information either about themselves or occupations, so that they are unable to make informed decisions. Another is that a person's interests may change over time; one is not necessarily locked into a particular personality type. Individual needs, as well as environmental options, alter with age, family status, and other factors. Thus, an initially congruent career choice may become incongruent, not so much because of changing circumstances as because of more fundamental changes in the individual. One of the strengths of Holland's congruence model is that it allows for such change.

Holland does not assume that career development is linear and sequential. It is not just a matter of choosing the right field, preparing for it, entering it, achieving in it, and retiring from it. Rather, a person's life can be viewed as a series of coded choices that can be studied for their patterns, stability, and mathematical relationships. Holland's most recent research findings indicate that career instability is fairly common until workers reach their late thirties; that older adults tend to demonstrate more career stability; and that this greater stability can probably be attributed not so much to congruence between personality and environment as to such external factors as job security, tenure, salary, and labor market considerations.

Holland's theory of vocational development is probably

the most widely used theory in organizational career development programs. The concept of congruence has been translated
into many workshops and individual counseling models. Interest
assessment using the Self-Directed Search or the Strong-Camp-
bell Interest Inventory, which also reports Holland's six types, is
a key part of the self-assessment component of many programs.

Holland's work, for example, is the basis for a self-directed,
self-managed resource center at NASA's Goddard Space Flight
Center (as in Figure 5). Employees begin their work in the center by completing a series of diagnostic questions; their answers
direct them to the appropriate learning station: Understanding
Self, Understanding the Environment, or Taking Action. As part
of the Understanding Self station, employees complete the Self-
Directed Search instrument. After determining their personality
types in Holland's classification, they look for matching occupations in the Occupation Finder and search for a fit among Goddard and/or federal government positions, which have been classified according to Holland's scheme. Figure 6 contains a
worksheet that guides employees through these diagnostic steps
and then to action based on the diagnosis.

Super: Development Stages. Super's theory is based on
the idea that career development progresses through a series of
stages, each of which is "characterized by the special importance of certain social expectations" (1975, p. 21). The stages
are as follows (pp. 21-26):

- *Growth stage:* As the child interacts with the home, neigh-
  borhood, and school, certain capacities, interests, and values
  are developed.
- *Exploratory stage:* From adolescence to about the mid
  twenties, the individual explores various activities, roles, and
  situations and thereby further crystallizes his or her interests, aptitudes, and values.
- *Establishment stage:* Most people in their mid twenties "find
  suitable paid employment," though some may "drift, floun-
  der, or explore for as many as ten years longer and some
  never achieve stable careers."

Figure 5. NASA Career Resource Center Model.

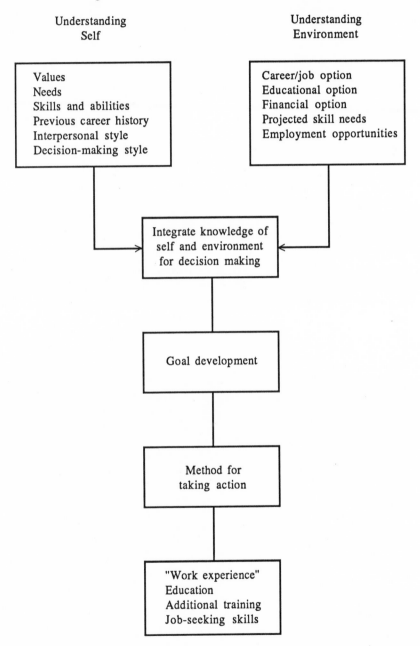

Figure 6. Worksheet Used at NASA's Career Resource Center.

FIND THE POSITIONS THAT MATCH YOUR INTERESTS

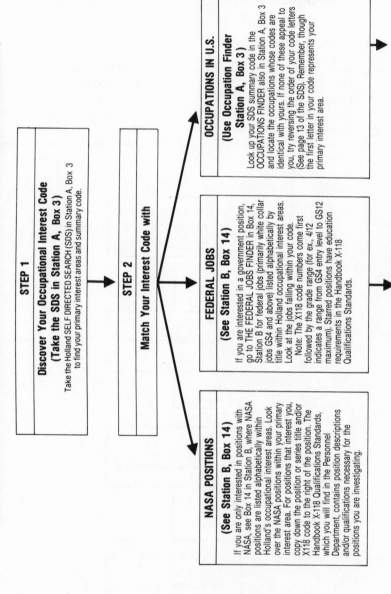

STEP 1

Discover Your Occupational Interest Code
(Take the SDS in Station A, Box 3)

Take the Holland SELF DIRECTED SEARCH (SDS) in Station A, Box 3
to find your primary interest areas and summary code.

STEP 2

Match Your Interest Code with

NASA POSITIONS
(See Station B, Box 14)

If you are only interested in positions with NASA, see Box 14 in Station B, where NASA positions are listed alphabetically within Holland's occupational interest areas. Look over the NASA positions within your primary interest area. For positions that interest you, copy down the position or series title and/or X118 code to the right of the position. The Handbook X-118 Qualifications Standards, which you will find in the Personnel Department, contains position descriptions and/or qualifications necessary for the positions you are investigating.

FEDERAL JOBS
(See Station B, Box 14)

If you are interested in a government position, go to THE FEDERAL JOBS FINDER in Box 14, Station B for federal jobs (primarily white collar jobs GS4 and above) listed alphabetically by title within Holland occupational interest areas. Look at the jobs falling within your code. Note: The X118 code numbers come first followed by the grade range (for ex., 4/12 indicates a range from GS4 entry level to GS12 maximum). Starred positions have education requirements in the Handbook X-118 Qualifications Standards.

OCCUPATIONS IN U.S.
(Use Occupation Finder
Station A, Box 3)

Look up your SDS summary code in the OCCUPATIONS FINDER also in Station A, Box 3 and locate the occupations whose codes are identical with yours. If none of these appeal to you, try reversing the order of your code letters (See page 13 of the SDS). Remember, though the first letter in your code represents your primary interest area.

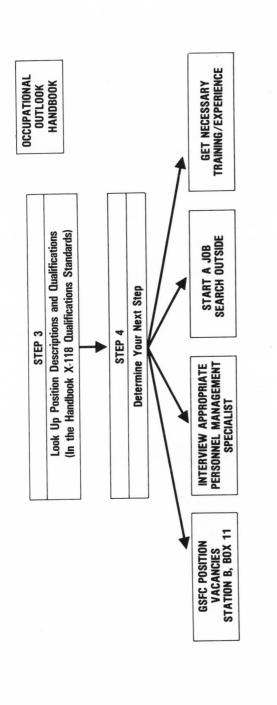

OCCUPATIONAL OUTLOOK HANDBOOK

STEP 3

Look Up Position Descriptions and Qualifications
(In the Handbook X-118 Qualifications Standards)

STEP 4

Determine Your Next Step

GSFC POSITION VACANCIES STATION B, BOX 11

INTERVIEW APPROPRIATE PERSONNEL MANAGEMENT SPECIALIST

START A JOB SEARCH OUTSIDE

GET NECESSARY TRAINING/EXPERIENCE

- *Maintenance stage:* At about age forty-five, most people
  have settled into an occupation and even a particular job,
  and the tasks at this stage consist of "holding [one's] own
  against younger people, keeping up with new developments,
  forging ahead by breaking new ground . . . , or getting re-
  established in the work force."
- *Decline stage:* This is the retirement period, and those people who have carried over their occupational and avocational
  activities and who thus are able to "preserve the continuity
  of roles and of life" are most likely to find retirement satisfactory.

Building on the foundation of this stage theory, Super
further proposes that people play a number of different roles in
each of the life stages: child, student, worker, spouse, parent,
homemaker, citizen, leisurite, annuitant, and patient. The individual may move through these roles in sequence, but some
roles are played concurrently. Super describes "the simultane-
ous and sequential nature of these roles . . . waxing and waning
during the course of the life cycle . . . as a rainbow in which the
bands of color vary in width at any one cross section of the arc,
and each individual's arc varies in width as it goes from birth at
the left to death at the right with the rainbow" (p. 5).

Theorists like Super, concerned with the needs and tasks
associated with developmental career stages rather than the process of choice, indicate that employees in different developmental stages require different programs and approaches. Table
6 displays the task needs and socioemotional needs related to
early, middle, and late career development stages as identified
by Hall (1976). These tasks and needs can serve as guidelines
for interventions to facilitate the development of employees in
different stages.

Dalton, Thompson, and Price: Career Stages. Dalton,
Thompson, and Price (1977) found that many, though by no
means all, professional workers employed by relatively large and
complex organizations get lower performance ratings after age
thirty-five and that many also feel frustrated and uncertain

Table 6. Task and Socioemotional Needs for Career Stages.

Development	Task Needs	Socioemotional Needs
Early career	1. Develop action skills. 2. Develop a specialty. 3. Develop creativity, innovation. 4. Rotate into new areas after three to five years.	1. Support. 2. Autonomy. 3. Deal with feelings of rivalry, competition.
Middle career	1. Develop skills in training and coaching others (younger employees). 2. Training for updating and integrating skills. 3. Develop broader view of work and organization. 4. Job rotation into new job requiring new skills.	1. Opportunity to express feelings about midlife (anguish, defeat, limited time, restlessness). 2. Reorganize thinking about self (morality, values, family, work). 3. Reduce self-indulgence and competitiveness. 4. Support and mutual problem solving for coping with midcareer stress.
Late career	1. Shift from power role to one of consultation, guidance, wisdom. 2. Begin to establish self in activities outside the organization (start on part-time basis).	1. Support and counseling to help see integrated life experiences as platform for others. 2. Acceptance of one's unique life cycle. 3. Gradual detachment from organization.

Source: From *Careers in Organizations*, by D. Hall, p. 90. Copyright © 1976 by Scott, Foresman and Company. Reprinted by permission.

about their careers and confused by the changing demands made upon them. On the basis of interviews with a group of 550 professionally trained men, which included both high-rated and low-rated performers, they defined four distinct stages in the careers of these "knowledge workers."

Table 7 lists these four stages in terms of the central activity the individual is expected to perform well, the primary type of relationship engaged in, and the major psychological adjustments to be made.

Dalton, Thompson, and Price point out that their model is intended only as a general description of the career development of professionals. Among the many exceptions are people who skip the apprentice or the colleague stage or return to an earlier stage (for example, to a colleague position after having been a mentor) without adverse effects. In addition, many people do not advance to the mentor stage, and most never reach the sponsor stage.

The Dalton, Thompson, and Price career development model is widely accepted, even though it is derived from a study limited to professional men (that is, men with graduate as well as undergraduate degrees) who worked in fairly large organizations. The model has been used to give professional workers a conceptual understanding of the stages of career development and what happens in each stage; to help professional workers understand the shift from individual contributor (or apprentice) to mentor; to design orientations that help new employees move successfully through the apprentice stage; and to help managers better understand issues affecting new employees.

Career Choice and Development Theory: Summary Implications. Career choice and development theory suggests such important points as the following:

- To promote best fit between people and jobs, multiple interventions are needed for helping employees conduct self-assessments and obtain adequate information on career options.
- For employees at different career stages, different approaches

Table 7. Four Stages in Careers of Professionals.

	Stage I	Stage II	Stage III	Stage IV
Central activity	Helping Learning Following directions	Independent contributor	Training Interfacing	Shaping the direction of the organization
Primary relationship	Apprentice	Colleague	Mentor	Sponsor
Major psychological issues	Dependence	Independence	Assuming responsibility for others	Exercising power

Source: Reprinted by permission of the publisher from "The Four Stages of Professional Careers" by G. W. Dalton, P. H. Thompson, and R. L. Price, *Organizational Dynamics*, Summer 1977, p. 23, © 1977 American Management Association, New York. All rights reserved.

are needed; for example, orientation programs for new employees and opportunities to mentor others for established employees.

- Employees need specific programs to assist them with such transitions as the move from technical specialist to manager or the move to retirement.
- Workers who stay in the colleague stage for long periods of their careers need programs that will help them maintain their technical currency.

Learning Theory

Learning theory data focus on responses to the variety of learning needs of employees.

Kolb and Plovnick: Managing Change. Kolb and Plovnick's (1977) experiential learning theory is constructed on the assumption that the central task of adult development is managing and adapting to change and that learning, therefore, is a central activity throughout adulthood. Kolb and Plovnick see learning as a four-stage cycle, as illustrated in Figure 7. Concrete experience leads to observation and reflection, which produce concepts that suggest implications for action, which leads to future concrete experience.

Kolb and Plovnick also see that—as a result of socialization, heredity, and past experiences—most people develop dominant and different learning styles, related to the four stages of the learning cycle. For example, some people learn best through abstract conceptualization; others, through concrete experience. Kolb and Plovnick developed the Learning Style Inventory, an instrument that can help identify an individual's dominant learning style.

Data from the Learning Style Inventory make it possible to design career programs that build from individual learning strengths. The approach to teaching used most often in organizations reflects traditional academic settings and emphasizes abstract concepts and theory formation. But this kind of teaching not only puts those with other learning styles at a disadvan-

Figure 7. The Experiential Learning Model.

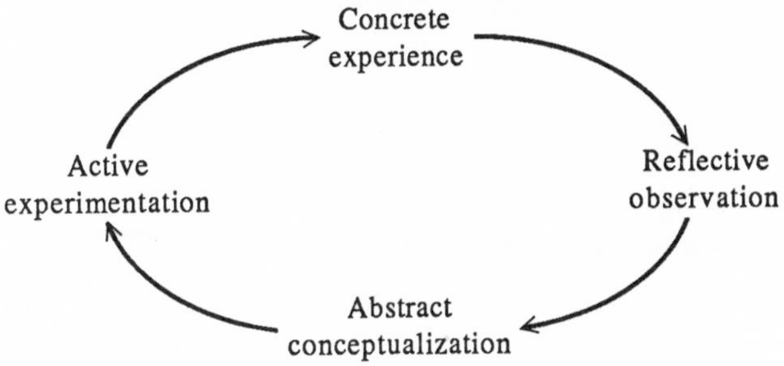

Source: Adapted from Kolb and Plovnick, 1977, p. 68.

tage; it also is increasingly seen today by organizations as both uneconomical and impractical. The current trend is toward alternative ways of learning and acquiring new skills, such as on-the-job experiences and self-directed activities. Whatever the setting for learning, those familiar with a variety of learning style approaches will be better able to design programs that meet employee and organization needs.

Two recent models based on Kolb and Plovnick's work may be helpful in planning career development programs. Hagberg and Leider (1978) see the four styles of learning as enthusiastic, imaginative, logical, and practical; Ward (1983) sees them as idealistic, pragmatic, realistic, and existentialistic.

Learning Theory: Summary Implications. Learning theory approaches suggest several key points to consider:

- Multiple approaches are needed in order to respond to multiple learning styles.
- Assessing the learning styles of employees means being able to design better programs and meet employee needs more effectively.
- Knowledge of the learning styles of top managers might provide important data for designing, implementing, and evaluating a program's effectiveness. For example, if the division chief learns best through reflective observation, anecdotal

and testimonial data would be most likely bring about an understanding and appreciation of the feelings of program participants.

Organization Theory

Organization theory provides a perspective on balancing individual needs and strengths with the realities of an organization, a balance (or match) that is vital to any effective career development program.

Schein: Matching Processes. Schein (1978) sees career development as a two-way process, in which the organization changes and socializes individuals and individuals change and create innovations within the organization. Organizations have the most influence on employees in the early stages of their careers, Schein says, and employees have the most influence on organization environment in later stages of their careers.

He envisions the organization as a three-dimensional cone, as shown in Figure 8. Within the organization cone, employees make external moves while simultaneously making internal moves through a series of career and development stages (similar to those described by Super, 1975). Among the kinds of external moves that employees make are hierarchical moves (mostly up, as a result of promotion), functional or technical moves (along the dimension of functional or technical expertise), and moves toward the inner circle (these more subtle moves toward membership and inclusion are often characterized by access to organization privileges and secrets).

Schein sees employees as making internal moves through career and development stages that range from a growth, fantasy, exploration stage (age birth to twenty-one) through full membership at midcareer (age twenty-five and over) to retirement. Each stage has its own general issues to be confronted and specific tasks to be performed. How Schein sees individual needs interacting with and matching organization needs is illustrated in Figure 9.

During this two-way process, employees are also interact-

Figure 8. A Three-Dimensional Model of an Organization.

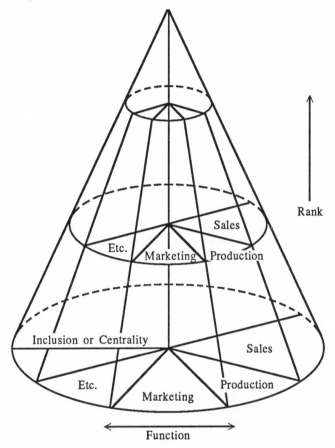

Source: Schein, 1971, p. 404.

ing with the work environment to create occupational self-con-
cepts—self-perceived talents and abilities, motives and needs,
and attitudes and values—that act as career anchors, driving and
constraining career decisions and choices. For example, when
employees move into positions that are not congruent with
their needs or that compromise their values, they are pulled
back, or anchored, to a more congruent choice. The five anchors
Schein identifies include technical/functional competence (concern with exercising technical abilities), managerial competence

Figure 9. Career and Development Stages.

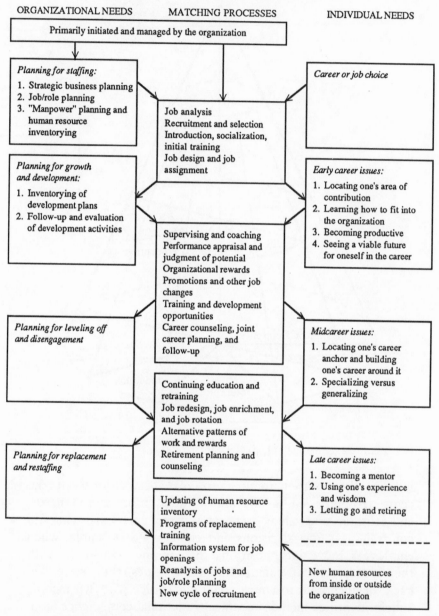

ORGANIZATIONAL NEEDS   MATCHING PROCESSES   INDIVIDUAL NEEDS

Primarily initiated and managed by the organization

Planning for staffing:
1. Strategic business planning
2. Job/role planning
3. "Manpower" planning and human resource inventorying

Career or job choice

Job analysis
Recruitment and selection
Introduction, socialization, initial training
Job design and job assignment

Planning for growth and development:
1. Inventorying of development plans
2. Follow-up and evaluation of development activities

Early career issues:
1. Locating one's area of contribution
2. Learning how to fit into the organization
3. Becoming productive
4. Seeing a viable future for oneself in the career

Supervising and coaching
Performance appraisal and judgment of potential
Organizational rewards
Promotions and other job changes
Training and development opportunities
Career counseling, joint career planning, and follow-up

Planning for leveling off and disengagement

Midcareer issues:
1. Locating one's career anchor and building one's career around it
2. Specializing versus generalizing

Continuing education and retraining
Job redesign, job enrichment, and job rotation
Alternative patterns of work and rewards
Retirement planning and counseling

Planning for replacement and restaffing

Late career issues:
1. Becoming a mentor
2. Using one's experience and wisdom
3. Letting go and retiring

Updating of human resource inventory
Programs of replacement training
Information system for job openings
Reanalysis of jobs and job/role planning
New cycle of recruitment

New human resources from inside or outside the organization

Source: Edgar Schein, *Career Dynamics,* © 1978, Addison-Wesley, Inc., Reading, Mass., p. 201. Figure 15.1. Reprinted with permission.

(concern with task, challenge, and responsibility), security and stability (concern with establishing trust in the organization), creativity (concern with creating a product or process), and autonomy and independence (concern with freedom from organizational constraints).

The value and strength of Schein's model lie in its view of the reciprocity between individuals and organizations, particularly as illustrated in Figure 9. The set of matching processes listed in the figure can strengthen career development programs. The link between the organization's planning components and the individual's career stages can effectively be used to integrate organization and individual needs. In addition, the questionnaire Schein developed to identify career anchors is a useful diagnostic tool to help employees assess their fit with organization needs.

Organization Theory: Summary Implications. Organization theory suggests several key points to be considered:

- Matching processes for organization and individual needs can be used or created to ensure a best fit between employees and positions, which benefits both organizations and individuals.
- In a career development program, links with human resource structures are of great importance.
- Assessment concepts such as career anchors are helpful for matching people to jobs as well as to short-term project teams.

A Final Word

Which theory or theories will be most useful for which career development effort or system? It depends on the specific needs and target groups, human resource structures, and organization culture that need to be accommodated, on whether a system or a single intervention is being designed. Certainly, exploring these theories—and others—provides a broader and more solid base for the essential visions of the future.

Chapter Five

Selecting Effective Employee Interventions

"Successful people have at least one experience in common. Somewhere, sometime, someone cared about their growth and development" (Miller, 1981, p. 47).

Career development interventions for employees abound. Which will work best to connect employees with those persons who will spur them on, to bring success for each employee, to produce growth and development? The second task in determining new directions and possibilities is to choose employee interventions.

Many of the criteria that can guide the decision already have been considered: the specific needs and key target groups (Chapter One), available human resource structures (Chapter Two), the kinds of support to expect from the organization's culture (Chapter Three), and a realistic vision and the implications of theories and models (Chapter Four). Other criteria include the program designer's expertise and familiarity with the various interventions and available resources and budget.

What should be clear from the overview of theories, in Chapter Four, is that multiple interventions should be considered, because employees in any target group will most probably differ in development and career stage, if not in learning style. In addition, differences in culture among and within organiza-

94

tions also calls for multiple interventions. In general, only a wide array of strategies, techniques, and approaches will uncover the best interventions for career development within the unique setting of each organization and provide employees with what they want most: interventions that fit best with their own styles of learning and stages of development.

This chapter first describes a four-question framework for focusing precisely on the career skills and learnings that target employees need. This model serves as a guide for the design and conceptualization of appropriate interventions. Subsequent sections discuss the three major categories of interventions: group activities, support-oriented activities, and self-directed activities.

What Targeted Employees Need: Four Critical Questions

For effective career development, employees must acquire several kinds of career skills or learning. Crites (1973) describes these as self-appraisal, occupational information, goal selection, planning, and problem solving. Holland (1973) sees the required career skills as self-assessment, environmental assessment, and action planning.

The model in this section, based upon these necessities and extensive interviews with employees and managers, is built on four questions:

- Who am I?
- How am I seen?
- What are my alternatives and goals?
- How can I achieve my goals?

Because employees must fully answer these four critical questions if they are to plan their careers successfully, the questions are used in designing and conceptualizing effective interventions. For example, the program can begin with such interventions as counseling, project teams, or resource centers. In them, employees can learn skills and strategies related to the four questions, so that they will understand the notion of best fit, so that they will appreciate the importance of answering the questions in order, and so that they can be sensitized to the notion of setting multiple goals within the context of current organizational realities. Managers also play key roles in helping employees explore these four critical questions. (Ways to make sure managers are involved are discussed in Chapter Six.)

Who Am I? The first question is directed toward making a self-statement. Self-knowledge, self-assessment, is basic to career planning. What employees consider as they answer this question are follow-ups to such statements as:

- "I'm not sure what I'm good at."
- "I've reached a dead end in this job. I don't know what to do."
- "I don't seem to enjoy my work anymore. I'm considering whether I'd fit better somewhere else."
- "The extra demands I have at home right now seem to interfere with my work. I need help balancing everything."

Interventions can be designed to give employees help in identifying their values, interests, strengths, and skills.

How Am I Seen? This second question focuses on reality checking. Employees need feedback on their performance and their potential based on their self-statements. What they explore here are such questions as:

- "I don't feel as if I'm effective in my job. What could I do to improve my performance?"
- "Does my manager think I'm ready for a promotion?"
- "Do my colleagues and my manager see me the same way I see myself?"

Interventions can be planned that help employees get needed validation and information from their managers and find out if their managers and fellow employees see them in the same way they see themselves.

What Are My Alternatives and Goals? The third question aims at investigating options and setting goals. Employees need to get information about the possibilities in the organization by asking such questions as:

- "What other career areas or options am I suited for?"
- "What areas in the organization are growing or declining?"
- "What would happen if I refused a promotion?"
- "What jobs are available?"
- "What are the implications of future changes in the organization for the work in my department?"

Interventions can be designed to help employees decide what makes sense in view of the information they have gathered about themselves and their options, so that they can set realistic, obtainable goals.

How Can I Achieve My Goals? The fourth question leads to making a career development plan. Employees need to detail the specific steps required to carry out their plans, to make their goals a reality. Interventions can be designed to help them answer such questions as:

- "How do I find out about training opportunities?"
- "How do I move from one department to another?"
- "How can I get more responsibility and more recognition in the job I have?"
- "How do I sell myself to a prospective manager?"

Employee Interventions: What Is Possible

Many kinds of interventions are available to help employees answer the four questions; that is, to help them gain self-understanding (including assessing their skills, abilities, values, preferences), solicit feedback, study the organization, set career goals, and undertake development activities. A convenient framework for viewing employee interventions, as new directions and possibilities are designed and conceptualized, separates them into three general approaches or broad categories:

- *Group activities:* Interventions in which individuals work in groups to learn about and plan for career development
- *Support-oriented activities:* Interventions in which one individual is assisted by another in career development planning and implementation
- *Self-directed activities:* Interventions in which career development activities can be undertaken by an employee working strictly alone

Creative combinations of activities also can be developed from some or all of these three categories to form still other categories of self-tailored activities. Figure 10 demonstrates the interrelationship among these categories and the gen-

Figure 10. Interaction of Career Development Activities.

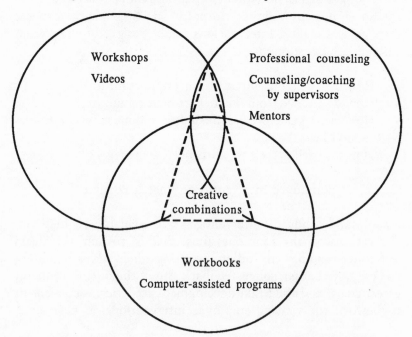

Workshops
Videos

Professional counseling
Counseling/coaching
  by supervisors
Mentors

Creative
combinations

Workbooks
Computer-assisted programs

eral activities that may be undertaken with each. Each of these categories and activities will be described in the following sections.

Group Activities

Among group activities are such interventions as workshops, formal training sessions, informal discussion groups, videos, and project teams. This section explores two of these: workshops and videos.

Workshops

Workshops are the most widely used group activity intervention for encouraging employees to think about and plan for their future progress. In a recent survey of career development techniques, 78 percent of organizations reported using career planning seminars or workshops (Gutteridge and Otte, 1983).

Workshops also have a great potential for setting the stage for other interventions. With an integrative approach, for example, employees might be asked to complete a workbook or career preference test and then attend a workshop; or they might be given the workbook at the end of the workshop, so that they can further investigate special career considerations on their own.

Workshop Advantages. Workshops get the message across to large numbers of people at one time—which means that costs are lower per employee than other types of interventions. The workshop setting, with its small group work and reliance on participant interaction, can inspire valuable networks and support among peers, even across the boundaries of job levels and functions. The workshop setting is also a source of vital information on career planning and the organization in general, particularly when participants work in different areas. Further, by career planning in the company of others, employees can take advantage of "groupthink," about career futures in general as well as about their own personal abilities and interests.

Workshop Disadvantages. Not everybody flowers in a group. Workshops best engage those participants who work well in groups; others may feel overwhelmed. With many people addressing the same topic together, time may not be sufficient to attend to each and every individual's need or questions. Some participants may not get enough "air time" to express opinions or concerns. Workshops have to start someplace, but that place may not be right for everybody. Some participants may need more preparation and background information than the workshop starting point assumes. Mismatch can be a problem in workshops if participants work in small groups or pairs with people too dissimilar for real mutual benefit. Workshops cannot be scheduled to best meet the work or personal needs of every participant, and because workshop participants may need to be away from their jobs for a large block of time, their managers may discourage participation. Finally, workshops are delivered only once and therefore do not encourage follow-up and continued learning and practice.

Workshop Components. Most frequently, the workshop allows groups of employees to work collectively on career and life planning issues. A career development workshop, or series of workshops, generally lasts one to five days and may launch a comprehensive effort that will ultimately include additional interventions.

The first workshop component imparts information to employees about the career development process, then quickly moves to exercises that help individuals answer the first question (Who am I?) by defining their skills, experiences, personal attitudes, and career preferences. This self-analysis results in individual self-statements, and participants are generally afforded ample opportunity to discuss their personal assessments.

The second workshop component involves checking the reality of the personal profile information developed in the first component. Employees are encouraged to check out their self-perceptions with others in the organization or in their personal network who can give them accurate, candid feedback. One effective method is to suggest that, before they ask for such feedback, employees consider what they think others may say. Employees should be encouraged to seek feedback from superiors and as many others as possible.

The third component forms a transition to goal setting. It includes an organization study in order to emphasize to employees that understanding their own environment and context is critical in selecting appropriate career goals. Written materials —from organization charts to reports on strategic plans—and information about future trends, pressing problems, and organization norms and culture may be presented by organization representatives and then discussed by employees to determine implications for their career futures.

The fourth workshop component centers on selecting career goals, testing these goals on others, and receiving help in formulating goals that are specific and attainable. In selecting goals, workshop participants need to be made aware that upward movement is not necessarily synonymous with career goals. In addition to vertical moves are lateral moves (for individuals who want to broaden their experience), job enrichment (by increased challenge, greater exposure, use of new competencies, and other experiences that build toward the future), temporary exploratory moves (to learn more about the organizational options and clarify future choices), realignment moves (downward in the organization to a different career track), and relocation moves (out of the organization).

Key Questions in Conducting Career Development Workshops. When an employee career development workshop is conducted, the following key questions should be resolved as early as possible—although answers will be affected, and altered, depending on the specific needs and key target groups:

- *Should participants comprise a homogeneous or heterogeneous group?* Taking employees from one level or type of work may seem to increase the peer aspect of the workshop and generate ease and comfort during discussions. However, heterogeneous groups can contribute a wider range of organizational experience to any given discussion and enrich the collective learning about the organizational environment.

- *How should employees be selected to participate?* The two major selection methods are self-selection and selection by managers. Employee self-selection generally results in participation by those who are motivated to undertake career development, although it could draw some employees who simply want a break from work routine. It also means that employees who might benefit most may not attend, and control of the number or mix of participants may be difficult. Selection by managers, on the other hand, means that some employees who desire and could benefit from career development workshops may not be selected, because they are needed at the workplace, because the manager is unable to assess accurately the benefits of the workshop, or because the manager fears losing them. While this selection approach involves managers in the career development of their employees, it may have drawbacks in terms of widely dissimilar, even inequitable, selection procedures by various managers.

• *Should workshops be scheduled on the organization's time or the employees' time?* Both the organization and the employee stand to benefit from career development; therefore, an arrangement for shared time usually seems most equitable. When both contribute time to the process, it is likely that both will feel committed to realizing its fullest possible benefits.

• *How can momentum for career development be maintained after the workshop?* Action plans that truly are action oriented, with built-in steps and timetables for implementation, will help motivate follow-up but generally are not enough in themselves. One of the best ways to maintain career development momentum is to build a system that keeps participants in contact with those who can encourage them to implement plans; for example, project teams or task groups drawn from participants and others to work on organizational issues that affect career development, or support groups that meet regularly to discuss progress and problems in career development activities.

Videos

A video is a particularly valuable intervention when an organization seeks to introduce a large number of employees to career development in a relatively short time and in a very consistent manner. All employees see and hear exactly the same message. However, although videos are effective, and cost effective, for explaining and introducing career development, they should not be the only approach. Videos cannot substitute for other approaches in actually implementing career development, and, at their best, they are combined with such other interventions as workshop group discussions, workbooks, and career counseling.

For example, when National Semiconductor used a video to introduce its managers worldwide to career development, it also used pre- and postviewing discussions, structured according to a Video Leader's Guide, which included a format for generating participant activities and questions. These brief pre- and postvideo workshops consolidated and multiplied the effectiveness of the video's content, which included a discussion of the organization's philosophy, a message from the president of the corporation, an explanation of a career development model, pointers on how to and how not to implement career development, and skits on what makes for good and poor development discussions. The video was further supported by such other interventions as career paths, job posting, training programs, tuition reimbursement policies, and performance appraisal systems.

Support-Oriented Activities

Support-oriented activities, in which an employee can discuss career issues with just one other concerned individual, are highly beneficial. Many employees feel more comfortable discussing their career development with a single knowledgeable person rather than in larger groups, which may seem intimidating. In addition, given the variety of ages, career and development stages, and needs, employees often require tailor-made advice on starting or maintaining their career development.

But this type of career guidance requires intensive use of staff and time and cannot reach as many employees as quickly as group activities. This means that such support-oriented activities as career counseling and mentoring, both of which are discussed in this section, are best utilized in combination with one or more other interventions.

Career Counseling

Career counseling can be undertaken at any or all steps in the four-question career development model described earlier in this chapter. As just noted, since resources are rarely sufficient to guide each employee personally through all that must be accomplished to complete each step, counseling is most often used as an effective supplement to such other interventions as workshops, workbooks, and videos.

Unfortunately, the very term *counseling* can cause resistance among those for whom it signifies psychotherapy and is thus reserved for those with "problems," according to Gutteridge and Otte (1983). When this is the case, some individuals will be reluctant to use this intervention. Possible solutions include multiple interventions—and use of the term *career discussion* instead of *career counseling* (Gutteridge and Otte use them interchangeably).

Furthermore, career counseling is often viewed as facilitating the career development process, rather than actually being the process. For example, as Meckel (1981, p. 65) elaborates, "Every person is concerned with the question What do I want to do with my life? The process of deciding one's career goals is difficult, and it is not easy to arrive at a satisfactory answer alone. Appropriate career counseling facilitates this process. Because of an increase in the number of choices available, changes in the meaning of work, emphasis on satisfaction and recognition, etc., career counseling is especially needed now to help persons cope with and utilize their new opportunities."

Career counseling, or career discussions, may be undertaken by counselors outside the employee's immediate workplace—either professionals from outside the organization or personnel on the organization staff—or by managers, who discuss career development with those they supervise. A survey by Gutteridge and Otte (1983) found that nearly 75 percent of those using career counseling relied on personnel within the organization, either specialized counseling staff or staff in personnel or training departments who performed counseling duties part time. Approximately 13 percent used career discussions by managers; only about 3 percent relied on external counseling staff; and others used some combination of these counseling arrangements.

Using Professional Counselors. Professional career counselors, even those with other personnel-related duties within the organization, have at least some training or experience in this capacity, in contrast to managers acting as counselors. They also have distance. Since they do not work directly with those employees they counsel, they are often able to create an atmosphere of greater ease and candor. In addition, individuals being counseled feel that a professional knows more and can be taken seriously.

Professional career counselors, however, must start at a point where they know little about the employee and his or her work environment. They must probe for information—and they get only one view of the situation at hand. They are frequently not able to do much follow-up because of their counseling load.

Using Manager Counselor/Coaches. Managers who act as career counselors, or coaches, are most often knowledgeable about the employee and his or her demonstrated abilities, past experiences, and skills. They also are quite knowledgeable about the work environment and the developmental activities within it. In addition, they are able to check back frequently on the employee's career development progress, to facilitate as well as advise career directions.

Many employees, however, may not want to open up to their managers and may be wary about ramifications of counseling sessions. They may also have a hard time taking seriously advice that comes from a nonprofessional. Further, even with a comprehensive effort to interest and train all managers in employee career counseling, which can produce extensive and relatively inexpensive coverage through an organization, not all managers are skillful in conducting career discussions and helping employees undertake the steps in the development process. Some managers will excel to a greater degree than others; some will simply decide they have neither the time nor the interest to utilize what they have learned.

Yet it is essential to make every effort to involve managers in this way. One of the characteristics of an effective career development effort, according to research by Souerwine (1981), is that it always incorporates discussion between managers and employees, particularly for reality checking. Among the benefits employees receive when coached by their managers on career development are better understanding of their personal strengths and weaknesses, access to current information that keys them to future opportunities within the organization, feelings of greater commitment to organizational purpose, more open communication with managers about developmental possibilities, and a recognition that career growth begins on the current job. (Ways to involve and prepare managers for counseling are described in Chapter Seven.)

A Career Counseling Model. In career counseling, probing questions, discussion, and advice are used to lead the employee to undertake the career development steps (as in the four-question model), verbally or in writing. Figure 11 shows the natural flow of counseling questions and how they relate to the career development steps, from self-assessment (Who am I?) to implementation (How can I achieve my goals?). Workbooks, self-assessment tests, and background materials about career development and the organization are useful supplements to the counseling discussions.

The counseling itself, according to Burack and Mathys (1980), generally progresses through three major stages: opening and probing (rapport is established; the counselor particularly needs to use effective listening skills in order to promote a discussion of ideas and values), understanding and focusing (the employee is assisted in self-assessment and planning; the counselor helps the employee develop goals and plans for his or her career future and check them against reality), and programming (support is provided for implementing activities toward career goals; the employee knows that someone cares about his or her progress).

Whether professionals or managers, career counselors for employees need skills to facilitate each of the counseling stages. It is particularly important to structure the counseling in such a

Figure 11. Career Counseling Model.

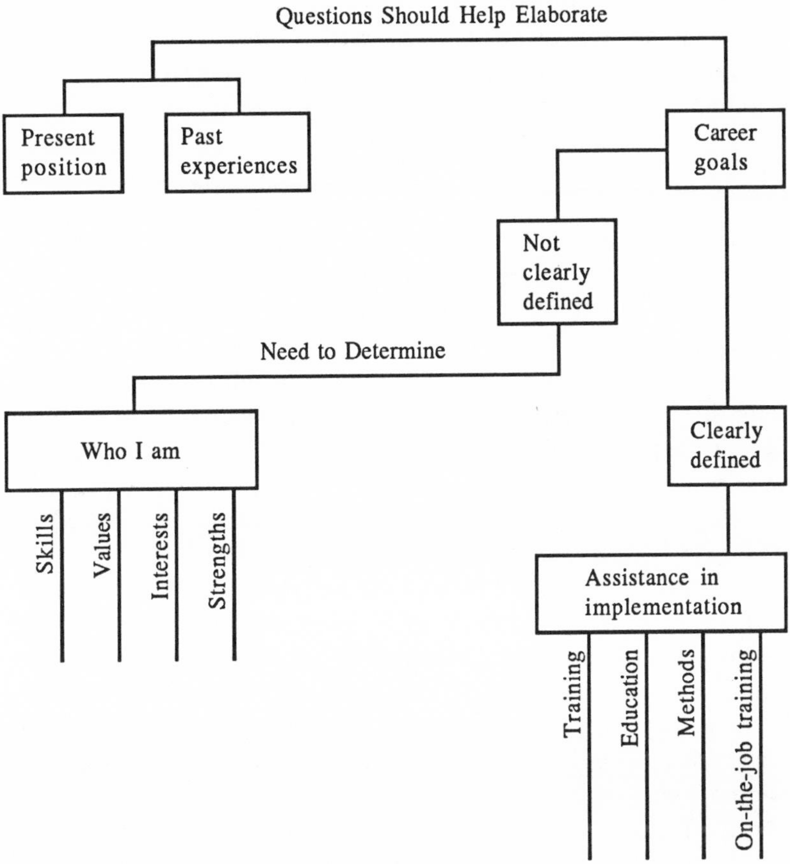

Questions Should Help Elaborate

Present position	Past experiences				Career goals

Not clearly defined

Need to Determine

Who I am

Skills   Values   Interests   Strengths

Clearly defined

Assistance in implementation

Training   Education   Methods   On-the-job training

way as to emphasize activities to follow up the one-on-one discussions.

Mentoring

Although interventions such as workshops and counseling can encourage development and teach employees how to take initiative and pursue plans, they may not get employees to take action. Many employees need a link between the plan and the payoff. A mentor, by offering continuous support, caring, and advice, often can create that link.

The word *mentor* has been defined and redefined in books and articles on the subject. Levinson (1978), for example, says that the term is most often used to mean teacher, adviser, or sponsor. He enumerates the roles of the mentor as teacher (to help increase skills and abilities), sponsor (to assist in career entry and advancement), host and guide (to acquaint an individual with key people and the organization culture in general), exemplar (to provide a model whom the protégé employee may emulate), and counsel (to offer support and advice).

Most mentor situations are informal relationships between two people who work together, generally initiated by the mentor. These informal situations usually have the advantage that a level of trust and comfort is established, or at least sensed, even before real mentoring begins. However, they have the disadvantage of benefiting only those fortunate individuals who somehow stumble into them. Other employees simply may not happen to work around individuals who are prepared or willing to be mentors.

Setting up formal mentoring arrangements can assure inclusion of greater numbers of employees. These formal programs generally require some training of volunteer organization veterans, who form a pool of mentors to be assigned to relatively new employees. Much of the involvement of mentors with employee protégés, even under a formalized system, entails informal encouragement and coaching, although it may also include meeting in structured sessions and learning situations, where mentors carry out specific assignments with their employee protégés.

Mentoring benefits the employee protégés, the mentors themselves, and the organization. Employee protégés benefit from mentoring through increased access to informal communication networks, relatively objective assessment of their strengths and weaknesses, encouragement for career development, positive reinforcement for achievement, increased understanding of the formal and informal networks in the organization, advice and feedback about developmental activities, expanded opportunities for visibility, and an expanded network of contacts who can be key to career development. Mentors gain through psychological rewards for developing talent, new insights into organizational issues, and expanded personal and professional networks. Organizations stand to benefit by establishing motivation and loyalty early in an employee's career, as well as a system for passing on organization norms and goals.

Mentoring, however, may not be right for every organization. For example, when mentors are assigned to protégés they do not know, the essential good chemistry may not develop. Volunteer mentors may be disappointed over what they can deliver in the program because of the limited time available. Or mentors assigned to several employee protégés may find it difficult to meet the differing needs of each protégé. In addition, a formal mentor program may perpetuate the myth that having a mentor is the only route to success, causing jealousy among those employees who have not been assigned to mentors.

The organization that is willing to work to overcome limitations of mentor programs can accrue substantial payoffs if the program is designed carefully. Among the principles for success of a mentor program are the following:

- Assure that participation of mentors is strictly voluntary.
- Allow mentors freedom to work with employee protégés in ways that best suit their own styles and time constraints.
- Develop, through mentor-protégé assignments, arrangements that maximize networking possibilities for the employee protégés.
- Assure that mentors and employee protégés share their expectations, in order to reduce problems of overly high expectations.
- Develop rewards, especially through feedback and visibility, for mentors.
- Keep the manager of the employee protégé closely informed about program activities and individual development.

Self-Directed Activities

Self-directed activities put the responsibility for working on career development squarely on the shoulders of the employees themselves by allowing employees to tailor the career development process to their own needs and to undertake career development at their own pace in accordance with their own desires.

Most organizations with career development programs provide an organizing framework within which employees map out their own developmental strategies. The framework can be a single workbook that guides exercises and plots steps or a sophisticated career resource center that includes video presentations, self-administered inventories, background reading, and other aids to self-direction. More and more frequently today, the framework for helping employees plot and pace their own career development is provided by a computer. These three self-directed activity frameworks are discussed in this section.

In addition to the obvious advantage that motivated employees can participate in career development at their own speed and selection, an organization that relies on self-directed activities requires a lower commitment of financial and personnel resources than might otherwise be necessary. In fact, self-directed activities make it possible for some organizations to even contemplate career development programs for their employees.

But self-directed activities are not for every employee or every organization. Some employees will not have the necessary motivation. Others require verbal feedback and communication in order to progress; therefore, unless self-directed activities are combined with other interventions, these employees may have nowhere to turn for assistance or for additional materials. Further, the lack of visibility of self-directed activities in an organization can also be a drawback. Success may not be readily apparent—and it can be difficult to involve managers.

As with other interventions, self-directed activities are most effective when they are appropriate to the organization and precisely designed for target groups.

Workbooks

Workbooks for self-directed career development activities can be developed within the organization, or off-the-shelf publications prepared for general organization settings can be used.

Both kinds include diagnostic materials that allow employees to assess their own strengths, weaknesses, skills, and work preferences and assignments that require employees to map their career paths to date, clarify goals, and develop plans for action.

Workbooks that are developed for a specific organization tailor their information and exercises to the organization and include the following items (see Burack and Mathys, 1980, pp. 234–235):

1. A statement of career policy, procedures, organization, and the means by which people can secure information
2. World-of-work vocabulary, covering terms such as job analysis, job description, wage structure, appraisal, assessment
3. General orientation to organization job structure, career paths, and general job qualifications
4. Orientation to the career exercises and skills needed in conjunction with the exercises
5. Skill exercises for
   Developing goals and values
   Developing means of achieving goals
   Developing alternatives
   Selecting among alternatives and evaluating them
   Expressing personal preferences
   Determining priorities
   Forming career paths
6. Planning exercises on
   Life goals
   Personal preferences, likes, and dislikes
   Priorities
   Work goals (general)
   Job goals and alternatives
   Time planning
7. Reference sources, including names, addresses, and phone numbers

Workbooks are most often used in combination with one or more other career development interventions, including counseling, workshops, and meetings to explain why the organization believes that career development is important. For example, a large telecommunications organization offers a career management program that supplements three sequential employee workbooks with discussion periods, in which managers meet with individual employees at least three times to discuss self-assessment, goal setting, and development planning. Completion of the first booklet leads to a personal profile detailing employee skills, values, interests, and style. Using the second workbook, employees compare their profiles against requirements of certain positions and identify two career targets. The third workbook guides employees in the creation of a detailed action plan based on their career goals and information drawn from various developmental activities. Managers are also provided with a booklet to guide them in working with employees.

Career Resource Centers

Most often, career resource centers are set up at a central location to serve as the focus for all employee self-directed career development. An array of skills inventories, planning exercises, and audio and video presentations allow employees to learn about career development, understand their own organization (including its opportunities and limitations), conduct realistic self-assessment, and plan for future careers. These materials are arranged sequentially and designed to maximize employees' initiative in working through the career development activities at their own pace.

For example, a career resource center at General Electric takes employees step by step through the four-question model described earlier in this chapter by utilizing five major stations, each aimed at a crucial step in the career development process (see Figure 12).

The orientation station familiarizes employees with the career development process and encourages those who may be skeptical, possibly through a video presentation and background literature. Station A provides self-scored inventories and other materials that allow employees to understand their values, interests, skills, and abilities. At Station B, which may incorporate the organization's performance appraisal system, employees

Figure 12. Career Resource Center Stations.

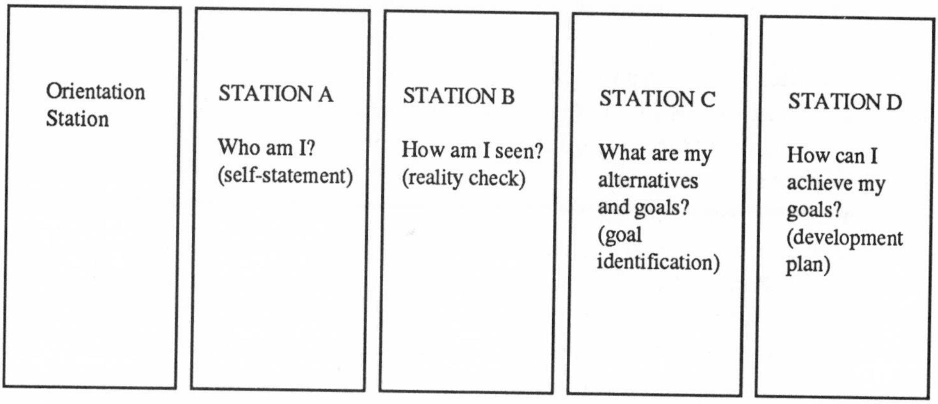

Orientation Station	STATION A Who am I? (self-statement)	STATION B How am I seen? (reality check)	STATION C What are my alternatives and goals? (goal identification)	STATION D How can I achieve my goals? (development plan)

complete forms and lists that require them to determine how others perceive their performance. Station C is tailored to the organization and provides materials such as career paths, organizational charts, department descriptions, projections of future personnel needs, and job skills requirements—all aimed at helping employees study the organization and determine the alternatives within it. This information, plus data collected at other stations, allows employees to set realistic goals for career development. Finally, at Station D, employees complete activities that require them to translate personal knowledge and career goals into plans for action (Kaye and others, 1984).

Computer-Assisted Programs

Computers, with their capability to provide and store information in a fast, compact, consistent, and accurate manner, can be used to assist self-directed career development activities by, for example, quickly scoring self-assessment surveys and displaying organization charts, career paths, and results of hypothetical career changes. Computers can also be programmed to facilitate the entire career development workbook process, interacting with personal data entered by the employee, giving answers to questions usually reserved for professional counselors, human resource specialists, or managers. This kind of programming is particularly useful for organizations that want to reach employees on swing shifts or in remote locations and that see computer-assisted interventions as quick, familiar, and easily accessible. Other organizations may see computer programs and interventions as inappropriate and impersonal.

Computer-assisted career development will, of course, work best in organizations that already have a general commitment to computerization, as well as the appropriate equipment. A major consideration continues to be compatibility among the many, and still proliferating, types of computers and the available software programs. Nevertheless, the use of computer-assisted career development is likely to expand in the near future, and it is an employee intervention that must be considered and planned for. Three successful, available computer-assisted interventions are OCIPS, DISCOVER, and MATCH.

OCIPS. The U.S. Army Research Institute for the Behavioral and Social Sciences sponsored the development of the Officer Career Information and Planning System (OCIPS) to provide officers with information about the U.S. Army and assist their professional development through reviewing such areas as aptitudes, training, interests, and experience. OCIPS consists of computer-aided experiences that allow officers to learn the principles of career planning, understand career progression systems, gain access to data relevant to career choices, undertake self-assessment exercises, set forth goals, and develop implementation plans.

DISCOVER. This software package contains five major modules integrated with specific organizational data: (1) Understanding Career Development and Change uses interactive exercises and a questionnaire to identify levels of job satisfaction and career stages; (2) Assessing Yourself identifies interests, skills, and work-related values; (3) Gathering Information develops a personal information needs profile and indicates where the appropriate information may be found; (4) Making Decisions sets goals based on a decision matrix utilizing information from the Assessing Yourself module; and (5) Taking Action develops an action plan and provides information needed for next steps (Harris-Bowlsbey, Leibowitz, and Forrer, 1982).

MATCH. Matching [one's own] Attributes to Career Happiness is divided into six segments: motivation, satisfiers, skills analysis, wants and wishes, prioritizing, and deciding and summarizing. These segments, which can be used all at once or in several sessions, are based on three precepts. First, each of us is very different in personal skills, individual motivations, and what really turns us on at work. Second, many of us spend too much time doing work that does not suit us, even though we may have become skilled at that work. Third, the best indicator of what we really like and are good at is what we have done well in the past and done with zest (Waterman, 1985).

Narrowing Down

Selecting the most effective and appropriate intervention from among the myriad available can seem confounding. The matrix in Exhibit 4 may help narrow the choices based on actual circumstances. General categories of interventions are already entered into the matrix, as are a few other interventions mentioned in Chapter One's discussion of specific target groups. (Referring back to that section of Chapter One may further narrow down the list.) Blanks are provided to add further and specific interventions under consideration. By entering the vision created for the specific needs and target group and then considering which category and kind of intervention best match those needs and that group, we are in a better position to achieve that vision and meet those needs.

A Final Word

This chapter began with a four-question model that can be used as a framework for designing and conceptualizing employee interventions. Whatever the group targeted for career development, its members need to answer these questions through self-assessment, reality checking, goal setting, and plan-

Exhibit 4. Intervention Assessment Matrix.

Instructions: In the left-hand column, list specific problems/needs and target groups. Rank the possible interventions for each problem on a scale of 1 to 5 (1 = unlikely to contribute to the solution of the problem; 5 = extremely likely to contribute to the solution of the problem).

Vision (for specific problems/needs and target groups)	Group Activities			Self-Directed Activities			Support-Oriented Activities			Other		
	Workshops	Videos		Workbooks	Career resource center	Computer-assisted programs	Counseling by professionals	Coaching by managers	Mentors	Orientation programs	Job enrichment	

ning next steps. The chapter also provided an overview of general approaches to consider (group activities such as workshops, support-oriented activities such as counseling, self-directed activities such as workbooks) and a matrix for narrowing down the choices.

Most important to remember is that a single intervention will rarely do the whole job. Creative combinations must be tailored, for example, to meet the needs of technical employees at different stages in their careers. Although so many different interventions are possible that they may seem overwhelming to those who must determine new directions and possibilities, this is also a blessing. Many career development efforts succeed and continue only because of the multiple choices available to meet multiple needs.

Chapter Six

Involving Managers in Employee Career Development

> "I'm too busy to think about the careers of my employees. I need to get the work out; besides, who looks out for my career? I've gotten to where I am on my own."

Despite such complaints, more and more managers today are being called upon to play an active role in the career development of their employees. For example, Washington Gas, as one component of its career management system, offers a career development seminar that both managers and employees attend. Aerospace Corporation uses middle managers as members of project advisory groups. Digital Corporation has a policy of having managers go through a career development program before their employees do. Gillette puts managers through three phases of its career program—involvement in a career life planning class, participation in a career discussion program for managers, and attendance at a skill development center for managers—before their employees participate. Rolm uses middle managers not only to design and develop its career development program but also to teach other managers about the process. These and other organizations are emphasizing the role of managers in career development because organizations in which managers help employees with career issues have realized a number of important benefits: better matches between employee abilities and organization needs, an identified pool of manager talent, increased attractiveness of the organization to potential employees, advancement from within, reinforcement and improvement of existing personnel systems, and improved long-range planning and forecasting.

Manager involvement is also, in fact, vital to the success of any career development system. As indicated in Chapter Five's discussion of counseling by managers, effective career development efforts always include a dialogue between manager and subordinates about the individual's career goals and how they match or do not match organizational reality (Souerwine, 1981). Because managers know the organization and "its philosophy, history, procedures, and its people, sources of information, help, [they are] in a position to make a realistic appraisal of organizational opportunities, timing, and possible limitations from both a factual and subjective basis" for their employees (Meckel, 1981, p. 65). They also know how their employees behave on the job over long periods of time as well as day to day (Bowen and Hall, 1977).

In this chapter, we explore how to tap this expertise, how to stimulate manager involvement in the career development of their employees, how to complete this third task in determining new directions and possibilities.

Helping Managers Get Ready to Assume Their Career Development Responsibilities

Managers need to assume a group of responsibilities—roles and behaviors—that will enable their employees to determine their own career development. When they have assumed these responsibilities, managers report that they have gained increased productivity in their own work groups, a reputation in the organization as a "people developer," increased confidence in their abilities to solve problems with employees on personal issues, and more focused development activities.

In fact, these career development roles and behaviors are an extension and enhancement of such traditional managerial functions as

Providing forums for discussion
Providing support and opportunities
Giving clear feedback about what employees should rea-
    sonably expect
Identifying employee potential
Providing growth opportunities consistent with employee
    and organization goals
Communicating the formal and informal realities of the
    organization
Providing exposure to employees
Linking employees to appropriate resources and resource
    individuals

These roles and behaviors are also highly consistent with
newer models of management behavior. Participative management models (Ouchi, 1981; Kanter, 1983), for example, point
to how critical interpersonal skills are in dealing with employees.
The shift described by Bradford and Choen (1984) from the
"heroic" model of management (which stresses managing, motivating, controlling, and coordinating employees) to a manager-
as-developer model (which emphasizes shared management responsibility) also indicates that managers in contemporary
organizations are moving to more interpersonal, consultative
patterns. Still other models, corroborated by profiles of today's
top managers, emphasize the increasing importance of interpersonal skills as managers climb the career ladder, as illustrated
in Figure 13.
    Two other trends increase the importance of managers as-
suming career development responsibilities. Human resource
functions traditionally were centralized and largely controlled
by a clearly defined staff within the personnel department; but,
according to Pinto (1981), the present trend is toward greater
ownership of human resource functions by line organizations.
The second trend is caused by the new-value workers identified
by Yankelovich (1981), who press for self-fulfillment in their
work (as noted in the Introduction) and, therefore, are more
active in developing their own careers. Both trends require managers who want to be successful and effective to become involved in the careers of their employees.

Figure 13. The Skills Necessary at Various Levels of an Organization.

Skills Needed

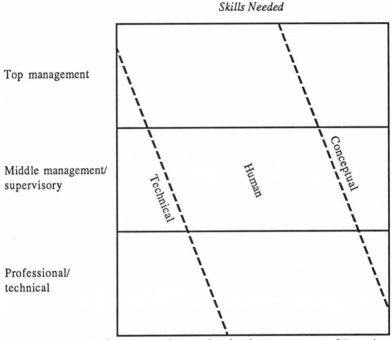

Source: Paul Hersey and Ken Blanchard, *Management of Organizational Behavior: Utilizing Human Resources,* 4th ed., © 1982, p. 6. Reprinted by permission of Prentice-Hall, Englewood Cliffs, New Jersey.

When they assume career development responsibilities, then, managers are benefiting themselves as much as they are benefiting their employees and the organization. Nevertheless, some managers refuse to realize the existence of these benefits, because involvement in employee career development may require changing long-established attitudes and behaviors. Counseling, for example, is a catalytic process rather than just giving advice (Miller, 1981). It means supporting an individual in the processes of self-assessment and goal setting and giving that employee "permission" to change instead of engaging in short, intense efforts to solve problems. It represents longer-term, more passive behavior than the generally "reactive" behavior that focuses only on final results.

Particularly those managers who once were technical employees will need a great deal of encouragement (see the discussion in Chapter One of programs assessing the movement of technical employees into management). These managers may feel quite uneasy in sessions with employees, which can lead to frustration and consequent rejection of career development (Byham, 1977).

One of the first steps to take is to educate managers about career development and explain, for example, that it includes several different kinds of movement (lateral, down, out— as well as up), that it is a way to keep their employees motivated, and that their role can be built into their everyday behavior. This helps explode the myths, identified by Souerwine (1981), that career planning is only for upward mobility, that individuals who stay in the same job too long are either not ambitious or will in the long run lose their motivation to keep performing effectively, that career planning is a waste of time for anyone but star performers, and that career planning is time consuming. Another first step is to consider the careers of the managers themselves.

The Manager's Own Career

This critical factor is often overlooked in thinking about the involvement of managers in the career development of their employees. Managers themselves progress through their own career cycle and, at certain times in that cycle, are in better positions to develop their employees. When managers are secure and confident, they generally feel strong enough to offer a helping hand to employees; but those who, for example, feel stuck in their own jobs or who are new to their roles may not be able to help others. We need to look at these and other career issues before we look at specific approaches and models for manager involvement.

The Plight of Middle Managers. This group is often characterized as caught in the middle. They have to balance employee needs against organization needs at the same time that they have to get the job done on time and within the budget, sometimes with scarce resources. They are expected to be in control of the situation and resourceful enough to devise solutions to whatever problems may arise; but they cannot always meet these expectations. As a result, middle managers often suffer from significant role isolation as well as the myth of competence, and their "discontent . . . is growing at an alarmingly unhealthy pace" (Opinion Research Corporation, 1980). Before these middle managers can become involved in employee career development, some of their problems should be addressed; for example, job redesign and an improved recognition system.

Plateaued Managers. In a longitudinal study of the lives and careers of AT&T managers, 422 participants were assessed between 1955 and 1960, with subsequent follow-ups eight and twenty years later. When scales were administered to assess the career expectations and the need for advancement of the 270 still active managers in the twentieth year of the study, it was evident that expectations as well as advancement desires had faded "gradually, gracefully, and, for the most part, fairly early" (Howard and Bray, 1980, p. 5). Two scales of the assessment—Achievement and Autonomy—were significant, and identified factors that could motivate these plateaued midcareer managers. This finding indicates that if there are opportunities for job challenge, task accomplishment, and freedom and independence, midcareer managers can continue to be motivated and productive. Involving these managers in career development could be beneficial for them as well as their employees.

Career Stage Relationships. The ability of the manager to meet the career needs of individual employees depends on the relationship between the manager's career stage and that of the employee, a relationship that changes over time. According to Baird and Kram (1983), as managers and employees progress through the career stages (establishment, advancement, maintenance, and withdrawal), each has specific personal needs that must be fulfilled by the other. Table 8 details what employees need from their managers and what managers need from their employees. It is noteworthy that only in the maintenance stage are managers psychologically prepared to provide the range of

Table 8. What Employees and Managers Need from Each Other
in Different Career Stages.

Career Stage	Employees' Personal Needs from Managers	Managers' Personal Needs from Employees
Establishment	Coaching Feedback Training A role model Acceptance and confirmation Protection	Technical support Psychological support
Advancement	Exposure Challenging work Sponsoring Counseling	Loyal fellowship
Maintenance	Autonomy Opportunities to develop others	Opportunities to mentor
Withdrawal	Consultative roles	Consultative roles

Source: Adapted from Baird and Kram, 1983.

support needed by employees, particularly those employees in early career stages; and when, for example, manager and employee are both in the establishment stage, the career development relationship will probably not be successful. Helping managers become familiar with the career stages they and their employees progress through can facilitate their involvement in career development.

Breyer's (1983) study of the level of managers' involvement in work relative to other important aspects of their lives seems to corroborate the difficulties of successful involvement in employee career development early in a manager's career. He found that, early in their careers, managers were under double stress because of high demands from both their families and their jobs. For middle and upper managers, Breyer found the relationship between these aspects of life complex and shifting. The most successful managers were those able to accommodate the shifts in needs.

New Managers. Those who have just become managers, and are in the establishment career stage, must proceed through five phases (and tasks) in order to take charge of their new role (Gabarro, 1985): taking hold (developing an understanding of the new situation, shaping an initial set of priorities, developing expectations and working relationships with employees), immersion (developing a deeper, finer-grained understanding of the situations and the people, reassessing priorities), reshaping (dealing with underlying causes of problems, being open to unanticipated problems), consolidation (following through on reshaping actions, remaining open to new developments), and refinement. Designing interventions to help new managers negotiate these phases and tasks that need to be accomplished during the establishment career stage will also help new managers understand that the transition to a management job is a long process.

Helping Managers Become Effective Career Developers

Can most managers become effective career developers? Probably yes; but, as is evident from looking at the manager career cycle and other issues, managers will be far more effective at some times and at some stages than at others. To promote effective involvement, we can educate managers about the benefits and realities, as opposed to myths, of career development. We can involve managers actively in career development by enlisting them in the data collection phase of a career development program (as suggested in Chapter One) and in its implementation. We can design interventions to help the careers of managers when they are plateaued or when they are new to the role. We can also help them develop career counseling and coaching skills.

Essential Skills: A Four-Role Model. To learn what behaviors distinguish managers who are effective career developers from those who are not, Leibowitz and Schlossberg (1981) held a series of "critical incident" interviews, in which employees were asked to describe how their managers had helped them with their careers. Comments indicating effective managerial behavior included:

- "He introduced me to other people in the field."

- "My supervisor worked behind the scenes on ways to help me move up."
- "I wasn't sure I could do the assignment, but she encouraged me to try it."
- "We would talk about what I would be doing in the future, not just about specific tasks."

From the interviews and subsequent data collection and factor analyses, four key roles for managers in career development were identified: coach, appraiser, adviser, and referral agent. The emphases of each of these roles are listed in Table 9.

Table 9. Emphases in the Manager's Four Roles.

Coach	Appraiser	Adviser	Referral Agent
Listens	Gives feedback	Generates options	Links employee to resources/ people
Clarifies	Clarifies standards		
Probes		Helps set goals	
Defines concerns	Clarifies job responsibilities	Recommends/ advises	Consults on action plan

A manager who is an effective career developer will use all four roles as appropriate, but each role relates particularly to one of the four critical questions that employees must ask in career development (and that, as suggested in Chapter Five, can be used in conceptualizing and designing employee interventions). Table 10 illustrates the relationship of the manager's role to the employee's question. The table also indicates a result or output required from the employee in order to answer the question, a result or output that ensures the success of the career discussion. The manager's behavior or skill varies according to his or her role.

In the role of *coach*, managers draw on their communication skills to assist employees in identifying strengths, weaknesses, interests, and values; that is, in answering the question "Who am I?" They maintain open communication, listen actively, and provide ongoing encouragement. At all times, they strive to encourage a two-way dialogue, asking questions that draw

Table 10. Career Development Model.

Employee Question	Manager Role	Result or Output from Employee
Who am I?	Coach	Self-statement
How am I seen?	Appraiser	Reality check
What are my alternatives and goals?	Adviser	Goal identification
How can I achieve my goals?	Referral Agent	Development plan

out and encourage employees to really think about themselves and their life experiences. Employees are expected to provide a self-assessment statement.

Important questions managers need to find answers for in the role of coach include

What are the employee's primary interests?
What are the employee's important career requirements? What does he or she value?
What are the employee's primary skills? How have they been exhibited?

In the role of *appraiser,* managers evaluate performance and relate it to potential opportunities. They seek to help employees answer the question "How am I seen?" They give specific, frequent, and timely feedback. They also back up their thoughts with specific examples of when, how, and where an employee may not have displayed the kind of behavior the manager felt was appropriate. The more opportunity a manager has to observe an employee, the more likely it is the manager will be comfortable in the role of an appraiser. Employees are expected to provide reality checks of their self-statements.

Questions to find answers for in the appraiser role include

What are the critical elements of the employee's job?
What standards are being used to judge the employee's performance?
How does the employee's current performance tie to future development?

In the role of *adviser,* managers provide employees with organizational information that will help them set multiple, realistic career goals; that is, help them answer the question "What are my alternatives and goals?" Managers who are able to share the knowledge they possess about the informal, as well as the formal, organization are particularly helpful in this role, especially when they shed light on opportunities and limitations inherent in the organization itself. By helping employees understand the value of multiple career goals, advisers help employees think about ways to move and grow in the organization. Employees are expected to list their identified goals.

Important questions to find answers for in the adviser role include

> What are the "hot" problems or trends in the organization that the employee must take into account in planning for professional growth?
> What are some unwritten rules in the organization that relate to career growth?
> What is the most appropriate professional development goal for the employee at this point?
> What would be an appropriate fallback goal?

In the role of *referral agent,* managers help employees develop action plans to meet their goals. That is, they help employees answer the question "How can I achieve my goals?" In this role, managers can provide advice on specific opportunities for exposure or visibility on the job. Managers can also refer employees to particular resources or training programs that can prepare them to meet their goals. Managers who are well informed about a host of development activities, and who have good connections in the organization, can be of great help to their subordinates in this role. Employees are expected to prepare action plans for achieving their goals.

Questions for managers to find answers for in the referral agent role include

> What primary obstacles keep the employee from achieving his or her goals?

What resources can be utilized?

What specifically must the employee do to pursue his or her goals?

What is the first step?

What is a reasonable deadline for completion of the first step?

What is a reasonable deadline for attaining the goal?

When will the next discussion take place?

Tying the Roles Together: A Discussion Framework. During any career discussion with their employees, managers will move in and out of each of the four roles, with the communication skills of the coach role particularly important throughout. A framework for tying the roles together within each career discussion with an employee is laid out in Table 11. The four steps

Table 11. Four Stages of a Career Discussion.

Steps	*Goal/Purpose*
Climate building	Establish a relaxed, open environment and a collaborative problem-solving atmosphere
Clarifying	Decide and agree on goals and time constraints
Collaborating	Manage a two-way discussion that achieves the agreed-upon goals
Closing	Gain clarification, commitment, and responsibility for next steps

(climate building, clarifying, collaborating, and closing) encompass a process that produces effective career discussions for the question (Who am I? How am I seen? What are my alternatives and goals? How can I achieve my goals?) focused upon. Using this framework will mean that managers are assured of progressing through essential discussion steps.

Sessions for Developing Role and Discussion Skills. To boost the counseling and coaching skills of their managers, many organizations put them through training programs. Most have certain basic dimensions and topics corresponding to the roles and framework just described. A program at Westinghouse (described by Miller, 1981), for example, included environment/ climate setting, enhancement of person/job fit, provision of timely and accurate performance feedback, provision of support for self-assessment, and provision of information about alternatives that will help employees prepare for change.

A sample training design for a two-day program based on the four roles (coach, appraiser, adviser, referral agent) and the discussion framework (climate building, clarifying, collaborating, closing) is presented in Exhibit 5. Such a program as this

Exhibit 5. Manager as Career Developer: A Sample Training Design.

Day 1

Overview of Program
Goals and Objectives
The Career Development Model
Assessing Manager Strengths in Career Coaching
The Role of the Coach
Practicing Coaching Skills and Behaviors
The Role of the Appraiser
Practicing Appraising Skills

Day 2

The Role of the Adviser: Understanding the Organization
Multiple Goal Setting
The Role of the Referral Agent: Force Field Analysis
The Development Plan
The Four C's of Career Discussions: Climate Building, Clarifying, Collaborating, and Closing
Closure/Evaluation

---

has a dual purpose: It teaches managers effective career development skills while it attends to their own careers. The suggested activities use the managers' own experiences and data for demonstration purposes, which means that managers experience first hand the benefits of career development for their own careers while refining skills to help their employees.

Variations and follow-ups for this and other training designs for managers include such components as the following:

• Learning coaching and communication skills by breaking skills into component parts (active listening, open and closed questions, probing questions) and by teaching others through a micro teaching model.

- Learning appraising skills by studying the role of the appraiser and reviewing their organization's performance appraisal system, to see how it supports career development, as well as the progress of one of their fast-track employees.
- Learning more about the adviser role by thinking about the future of the organization through studying the ten megatrends (as in Naisbitt, 1982) and considering how each might affect the organization.
- Sharpening the development planning skills needed for the adviser and referral agent roles by plotting career goals for both a marginal employee and a high-performance employee.
- Sharing with each other the ways in which they had learned particular development skills that helped them to be better prepared to discuss employee development needs.
- Having pairs of managers practice discussions with employees who work in neither of their departments or divisions (as General Electric has done), thus giving both managers necessary practice before they work with their own employees.
- Setting up trouble-shooting sessions six weeks after the initial program.

Providing Recognition and Accountability

If managers, and their employees and organizations, are to receive the fullest benefits from career development, organizational mechanisms for recognition and accountability need to be firmly in place. Ongoing, visible reinforcement of managers for their career development roles is essential.

Top management's support for managers' involvement in career development must be in evidence through verbal communications and through development activities with top management's own staff. More subtle forms of recognition (described by Pinto, 1981) include giving managers who are involved in career development first priority on trainees, increasing their staff or budgets, and reinvesting the savings realized from career development back into the managers' departmental budget. Managers who are effective in developing their employees also need tangible rewards and recognition for their efforts—for example, a pay increase or a bonus.

Continuing emphasis on accountability for career development responsibilities is also essential. One of the most direct organizational mechanisms for accountability lies in the performance appraisal system, which can link a manager's performance in the area of career development to subsequent promotions and pay increases. Another is to institute a policy stating that supervisors cannot be considered for promotion until they demonstrate that at least one of their employees is ready for promotion (Morgan, Hall, and Martier, 1979). This can be augmented by, for example, giving managers an opportunity to meet with top management to discuss action plans for their departments and obstacles that they think prevent them from working on career issues.

In addition, the organization must provide the continuing information that managers and employees need on such issues as new product lines and the development of positive or adverse business conditions. The organization also must ensure employees easy access to self-appraisal and planning tools, such as workshops, computer-assisted programs, and self-directed career resource centers that contain a variety of workbooks and informational materials. Finally, the organization must make a commitment to implementing changes in structures and policies, so that organizational obstacles to career development, identified in discussions between managers and employees, can be eliminated—through, for example, initiating or revising job posting systems, setting up rotating programs, providing better tuition aid, or considering new compensation schemes.

A Final Word

Managers are a vital resource in any organization's career development effort. In order for their involvement to be effective, however, their own career needs must be addressed, benefits and responsibilities established, and adequate training and resources provided. Equally important, key organizational components, such as reward systems and sources of information, must be in place. When all of these conditions are met, managers can, indeed, become key participants in the career development of their employees.

Chapter Seven

Building on Existing
Human Resource Programs
and Practices

"High-performing organizations involve human resource structures appropriate to their vision."

What human resource structures must be in place for the vision
to become reality? For the specific needs of the key target
group to be met effectively? The fourth task in determining
new directions and possibilities is to decide how the structures
(the policies, procedures, practices, and formal systems) now
existing under the organizational umbrella of human resources
can be strengthened, redesigned, updated, linked with, or integrated into the career development system. In order to assure
that specific needs and target groups are addressed, we have to
choose—and create. For example, because survival in an increasingly competitive environment depends on an open flow of
communication among functional units and on rewarding innovative marketing ideas, a small, nonprofit association created a
high-level steering committee to support and reinforce these
goals. The makeup of the steering committee and the rewards it
presented were in themselves innovative, since they, too, crossed
functional lines. In another example, a leading hotel chain,
which believes in promotion from within and in maximizing career opportunities, chose to create a new job posting system for
both exempt and nonexempt positions; in this new system, a

bulletin listing open positions is circulated to all employees weekly, and posted jobs are open to all people with satisfactory performance ratings.

Making the Transition to the Future

The transition from the present system to the future, envisioned system is not necessarily simple and straightforward. Most people, according to Nadler (1979), view the movement from the current to future state as a mechanical or procedural detail. They concentrate exclusively on the vision of the future and overlook the inevitable transition. Yet, going through a transition state is the only way to get from the current state to the ideal future state. It is necessary to think about building intervening, transitional structures to help smooth the path between the present structures and the future state's formalized new structures. Proper planning now will make the vision a lasting reality.

Table 12 outlines the process Holiday Inns, Inc., used to meet the specific needs of several hundred reservation agents who were plateaued and felt they had no place to go. The nature of the job meant that the reservation agents were geographically separated and that they interacted mostly with customers, which put severe limitations on their ability to form networks. They needed lateral mobility as well as job enrichment. Some intervening or transition program had to be designed to get them interacting with their peers and make them more visible in the organization.

Two such transition structures were included in a Career Directions program designed for the reservation agents. One was the four-page application form called *The Starting Line,* that required reservation agents to interview people outside the division in order to be accepted into the program. In essence, they were given permission to gather information about other areas and were provided with a set of questions that supported their information gathering. They began to build external networks. The application form produced dramatic results. Nearly a dozen of the initial 103 applicants in the program received new posi-

Table 12. The Transition Process.

Vision	Current State (Organizational Structure)	Transition State (Program)	Ideal Future State (New Formal Structure)
To provide lateral mobility and job enrichment for plateaued reservation agents; to assure retention of valuable employees.	Job structure and design limit physical mobility, networks, and access to organization information.	• Application to Career Directions Program requires two informational interviews. • Project groups study the organization for eight weeks during the program. • Final presentations empower reservation agents and make them visible to cross section of the organization.	Career resource center is set up to contain research projects; give tips on informational interviewing; act as a clearinghouse for information on organization opportunities and career paths.

tions in the company as a result of the information interviews they conducted. Most did not participate in the program beyond this first step: They were no longer "stuck."

The second transition structure in the program involved project groups into which the participants were divided. These groups gave the reservation agents an opportunity to disconnect the phones and connect with each other. Each group selected a project from among a list of research topics developed by the program's advisory group with an eye to improving leadership and problem-solving abilities as well as presentation and networking skills.

The research projects chosen by the initial groups included gathering case histories of successful lateral moves, developing a career movement chart, revising the organization's orientation handbook, creating a reservation agent survival kit, cataloging resources in reservations (special skills, talents, and hobbies of agents), and producing a dress-for-success sourcebook. Project teams worked together for eight weeks interviewing, studying, and organizing data. The presentations of their findings to top management and their immediate supervisors were polished and creative—and made the reservation agents visible to a cross section of the organization. Participants felt empowered as they filled out a form, called *The Finishing Line*, at the end of the program. (See Chapter Eight for a description of the system model for the entire Holiday Inns, Inc., program.)

The envisioned new, formal human resource structure, a career resource center, now houses the completed presentations of the initial groups in the program as well as subsequent groups, who selected projects from lists freshly compiled by the advisory group. At the center, the reservation agents can continue to follow up on their initial work in the career program, and all organization employees, whether or not they participated in the program, now have access to the information gathered by the program projects. The center, organized around the four critical career questions described in Chapter Five, provides questionnaires, audiotapes, self-assessment inventories, guided study projects, reading materials, and organization charts for employee self-study, organization study, goal setting, and development planning.

As an ongoing formalized structure, the career resource center assures that the vision is a reality. A formalized structure is an institutionalized structure; that is, it holds lawful status and approval and is applied in a regular, systematic way. When such a new formal structure replaces the current structure, the transition has been completed and the cultural change will last over time.

Choosing Structures, Establishing Links

Current human resource structures to be incorporated into the career development system must support the vision. Some of these structures may need to be redesigned or deleted, and intervening structures or new formal structures may need to be added. Chapter Two already provided the answers to the first necessary question: Which structures are currently in place and are effective? Other necessary questions include

What structures must continue and what structures must be added if the vision is to be achieved?
Given the choices, what is realistic? Cost effective? Relatively easy to design and maintain?
What will management support?

Figure 3 (in Chapter Two) illustrates the support and interaction between career development and human resource structures. Human resource structures can be seen in four broad groupings encircling career development: (1) performance appraisal and career pathing, linked to individual information and planning; (2) job descriptions, job posting, and recruitment-transfer-promotion policies, linked to job acquisition and movement; (3) training, development, and education plus compensation and benefits, linked to development and reward; and (4) strategic planning, forecasting, succession planning, and skills inventories, linked to organizational information and planning.

Performance Appraisals. Performance appraisals are generally regular, periodic occasions for organizations to assess the accomplishments of employees. They provide employees with realistic information about themselves that can tie to future options. They provide organizations with information about employees that contributes to reasoned decisions about promotion and potential. Ideally, the appraisals include face-to-face meetings between managers and employees to review the performance against some previously agreed-upon standards and/or goals, so that employees have feedback on whether "they are missing, hitting, or exceeding performance marks [and, as a result, are] able to improve" (Levinson, 1981, p. 12). Performance appraisals may be used to help determine advancement, pay raises, transfers, and other areas of individual job-related change. They may also be used by individual employees to clarify expectations, job requirements, and approval of their work to date. Essential elements of performance appraisal dialogues are

> Observed behaviors and measurable results
>
> Existing and required competencies (knowledge and ability required for effective job performance)
>
> Descriptions of performance strengths and suggestions for capitalizing on them
>
> Descriptions of performance deficiencies and suggestions for correcting them
>
> Exchanges of mutual expectations between employee and supervisor
>
> Discussions and guidance pertaining to developmental and career opportunities
>
> Establishment of performance expectations and standards for the upcoming year

Performance appraisals can be vital links in meeting, for example, needs to increase bench strength in the management cadre, to select best-fit job candidates, to promote employee planning, and to improve manager skills in career coaching.

In enabling organizations to increase bench strength of management, performance appraisals contribute to a data base on the current performance of employees and help organizations decide who would be a prospective manager. Useful adjuncts to performance appraisal, used by a number of organizations, are assessment centers that provide raters an opportunity to judge participant performance on simulations and activities related to manager effectiveness.

Good performance data also help organizations select the right people for the right jobs (best fit) by providing clear, realistic pictures of employee strengths and limitations. This is particularly true when the standards used to measure performance are clearly stated, operationalized behaviors, rather than broad-based traits or judgments.

In the areas of employee planning and improvement of managers' skills in career coaching, the link between current performance and future development is inextricable. In order for employees to make sound, realistic decisions about their next steps, they must have candid, honest feedback about their current performance. This need for effective performance appraisal systems also provides a springboard for strengthening and extending manager skills in career development.

Further, linking career development to performance appraisals helps institutionalize career development. When career development discussions are made part of the performance appraisal system, according to Hanson (1981), it ensures "more action than an implementation scheme that is dependent [solely] on progressive managers who recognize its importance and the relationship to long-term organizational health." To date, however, "in most organizations the relationships of the parts of the career development system are neither recognized nor dealt with as priority issues" (p. 89).

A further point to consider is whether employee-manager career development and performance appraisal discussions should be held within the same session. The two roles played by the manager, as judge and as helper, are clearly in conflict. Current practice points to separating the two annual discussions by six-month intervals (for example, holding performance appraisal discussions every April and career development discussions every October), although human resource professionals strongly emphasize the importance to employees of continual feedback as well as access to development discussions.

One method for assuring the performance appraisal/ career development link is to have participants in a career development program fill out their own performance appraisals at the close of the program. At one General Electric company, for example, the appraisal form has three major categories: career interest (next and longer range), qualifications (technical, managerial, interpersonal), and development actions and plans. Employees then discuss these appraisals with their managers.

Career Paths. Career paths, which present realistic, sequential lines of progression within an organization, provide valuable information for employees on job opportunities. A career path demonstrates clearly the network of alternatives related to an individual employee's experience and training—and helps employees understand the fit among a variety of experiences, tasks, and jobs. Career path information also helps employees identify training needs and visualize options other than promotion: lateral moves, downward moves, and moves to other departments that may have previously seemed too different to contemplate. Career paths, together with job descriptions, job posting, and recruitment, transfer, and promotion policies, help employees discover realistic options in the organization.

Career paths can be built in two ways, according to Sheppick and Taylor (1985): a traditional/political approach and a job/behavior approach. The traditional/political approach uses past movement of employees to map future career development. The job/behavior approach analyzes knowledge, skills, and abilities required on the job as well as similarities and differences among jobs. This approach often results in clusters or families of jobs and can open up new avenues for employees, thus supporting one of the key objectives of career development.

Job/behavior career paths, although more difficult to create and dynamic to maintain, require, first, analyzing jobs for content and tasks performed and then grouping into clusters those jobs with related activities requiring similar skills and knowledge and representing transferable experience. Table 13 illustrates the job content analysis and Figure 14 the clustering of jobs for a job/behavior career path in the text processing areas of Aetna Life and Casualty. Both the table and the figure are included in an employee handbook. The handbook is divided into fourteen sections, each of which describes one of the principal job clusters within the organization. In each section, the field of employment is described, including general skills and responsibilities, thus giving employees an understanding of jobs and job clusters outside their current divisions or departments. A chart, like that in Figure 14, depicts typical career progression within each field; and written information, like that in Table 13, details career steps.

Table 13. Job Descriptions for Text Processing Services.

A person normally enters this career path at the typist or transcriptionist level. Progress depends on performance, experience, and the number of opportunities and openings that occur in the area.

Text processing employees who like to work with people and have time management and organization skills may move into the secretarial career path.

Supervisor: Supervises a unit of Text Processing typists. Job class and responsibilities vary from unit to unit.

Senior Word Processing Typist: Sets up and operates automatic text editing typewriters. Prepares master magnetic tapes for reports and company systems manuals for storage and subsequent editing and updating. Gives advice and counsel to customers on the most efficient way to format data.

Senior Transcriptionist: Transcribes voice recordings with a minimum of supervision and guidance, using format described by principal. Work requires a high degree of concentration, comprehension, and accuracy. Requires a thorough knowledge of English grammar, punctuation, spelling, and an extensive vocabulary.

Transcriptionist: Transcribes telephoned voice recordings of routine documents transmitted from all divisions of the company.

Senior Typist: Uses a typewriter to make copies of various material. Types copy from handwritten or typed drafts. Sets up tabulations, outlines, and scripts from general instructions. Types insurance policies requiring knowledge of applicable instructions. Types material in final form when it involves combining material from several sources. Types manuals for reproductions following specific setup. Corrects spelling, punctuation, and grammatical inconsistencies where appropriate.

Word Processing Typist: Operates automatic text editing typewriters. Receives basic copy and instructions from various departments, usually a letter or form with a fixed formal and variable information for each copy requested.

Typist: Uses a typewriter to make copies of various material. Types copy from handwritten or typed drafts. Sets up routine tabulations, outlines, and scripts from general instructions. Corrects spelling, punctuation, and grammatical inconsistencies where appropriate.

Source: Aetna Life and Casualty, 1979.

Figure 14. Career Path for Text Processing Services.

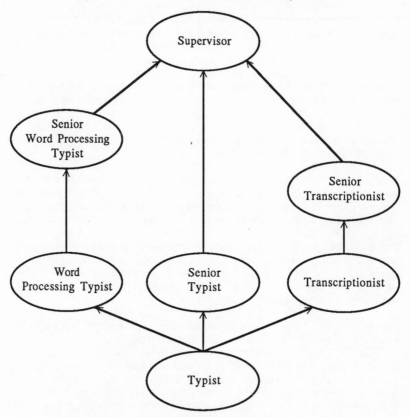

Source: Aetna Life and Casualty, 1979.

Career paths are particularly useful in responding to the specific needs of plateaued employees and technical employees who may not want to move into management. Looking at non-traditional paths (for example, at the case histories of successful lateral moves made by the reservation agent project groups mentioned earlier in the chapter) can generate ideas for alternatives. The organization's human resource staff can also interview those who have moved in nontraditional ways, report their findings, and demonstrate possible atypical, nontraditional paths. By looking at paths other than the ones they already know, employees can visualize still more alternatives. Career paths can also be a vital link in providing a framework to guide career discussions as well as a framework for employee self-assessment in preparation for career discussions (Burack and Mathys, 1980).

In order to make the most of career paths in a career development system, it is vital that the paths be communicated openly to all employees, as in the Aetna Life and Casualty handbook, and that employees be encouraged to examine paths other than just those that start at their current jobs.

Even with up-to-date career paths, broad information still can, and should, be made available—information that shows barriers and aids to various career routes. For example, this information might simply include numbers of employees in a given field and the percentages of those who reach various higher levels of that field or the amounts and percentages of experience and training among those who have reached various levels or certain areas of the organization. Such information at least demonstrates to employees what is and is not likely to be possible.

Job Descriptions. Job descriptions are generally one- or two-page summaries of the tasks and competencies required on the job. They provide employees essential data for realistic exploration of options. They are also the building blocks for such human resource structures as career paths, job posting, training and development, and performance appraisal.

Job descriptions allow the development of job specifications; that is, the summary of the necessary qualifications for the job. These, in turn, help locate the best candidates for a job. They are useful in personnel planning and recruitment and assure compliance with EEO standards. They are "the basic documents used in developing performance standards" (French, 1974, p. 211). Thorough job descriptions are the result of careful analysis of the tasks performed on the job and the competencies necessary for successful performance of those tasks. They include information about day-to-day work factors and information about the personal level of achievement necessary. Thus, complete job descriptions include both job duties and job requirements. Job duties comprise a specific, written listing of all tasks, all day-to-day work factors, required of the employee, such as keeping abreast of particular issues, writing reports, and maintaining certain records. Job requirements address the employee's personal level of achievement, the knowledge, education, skills, and experience necessary, such as supervisory ability, computer skills, and knowledge of statistical methods. To be fully useful, job descriptions must be

> Updated regularly to reflect any change in duties or competencies
>
> Written in clear, concise language that can be readily understood even by those not familiar with the agency or department concerned
>
> Specific enough to include all possible tasks and competencies and reflect the performance requirements and behavior expectations
>
> Accessible not only to employees in the jobs but also to any others who want to review them for background information and future planning purposes

Job descriptions link directly to career development in two important ways. First, by examining the present and past descriptions of their jobs, employees can identify their own competencies and devise accurate profiles of their current abilities. Second, by examining descriptions of jobs throughout the organization, when they are readily available, employees are better able to determine a variety of career options and assess whether their own skills and experiences might realistically fit certain job opportunities. Only by such job descriptions can employees determine alternatives and plan developmental activities. Thus, they can also test their preconceived notions about what it means to be, for example, an administrative analyst, a research assistant, or an accounts manager. In fact, a thorough review of job descriptions frequently shows employees that they really know very little about the exact duties associated with many titles.

To give employees the important ready access to complete descriptions of a wide variety of jobs, Holiday Inns, Inc., provides a booklet for its employees. The booklet, called *Career Directions,* contains specific job information developed from a job analysis questionnaire completed by over 700 exempt employees. It is in two parts. The first describes the scope and primary responsibilities of each exempt job; the second lists specific competencies for each job. Employees checking out various career development and movement options are advised to look first at the statements concerning the scope and primary responsibilities of the jobs that interest them and then to examine the competencies required for that particular job. Under Sales, for example, they find that the competency required under personal performance management "has to do with maintaining one's own level of performance. It includes the ability to (1) maintain performance in stressful situations, (2) shift priorities when conditions change, (3) complete projects and programs, (4) plan and conduct multiple activities within a specified time frame" (Holiday Inns, Inc., p. 84).

The booklet contains the following useful listing of these and related skills (pp. 84–85):

- Ability to follow through on specific projects and programs until completion
- Ability to maintain performance in stressful situations
- Ability to set priorities when faced with conflicting alternatives and varying conditions
- Ability to plan and conduct multiple activities within a specified time frame in order to ensure goal/deadline achievement
- Ability to shift priorities in response to changing schedules or conditions
- Knowledge of factors which are related to successful job performance
- Ability to evaluate project status in relation to plans and schedules

Another strategy to make job descriptions accessible to employees interested in their career futures is to arrange, and possibly restate, the descriptions in a well-organized file at a central location, such as a career resource center.

Job Posting. Job posting helps identify most of the real possibilities in an organization; it is particularly valuable for plateaued employees and in preventing the loss of any high-potential employees. "Job posting is not just a simple matter of tacking a notice on a bulletin board," according to Dahl and Pinto (1977, p. 40), "but rather is a complicated system for employee self-development as well as [for] reducing external recruitment costs and uncovering hidden talent."

Logistically, job posting can include dissemination of individual bulletins or even development of a phone-in recorded message system announcing openings. Conceptually, it can include information not only describing a job but also detailing related skills, experience, and anticipated career progression.

To be effective, a job posting system must not only encompass all jobs but those jobs must actually be available. If the jobs posted are already "wired" for a specific candidate, and the posting process is an exercise carried out only to fulfill regulations, employees catch on immediately and stop applying for, or even reading, posted job announcements—and the organization loses a pool of talent to draw from.

Although job posting is primarily to alert applicants to specific openings, posted jobs also assist employee career development by providing information about the range of opportunities that might be goal alternatives. For example, for a hotline providing recorded telephone messages about available jobs throughout the University of Utah, jobs are categorized as technical, administrative, and clerical; and a different time of day is reserved for the recording in each category. Included in the recorded messages, which are updated weekly, are job titles, brief descriptions, and application deadlines. More detailed descriptions are posted at the personnel office. Employees can thus easily obtain not only information about present options but also ideas for future options.

Similarly, in the job posting system at Holiday Inns, Inc., each employee is provided with a job posting bulletin each week.

The bulletins include salary ranges and job descriptions for entry-level up to director-level positions.

In addition to listening to recorded messages and reading bulletin boards and bulletins, employees searching for goals and alternatives also find that job postings from the recent past can provide useful information about trends and opportunities that influence career choices, particularly if these postings are filed in a central location or career resource center.

The very fact that jobs are openly announced signals to employees that internal recruitment and development are important to the organization and serves to motivate them to take major responsibility for their own career development efforts.

Recruitment, Transfer, and Promotion Policies. As job descriptions and job posting link directly to the job acquisition and movement aspects of career development, so, too, do organization recruitment, transfer, and promotion policies. These policies can provide the procedural support for movement, particularly in nontraditional ways, for employees who have reached a dead end or plateau.

These policies vary from organization to organization, division to division. Recruitment may be "first from within" or generally from outside the division or organization. Transfers may be made "from one job to another, one unit to another, or one shift to another, and they may involve a new geographical location" (French, 1974, p. 336). Promotions may be made by incremental steps in some departments or organizations and by less regular leaps from one level to another in others. Promotions may also increase responsibilities or future potential more than pay.

Employees cannot realistically contemplate career directions without a clear understanding of the organization's policies in recruitment, transfer, and promotion. They need to know if the career goals they set for themselves are within the realm of possibility or simply fantasies, and the difference often hinges on the policies and practices related to recruitment and movement within the organization. Lateral transfer programs within an organization, for example, indicate opportunities for employee development and learning that do not involve upward moves, opportunities for employees to try a number of possibilities.

For greatest benefit to career development, these policies may need to be formalized and clarified. In any event, the policies must be widely known. To reiterate: It is impossible for employees to plan for their career futures unless they know about organizational policies and practices that might affect those plans.

Training, Development, and Education. Training, development, and education enable employees to update skills, acquire new capabilities, enrich current jobs, and, in general, pursue their career goals successfully. Therefore, employees need full information about their options for training, development, and education. Table 14 gives an example of one method for letting employees see what skills are covered in various training programs. In this case, the matrix lists thirty-four skills, ranging from organizing presentations and interviewing to salary administration and reprimanding, and indicates which of eleven training opportunities will help develop each skill. (Only a portion of the matrix is included in the figure.)

Organizations need to link such offerings to employee needs and plans and/or to organizational plans. In the past, training and development programs have frequently been made available on the basis of a reward principle (attendance at seminars and conferences or benefits such as tuition reimbursement granted as performance rewards or promotion benefits), a nuts-and-bolts principle (training given only in skills needed for immediate tasks), or a smorgasbord principle (employees left to make their own selections from a miscellany of offerings). Training and development offerings should instead be based on full information about employee needs and plans, and participation in training programs should be part of carefully considered career development plans, not "because someone 'feels this would be good for him' or that 'we should send somebody to this program' " (Walker, 1973, p. 69). Offerings that are tightly tied to employee and organization needs are far more likely to be effective.

Table 14. Links to Training Information.

Skills \ Programs	Career development programs	Supervision skills training	The one-minute manager workshop	Leader effectiveness training workshop	Effective presentations workshop	Negotiation skills workshop	Managing meetings workshop	Written communications workshop	Time management workshop	Professional strategies for managers workshop	Performance appraisal: win/win workshop
Averting discrimination problems		✓									
Bank personnel policies		✓									
Basic principles of supervision		✓									
Career management	✓										
Communicating		✓	✓	✓	✓	✓	✓	✓		✓	
Conflict management		✓		✓						✓	
Correcting problem behavior		✓									
Counseling		✓									
Delegating		✓							✓		
Disciplinary action		✓									

Source: Security Pacific National Bank, 1984.

Training, development, and education link clearly to a wide variety of specific needs/problems and target groups. For example, employees whose skills are no longer current need training, development, and education so that they can progress in their careers and so that the organization does not have obsolete employees. Shifts in technology, particularly in relation to the automated office of the future, mean that clerical staff need updated skills as well as new career directions. Plateaued employees, faced with limited promotion potential, direct the focus of training, development, and education toward both enrichment and new directions.

Tuition reimbursement programs for these employees and others can be cost effective and beneficial to organizations, but only when they are tied closely to projected organization staffing needs. As one utility organization expressed it, "Why should we pay for one more person to complete law school when we only have one corporate attorney on staff?"

Compensation and Benefits. Compensation and benefits, traditionally viewed as pay (salary, bonuses, one-time cash awards, group awards for unit accomplishment) and extra fringe benefits (insurance plans, leave time, profit sharing), now include material and intangible items that might be sought after by employees: autonomy in the workplace, increased decision-making authority, interesting challenges on the job, status symbols (such as larger offices and free parking spaces), titles, and recognition by personal feedback or from the organization at large.

In most cases, all of these compensations and benefits are still considered rewards and, as rewards, are still linked to upward movement. Salary systems in particular, despite such labels as merit based, skill based, or performance based, generally tend to follow a hierarchical pattern in the organization.

It is challenging to create reward systems that can be linked to the variety of developmental possibilities, in addition to upward movement. For example, equal pay intervals must exist for dual career ladders if technical employees are to consider staying in a technical job a viable choice. Rewards also need to be linked to horizontal moves, temporary experimental moves, enrichment moves, and even downward moves, because if increased pay and other rewards are linked only to upward movement, employees will be encouraged to view career development only in that direction. They will ignore other valuable opportunities, and the organization will not receive any benefit from the rich variety of possible employee development experiences. For example, rewards for lateral moves could include learning opportunities and autonomy or a one-time bonus for the skills enhancement involved. Rewards for other types of moves could involve better working conditions or public recognition.

For any such strategy to be seen as a reward, it must not be presently available to the employee, and the employee must view it as personally important. A reward also has more impact if it is fairly immediate. When the goal of a career development is five years in the future, rewards during implementation steps will be more effective.

The key is to design compensation and reward systems that can promote the acceptance of multidirectional career moves. This requires understanding how rewards work, recognizing the options for developing reward systems, knowing what rewards the organization is currently using and with what results, and trying to understand employee perceptions of what actually is rewarding.

Strategic Planning. Strategic planning is one of four human resource structures (the others are forecasting, succession planning, and skills inventories) that attempt to reconcile in deliberate ways the future plans of the organization with its expected staffing requirements and its need to develop people for key positions. Together these structures form a powerful approach to such issues that affect employee career development as mergers and acquisitions, lack of bench strength (particularly among managers), shifts in technology or product lines, and turnover and its effect on the internal labor pool.

Strategic planning involves stating, and restating, organizational objectives and developing strategies for carrying out those objectives. Often viewed as the domain of top management, the strategic planning process goes through several steps: defining the organization philosophy, scanning the environmental conditions, evaluating the organization's strengths and weaknesses, developing objectives and goals, and developing strategies (Walker, 1980). These strategies for carrying out the objectives and goals generally involve developing new programs, determining an appropriate business mix, selecting from organizational structural alternatives, deciding on resource commitments, and devising relevant managerial policies and procedures. Strategic planning may imply major, long-term changes in direction or growth; and it is supported by shorter-term operational and tactical plans.

Stated in another way, "Managers at every level must ultimately agree on an integrated plan of action and identified priorities. They arrive at agreement through a series of steps starting with the identification of the [organization's] strategic direction to meet its future needs and conclude by publishing the coming year's operational plan" (Selin, 1984, p. 1).

Strategic planning gives direction to career development efforts; but organizations must share their strategic plans with employees at all levels, so that the employees can plan careers that fit with the organization's current and future directions. In particular, employee goals and training and development activities must match with strategic plans in order to prevent, for example, employees striving to become proficient in areas no longer important to the organization. The key is open communication of strategic plans to employees and managers, so that career development plans and organizational plans can be synchronized. In addition, communication of information on employee goals and training needs can provide valuable human resource input to those responsible for generating strategic plans.

Forecasting. Like strategic planning, forecasting provides information that helps assure that employee career goals will not be planned in a vacuum, that the organization and its employees will not be setting off in different directions. Forecasting, according to Walker (1980, p. 100), is a "central aspect of the human resource planning process, as it yields the advance estimates or calculations of staffing required to achieve the organization's stated objectives."

Clearly, knowledge about the availability of talent within the organization is essential in determining future human resource needs, and forecasting is strengthened when it uses career development information on employee abilities and aspirations. Similarly, forecasting information strengthens employee understanding of what kinds of talent the organization will seek in coming years, and this aids employees in setting realistic goals and planning effective implementation strategies.

In forecasting systems, most often maintained by those in human resource areas, current staffing patterns are analyzed and matched against the projection of future requirements, thus linking together information on current available skills and estimations of future skill needs, current and future attrition and mobility of the work force, current and estimated future staffing levels for various functions, upcoming succession needs and plans, employee current and future career interests and plans, current training and future estimated training needs, plans for organizational change (generated internally or externally), and estimates of human resource productivity (efficiency and effectiveness).

When human resource forecasting is done informally and only to check on supply and demand to meet needs over the coming year or within a few departments, it is rarely widely shared, making it much less valuable for career development purposes. An important point to emphasize is the impossibility for employees to make intelligent career decisions without such information (preferably intermediate and long-range—for five or more years). In addition, like strategic planning, without information about employee career plans and interests, the forecasting process itself misses crucial input.

Succession Planning. Succession planning, a natural step after strategic planning and forecasting, locates and grooms replacement candidates for future openings in key positions and serves as an implementation strategy for organizational plans and for decisions concerning human resource needs.

When succession planning is informal, it typically begins

and ends with an individual manager identifying and grooming his or her replacement. This next-in-line individual is given the title of deputy or assistant and granted appropriate responsibility and exposure in preparation for the next step. What informal succession planning fails to consider, however, are possible organizational changes, structural adjustments, or changing requirements for managerial talent. It also is generally a private process, neither widely known nor understood by others in the organization.

When succession planning is formal, it generally includes examination of strategic plans and human resource forecasts; review of data on all potential candidates, from biographical information to career development intentions; determination and clarification of managerial position requirements; development of plans for how upcoming managerial requirements will be met (who, how, when); determination of the training, development, and experience needs of those being groomed for succession; and review of recruitment and replacement needs down the line when those individuals advance to managerial positions.

A formal succession planning process thus benefits from considering more information, taking organization-wide needs and plans into account, and gaining greater credibility among employees, who feel part of the process. Formal succession planning connects with employee career development by utilizing information about individual skills, abilities, and career goals. Further, when succession plans are openly communicated to all employees, career goals and implementation strategies are more likely to be realistic.

For example, Kaiser Permanente's southern California region links formal succession planning to career development in an ongoing system for maintaining the necessary managerial depth to respond to future organizational needs and strategies. The program has three major phases: The first, a management replacement process, identifies potential candidates for immediate backup of key management positions and structures individualized development activities for those employees. The second, a succession planning process, provides for identification of potential candidates outside a functional area's direct reporting levels (crossing function, department, and entity lines) and designs development activities that emphasize preparation for movement regardless of function, department, or entity. The third, a high-potential identification process, involves early identification of promising candidates, generally from below the third reporting level of the organization. Development of these candidates involves increasing their understanding of opportunities within the organization, broadening their career knowledge, and thereby encouraging their retention (Botten and Hansen, 1984). Throughout the program, the organization not only identifies candidates for key positions but also contributes to their career development in order to increase their potential for succession.

Skills Inventories. Automated skills inventories support strategic planning, forecasting, and succession planning. These computerized compilations of data on employee skills, abilities, experience, and education give employees information on available and future options and give management data on current and future training and development needs and rates of turnover and advancement. Reliable up-to-date skills inventories enable organizations to take full advantage of inside talent in recruiting and are often used in making shorter-term project or rotational assignments. They can also be a critical adjunct to such career development needs as definition of work-force characteristics, compliance with regulations concerning equal educational opportunities, and shortage of promotable employees.

Kaumeyer (1979) sets forth the following as basic components of a skills inventory system: key words, work history, foreign languages, formal education, special courses, special projects, and vocational license. He sees skills inventories as valuable tools that allow better utilization of employee skills and benefit both the organization and the employee. Kaumeyer also believes that skills inventories increase overall efficiency and improve employee morale.

To ensure these results, we must take steps to see that the skills inventories are widely accessible and fully used by all managers making recruitment and other decisions. We also need to make sure that skills inventories are updated at least annually, and whenever employees pass through data-producing events. Such essential updating is the joint responsibility of employee and manager.

As for strategic planning, forecasting, and succession planning, the link between skills inventories and career development works in both directions. Through their answers to the question "Who am I?", career development programs generate information about employees' skills that is valuable to skills inventories. Additionally, career development efforts establish greater interest in keeping these inventories up to date, as employees begin to realize how important skills inventories are to their futures within the organization.

Functional and complete skills inventories can contribute much to employees' career development by providing them with records of their own skills and abilities, which they can match against the typical skills and abilities of those who hold positions to which they aspire. Thus, employees can begin to note areas in which they might need more training or experience if they are to attain their goals; and, as employees begin to acquire additional training and experience, the existence of a skills inventory helps assure that their efforts will be recognized and movement will be possible as the organization seeks to fill positions with qualified candidates.

Linking Structures to the Four Critical Questions

The preceding sections have described traditional human resource structures and their links to career development, as described in Figure 3. The human resource structures can also be tied back to the four critical questions that employees must answer in planning their careers. These links are as follows:

Career Development Questions	*Supporting Human Resource Structures*
Who am I? (self-statement)	Skills inventories Job descriptions
How am I seen? (reality check)	Performance appraisal

Career Development Questions	*Supporting Human Resource Structures*
What are my alternatives and goals? (goal setting)	Job posting Strategic planning Forecasting Succession planning Career paths
How can I achieve my goals? (action plan)	Training, development, and education Recruitment, transfer, and promotion policies Compensation and benefits

New Possibilities

When the traditional human resource structures seem inappropriate for a career development system, it may be time to design new structures. For example, at Carolina Power and Light, the vision was to facilitate mobility and job information for plateaued employees located at widely spread-out workplaces. Two new formal structures were designed: One was a career resource center (as described in Chapter Five). The other was a personnel representative system built into each functional unit, so that employees were linked to resources for job vacancies. In another example, the National Football League wanted to help find new employment for professional athletes faced with early retirement. Many of the players lacked degrees in higher education, contacts outside of the sports world, and knowledge of any other field; therefore, a resource network of retired players, categorized by geographical areas and different career fields, was formally hooked up to the new retirees through workshops and written directories.

Other new structures that have been specially created, formalized, and successfully used include the following:

- *Job rotation or work experience programs:* Employees have an opportunity to try out other functional work areas in this structure. At the Goddard Space Flight Center, for example, this approach enabled midlevel electrical engineers in declining areas to try working in expanding areas that could make use of their skills.

- *Project assignment program posting systems:* These programs give employees the opportunity to try out and develop new skills and to work in areas where they may not have had formal training. A program established by the Norton Company also provides managers with additional assistance for peak work periods and additional tasks. Managers post part-time assignments that will take six to twelve hours per week, and employees bid for the work.

- *Utilization committees:* The objective of these committees, which several organizations have established, is to oversee and ensure the best utilization of employees. If an employee and his or her manager agree that the employee is not in the best job, the employee's profiles and goals are forwarded to this committee. The committee then searches for other possibilities on a system-wide basis and brokers the employee to other jobs.

- *Competency assessments:* Many organizations have begun to establish competencies as a critical self-assessment tool for employees to compare themselves against. For example, in a large telecommunications organization, a set of marketing competencies was identified through a series of critical incident behavioral interviews with top-performing sales representatives. These competencies were then used as self-assessment tools for participants in a career management program established to help employees shift from a technical engineering orientation to a competitive marketing orientation. The competencies are now formalized in the system as part of the organization's selection process.

To respond to employee and manager needs for current, accurate career information, various organizations have used the following information dissemination structures:

- *Career fairs:* At fairs set up to help employees learn about the various areas in an organization, representatives from each division and department are on hand to talk with employees about opportunities in their areas. Such fairs often begin with an overview of the career planning process and general career tips. One organization then arranged a scavenger hunt, in which employees were given a set of questions and were told to find answers to these questions by interviewing the representatives of the different divisions and departments. Winners were given prizes.

- *Future forums:* On a regular basis, management panels share with employees future trends and issues in the industry, environment, and organization that might affect career choice and options.
- *Career advisers or functional representatives:* Representatives from each division in an organization are chosen to provide information to employees on job opportunities and requirements within their area. So that they have a context for the role they are playing, these representatives are generally given an overview of the career development process.
- *Videotapes:* Employees in different career areas are videotaped as they talk about such issues as how they got into the job, what skills it requires, what a typical day is like, and what next steps they are considering. Similar tapes have also been produced with top managers in organizations talking about their own careers and giving tips and advice for employees.

A Final Word

Human resource structures support the career development process; the career development process supports human resource structures. This chapter's overview of traditional and possible human resource structures helps us choose those structures that are most helpful in accomplishing a specific vision. The message of this chapter emphasizes that successful career development systems have human resource structures, traditional or newly created, firmly in place to support, complement, and supplement group, support-oriented, and self-directed activities and interventions.

Chapter Eight

Model Career Development Systems: Examples from Leading Companies

> "A good model is like a road map: It provides direction, landmarks, and a way to measure progress."

Models tie components together into a framework. They serve as guideposts for action, organize reality, provide a communication tool and a common language, and reduce anxiety and stress by presenting a clear picture of what is ahead (Ackerman, 1985). Models give us a way to blend our vision of specific needs and key target groups with employee interventions, ways to involve managers, and human resource structures to achieve a living, breathing reality.

The final task in determining new directions and possibilities is, therefore, to create a model for implementing the vision that responds to organization needs, involves managers and employees, builds from present human resource structures or establishes new ones, and fits the culture and norms of the organization. To help in this task, four systems models are described in this chapter. Models such as those—from a large telecommunications organization, Holiday Inns, Inc., Corning Glass Works, and First Chicago Bank—can be creatively adapted to other organizations, other needs.

Telecommunications: Account Management
Career Development Program

Target group: Account representatives; approximately 300.

Objectives/Visions:

- To identify critical skills in the sales organization
- To ensure the best fit between employee skills and the requirements of the organization
- To provide tools and materials for employees to assess themselves and determine career targets
- To provide support and structure for employee-supervisor career discussions

Background: Following divestiture, a large telecommunications organization was faced with a severe challenge, optimal utilization of its employees. The primary cause was a shift in emphasis from engineering to marketing, which necessitated a change in the skill mix required of employees. A secondary cause was the data from a survey completed in 1983, which indicated that employees wanted an opportunity to discuss their careers with their managers and create realistic career targets and that managers wanted a formal process to handle employee career development, as well as a mechanism to create staffing flexibility. Thus, employee and manager needs were arrayed against the organization's need to identify skills critical to effectiveness in marketing.

The first step was to reach consensus on those critical competencies. Based on skills already in use in the company's assessment centers, sixteen competencies were identified as essential to marketing, then ranked and scaled according to importance. The top three skills were initiative, persuasiveness, and oral communication. Critical incidents, examples of behaviors that illustrate the skills, were also identified. On the basis of these critical skills and incidents, three modules were designed: personal fit, organization fit, and better fit.

Model Components: The assessment modules and other components of the Account Management Career Development Program are displayed in Figure 15. Each component is as follows:

- *Orientation.* Managers are introduced to and briefed on the

Figure 15. A Large Telecommunications Organization's Account Management Career Development Program.

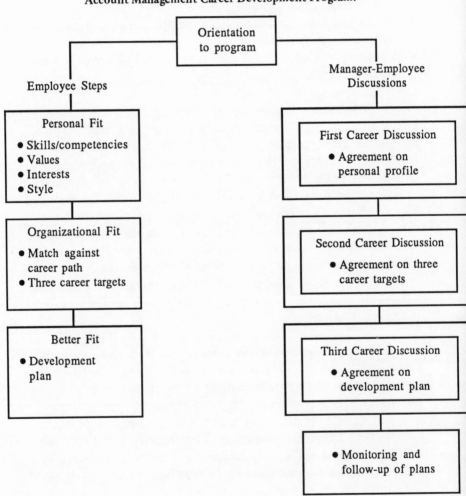

program. They in turn provide a briefing and orientation to their employees.

- *Personal fit:* Employees complete a personal profile that assesses their skills/competencies, values, interests, and style. This self-assessment becomes the basis for the first employee-manager discussion.

- *First career discussion:* Managers are given tools and guidelines for the discussion with their employees, as well as videotapes of employee-manager discussions. The major purpose of the discussion is to reach a consensus on employee personal profiles, to agree that those areas in which employees see themselves as good agree with the manager's assessment.

- *Organization fit:* Employees compare their personal profiles with career paths portraying moves and possibilities in the organization. Employees are encouraged to create multiple options and, as a result of completing this module, identify three career targets.

- *Second career discussion:* Managers are provided resource data on future trends of the organization to help judge feasibility of the three employee targets, which are also judged on their appropriateness to employee skills, values, interests, and current performance. The objective of this discussion is to reach agreement on both the reality and appropriateness of the employee's targets.

- *Better fit:* This final module gives employees a framework for designing an action, or development, plan. A step-by-step process helps them decide on activities that will bring them to their goals. Examples of development activities are provided that include both on-the-job activities and formal training.

- *Third career discussion:* The objective of the final discussion is agreement between manager and employee on the action plan: on the development activities chosen, the dates established for completion, and any assistance the employee may need. A schedule to monitor and evaluate progress is also set up.

- *Monitoring and follow-up of plans:* Future steps include institutionalizing career discussions on an annual basis, six months after performance appraisals.

Summary: Preliminary evaluation indicates that the program provides an effective means for employees to assess their strengths and development needs and consider where they fit best in the organization. In addition, the format provides a safe and appropriate environment for employees and managers to discuss career plans.

Holiday Inns, Inc.: Career Directions

Target Group: Reservation agents, approximately 400.
Objectives/Visions:

- To create lateral mobility for plateaued reservation agents
- To provide managers skill in coaching their employees on a variety of career moves
- To assure retention of valuable employees

Background: Holiday Inns, Inc., was faced with the loss of several hundred reservation agents, who felt that they had no place to move in the system. The organization was committed to retaining and continuing to motivate these employees.

An analysis was recently completed of most of the jobs in their organization to create data to form the basis for many of Holiday Inns, Inc.'s, human resource structures, including compensation, training, performance appraisal, and development (Doerflin, 1985). The analysis produced descriptions of skills for most jobs in the system. Because these descriptions were also viewed as invaluable career development tools, they were included in a set of Career Directions booklets that described families, or clusters, of jobs in Holiday Inns, Inc., detailed the skills required in each, and tied development activities to these skills. In order for the tools to be utilized by employees and their managers to best advantage, they also needed to be built into a process and system.

The system created is displayed in Figure 16. Each of the components is as follows:

Figure 16. Holiday Inns, Inc., Career Directions System.

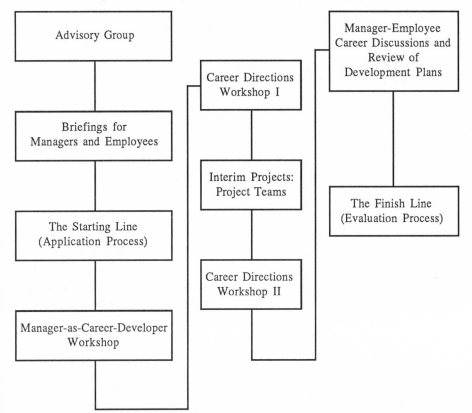

• *Advisory group:* The reservations division director put together an advisory group made up of managers, the division director, and several human resource consultants from the hotel division. The role of this advisory group was to consult and react to the various components of the program, make the final selection of applicants for the program, monitor the program for six months, and help redesign and add such other components as became necessary once the program started.

• *Briefing:* The division director briefed the thirty line managers who supervised the 400 reservation agents. The briefing included an overview of the entire program, selection criteria, the application process, the career development model, and an outline of the manager-as-career-developer workshop, which each manager would be invited to attend. Managers were then urged to give a similar briefing to all of their reservation agents and invite them to participate in the Career Directions program. Application forms were made available to all managers to hand out to their employees. This briefing not only demonstrated the commitment of the division director to the program but also gave her valuable data on the concerns and fears of managers at the beginning of the program.

• *The Starting Line:* The four-page application form, called *The Starting Line,* assured that the reservation agents would begin to answer some of the questions critical to managing their own careers. One of the key ingredients of this process was the requirement that each applicant perform two informational interviews with people outside his or her immediate area. One problem of the reservation agent's job was being confined to the telephone with little chance to converse with anyone but customers. The application process was meant to ensure that they started talking to other reservation agents, from whom they were geographically separated, as well as other Holiday Inns, Inc., staff members. Other questions asked them to examine, for example, what factors were critical to them on a job, what their jobs lacked, what were the special contributions they made to the service industry and to Holiday Inns, Inc. A unique aspect of the application was that the criteria for selection were stated publicly on the form: All applicants were assured admission into the program if they (1) got the application in on time, (2) completed each question, and (3) had been in the job for a minimum of one year. Over 100 agents applied for the first workshop. The first thirty that met the criteria were in the first program, the second thirty in the second, and so on. Employees said that filling out the form was a highlight of the program and really started them thinking. This component is an example of the transition structures that successfully intervene between current and future structures, as discussed in Chapter Seven.

• *Manager-as-Career-Developer Workshop:* This three-day program, which preceded all employee workshops, was offered for all managers of reservation agents and touched upon the basic skills needed in coaching and counseling employees.

The program also helped managers examine their own careers. Managers left the workshop eager to enter into discussions with their employees and clearer about some of their own career goals.

- *Career Directions Workshop I:* This two-day workshop focused on building a strong network of reservation agents and enabling them to take a hard look at themselves. Self-study instruments and exercises helped them understand their specific skills, strengths, interests, values, and career anchors. During the workshop, five-person teams were formed to work together on the interim research projects. These project groups were also an example of a bridge to ease the transition between current and future structures, as in Chapter Seven.

- *Interim projects:* The employee teams chose projects from a list developed by the advisory group. This component was designed to give the reservation agents an opportunity to work with each other for eight weeks and develop their leadership abilities, problem-solving abilities, presentation skills, and networking skills. The research projects included revising the Holiday Inns, Inc., orientation handbook, cataloging the factors that lead to success as a manager, and developing a dress-for-success sourcebook. These projects were completed and presented at the next gathering of the group, during the second workshop, as well as in print for continual use by other employees in the newly set-up career resource center. The division director felt that it was important to have employees make such contributions to the organization.

- *Career Directions Workshop II:* The second workshop, eight weeks after the first, entailed presentation of the research projects to the managers, goal setting, and development planning. The reservation agents were encouraged to discuss their career goals and development plans with their managers, if discussions had not already begun in the interim between the two workshops.

- *Career discussions:* Employees discussed their goals with their managers several times and got help and support for their development plans. Both employees and managers felt confident after these discussions of goals.

• *The Finish Line:* Six months after the second workshop, the entire group was brought together to evaluate the program. A form called *The Finish Line* let the employees note the progress they had made over the six months. A series of exercises allowed the reservation agents to talk about their accomplishments and new goals and acknowledge the support they received from their managers, the organization, and each other.

Summary: Overall, the program has been highly successful. Of the first 100 applicants, nearly a dozen received new jobs as a result of the interviews they conducted for *The Starting Line* application. Other agents moved into management; many of them moved into other parts of the organization. Managers felt supportive toward the agents and no longer felt threatened by employee requests for new job opportunities. The organization became even more productive, and the program is used as a model in many other divisions of the organization.

Corning Glass Works: Career Planning and Information System

Target Group: Approximately 1,400 nonexempt employees at corporate headquarters.

Objectives/Visions:

• To provide tools and techniques to assist nonexempt employees in managing their careers
• To organize and make available career information to assist employees and managers in career planning and discussions
• To build a career planning system from the current performance development and review process
• To provide managers the skills and knowledge needed to hold effective career discussions with their employees

Background: Following a company-wide attitude survey in 1984–1985, Corning Glass Works designed and implemented a Career Planning and Information System in its corporate headquarters. The survey indicated that nonexempt employees felt unrecognized and underutilized, had limited career opportunities, and lacked information to plan their careers. The professional employees expressed similar dissatisfaction, but the organization chose to begin with nonexempt employees because of the traditional neglect of this group.

The objective of the new system was to provide employees with the tools and skills needed to identify career goals and development plans that meshed with Corning Glass Works opportunities and needs.

In the new system, career planning is linked to the organization's strong performance appraisal system. In the past, career planning had been only minimally discussed in these sessions, but now developmental as well as performance objectives are set between managers and employees.

Model Components: Each division was supplied a human resource representative and the necessary organizational support to implement the program in the division. A steering committee of human resource representatives helped design the program. The system now in place is displayed in Figure 17. Each of the components is as follows:

- *Manager training as career coaches:* Before employees enter the career planning system, managers are provided training in how to hold effective career discussions with their employees. The training concentrates on such areas as coaching and counseling, setting career goals, and creating development plans. Managers are also given a framework for linking the career discussions and development plans to the current performance appraisal system.
- *Your Career Is Up to You:* This orientation videotape provides an overview of the career planning process for employees.
- *Discover 1-2-3:* Employees complete the first three computer-assisted modules (Current Satisfaction, Self-Assessment, and Gathering Data) to assess their skills, values, and interests and to identify opportunities within the organization.
- *Reality-check discussions:* Employee-manager discussions are scheduled to ensure that employee views of their skills are the same as manager views.

Figure 17. Corning Glass Works Career Planning and Information System.

```
┌─────────────────────┐                          ┌─────────────────────┐
│     Employees       │                          │      Managers       │
└─────────────────────┘                          └─────────────────────┘
          │                                                 │
          ▼                                                 ▼
┌─────────────────────┐                          ┌─────────────────────┐
│ Orientation Videotape│                         │                     │
│   Your Career Is    │                          │     Training as     │
│     up to You       │                          │   Career Coaches    │
└─────────────────────┘                          └─────────────────────┘
          │                                                 │
          ▼                                                 │
┌─────────────────────┐                                     │
│   Discover 1-2-3    │                                     │
│ • Current Satisfaction│                                   │
│ • Self-Assessment   │                                     │
│ • Gathering Data    │                                     │
└─────────────────────┘        ┌─────────────────────┐      │
          │            ───────▶ │   Reality Check     │ ◀────┤
                                │    Discussion       │      │
┌─────────────────────┐        └─────────────────────┘      │
│   Gathering Data    │                  │                  │
│  Career Directions  │ ◀────────────────┘                  │
│      at CGW         │                                     │
│  Career Matrix Book │                                     │
└─────────────────────┘                                     │
                                                            │
┌─────────────────────┐                                     │
│   Discover 4-5      │                  ▼                  │
│ • Formulate Career Goals│      ┌─────────────────────┐    │
│ • Develop Career Action Plan│   │  Development Plan   │ ◀──┘
│  How to Use All You've │ ─────▶ │    Discussion       │
│   Learned to Plan   │          └─────────────────────┘
│     Your Career     │
└─────────────────────┘
```

- *Gathering data:* This module is augmented by *Career Directions at Corning Glass Works,* a videotape that identifies different functional work areas, and a career matrix book that
  contains detailed information on position responsibilities,
  salary grades, skills requirements, sample career paths, and
  statistics on career movement. This information further
  helps employees create realistic career options.

- *Discover 4-5:* These modules—Formulate Career Goals and Develop a Career Action Plan—are supplemented by a final videotape, *How to Use All You've Learned to Plan Your Career.* Employees do computer searches for positions at Corning that would fit their unique skills and interests before preparing their plans.
- *Development plan discussions:* Managers provide support and additional information to further employee career plans. The final videotape helps employees prepare for this discussion.

Summary: A pilot program, run with a small group of managers and employees, resulted in a 47 percent increase in employees who had completed career plans and a 33 percent increase in managers who helped employees with career planning. A detailed plan has been created for wide-scale implementation of this system for nonexempt employees at other sites and localities. The wide-scale implementation includes collecting pre–post-program evaluation data. A similar system is also being planned for professional employees.

Among the system's key strengths are its useful, well-documented career information; its decentralized nature (so that it can be implemented in all the divisions); its multiple interventions (computer program, workbooks, videotapes, involvement of managers); and its integration of the current performance appraisal system with career development.

First Chicago:
Individual Career Planning and Development System

Target Group: Approximately 2,800 bank officers.
Objectives/Visions:

- To retain valued officers
- To reinforce the bank's overall commitment to excellence and its personnel
- To strengthen the internal job matching system

Background: First Chicago established an individual career planning and development system in response to several sources of data. A 1980 officer attitude survey, and results from subsequent feedback groups, indicated that 60 percent of the officers were concerned about career issues; exit interviews with former officers supported these data. For example, one officer stated, "When I talked to my manager about a career change, he said I was too valuable to the department in my current position to make a move—but I wasn't doing what I want to be doing, so I decided to resign." Furthermore, this group had a higher turnover in personnel than other groups in the bank.

In response to these needs, a system was established that viewed career planning as a voluntary activity, for which responsibility is shared by the individual, the managers, and the organization. Each officer is responsible for planning his or her career; each manager is responsible for counseling and helping develop the careers of his or her employees; and the organization is responsible for providing the system and support through which the officers and managers can fulfill their responsibilities.

Model Components: The program was introduced separately to managers and employees through a rolling implementation in eighteen departments. One hundred small group sessions, lasting thirty to sixty minutes and involving two to three dozen employees, introduced the program. Department managers or senior managers presided at these sessions. A model of the program is displayed in Figure 18. Each of the components for the individual employee is as follows:

• *Résumé/career planning worksheet:* As a first step, officers complete a career planning worksheet; it is for the individual's own use and need not be submitted to anyone, although officers are encouraged to share them with their managers if they feel comfortable doing so. The worksheets are designed to help officers organize their thoughts about their strengths, development needs, and short- and long-term goals and interests. As officers complete the worksheet, they can obtain information from their managers or the human resource staff on possible career options in the bank.

Figure 18. First Chicago Individual Career Planning and Development Process.

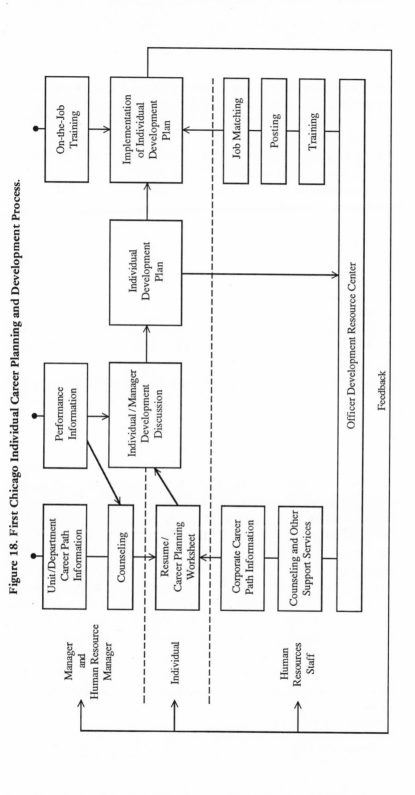

• *Individual-manager development discussions:* After completing the worksheet, officers conduct development discussions with their managers. In these, they discuss their short- and long-term goals, agree on an "earliest consideration," and identify any further development or training they may need to qualify for the next possible placement.

• *Individual development plan:* As a result of the development discussions, managers assess the reality of the officers' short-term goals, the next possible placements. After agreement is reached, the officers and their managers sign the plan, which is forwarded to the officer development resource center, whose staff serves as a clearinghouse between officers and the human resource managers assigned to various bank departments.

• *Implementation of individual development plan:* After submitting individual development plans, officers are entered into a job matching system, which includes posting and training (on or off the job). Officers are considered for open positions if they have expressed an interest in the particular position or that type of position, if they meet the basic qualifications, and if they are eligible for consideration. Individuals are notified when they are being considered for a job.

Summary: Since 1984, when the system was implemented, 130 officers have been matched with open positions. Twenty-five of the matches resulted in placements, sixteen of which were in new departments. Program expenses to date have been calculated at $175,000; and savings (based on the 30 percent search fee that would have been charged to fill the position from the outside) are calculated at $215,000—a net gain of $40,000 to date. Several factors contributed to the system's success: it responded to the concerns of officers and helped them take a more active role in planning their careers; it had the bank chairperson's up-front support; it augmented human resource structures, such as succession planning, staffing, recruiting, training and development, and staff credibility; and it gave managers an additional source from which to fill vacancies within the bank.

A Final Word

The four systems models presented in this chapter are designed to portray a variety of successful designs and approaches. They illustrate the importance of combining a variety of interventions in order to respond to the needs of the organization, involve managers and employees, build from existing human resource structures or establish new structures, and fit the culture and norms of the organization.

These criteria can guide the design of models in other organizations and can be adapted to accommodate such factors as limited resources, time, and acceptability. Advisory groups also provide useful feedback on these and other factors. (Other possible models to use as references are included in Resource B.) A final—and important—ingredient for the last task in determining new directions and possibilities is each developer's creativity and inventiveness.

PART THREE

Implementing Action Plans

Part Two discussed creating a vision, a desired state based on specific needs and key target groups. The time has come to focus on an action plan, the third essential element for creating change. Often, organizations stall at the vision: Part Three describes ways to decide on practical first steps to ensure that the vision will indeed be implemented. Among the strategies included here are those for assuring top management support, forming advisory groups, setting up a pilot project, and developing a career development system.

Some key questions must be answered to achieve this step:

- How can commitment and support for the project be built? What strategies help assure top management's endorsement and participation?
- What strategies bridge the gap between present needs and the vision of the future? What roles can advisory groups play?
- What steps need to be taken in setting up a pilot program? What options are there for developing a career development system? What skills are needed in a career development staff?

The first chapter in Part Three describes strategies for building and maintaining the critical involvement of top managers from the beginning. How to use advisory groups during all steps and phases is discussed in the second chapter. The third chapter covers what must be in place to ensure a successful pilot program and what approaches are useful in developing the career development system within an organization.

Chapter Nine

Gaining the Support
of Top Management

"Change has got to be top down and bottom up simultaneously [and] you must get top management support" (Thompson, 1983, p. 16).

This chapter addresses the essential task of assuring top manager support—not only in the first planning stages but also in defining needs, creating a vision, and throughout the process of maintaining change with a career development system.

All organizations, whether in industry, education, religion, or government, are made up of three groups: top managers, middle managers, and workers. Each group has unique and critical powers (Oshry and Oshry, 1977). Crucial for career development efforts are the powers of top managers. Top managers have the ultimate approval or rejection of a project, proposal, or idea in the organization. They are the policymakers who command the money and personnel resources that can legitimize the changes required by a career development system. Only if top managers lend their credibility, blessings, and support will career development programs be successfully implemented and will others in the organization be permitted to experiment with changes in current procedures, rules, forms, and practices. It is noteworthy that a characteristic of internal entrepreneurs, according to Kanter (1983), is the ability to get the blessing and sanction of top managers.

Only top managers, researchers Oshry and Oshry (1977)

found, can create a mission or vision for the organization that captures system energy, and only they can develop structures (policies, practices, procedures) that enable the mission or vision to flourish and be realized. If middle managers or workers—or human resource professionals—try to usurp this unique power, they are either sabotaged or ostracized, despite the most excellent ideas and best intentions.

But, if human resource professionals have no power to create missions or develop structures, they can move information, as can middle managers, Oshry and Oshry also found. They can be coordinators, stage managers, and facilitators; they can orchestrate the career development program in such a way that top managers are seen as mission setters and structure validators. To do this, in addition to their conceptual and intellectual skills, they need to call on their political and persuasion skills to gain the interest and commitment of top managers, to convince the managers to view the ideas and projects as their own.

To "sell" the vision means anticipating the needs and fears of the managers. Kanter (1983) developed the following list of characteristics of saleable projects:

- *Testability:* Can the vision be demonstrated in a pilot program?
- *Reversibility:* Can the organization easily go back to the old way or method?
- *Concreteness:* Will results be discrete, tangible, and easy to see?
- *Familiarity:* Is the vision in line with successes from the past?
- *Congruence:* Does the vision fit the current direction of the organization?
- *Publicity value:* Will successes be seen and recognized?

Another aspect also must be considered: how to sell top managers on support during start-up and on continuing such support and involvement throughout the effort. Useful strategies and techniques are described in the following sections.

Strategies for Building Top Management Support
from the Start

Top managers must feel they own the idea. If the career development program is to take place, essential top management interest and support must be built. Strategies for building such support include using a single-text approach, analyzing the competition, pointing to bottom-line possibilities, building a support network among top managers, pointing to results elsewhere, and using appropriate language.

Use a Single-Text Approach. No real change can be brought about without accommodating the basic interests that motivate people and underlie the hubbub of activities and discussions (Fisher and Ury, 1981). The basic interests of top managers must be addressed in any career development program, so that those managers will provide the requisite energy and momentum to see the project through; so that they will generate creative ideas and suggest structural possibilities; and, most important, so that they will feel a sense of ownership. Top managers must be made to realize that the career development program is in the organization's interest—in their interest.

A single-text approach is an effective strategy for uncovering what is important to top managers. In this approach, we first prepare a rough draft proposal for a career development system and share the draft with trusted allies in different parts of the organization. The objective is to garner advice on how the draft does or does not meet their interests, what they would like to add or subtract. Ask such questions as What is wrong with it? Why won't it work? Why might it work? What is your main concern? What do you really care about? What is needed for your involvement and support?

Based on the advice received, and with a clearer understanding of the underlying interests in hand, rewrite the draft to incorporate and accommodate those interests; then recirculate the rewritten text for a second round of advice. The process needs to continue, spreading to a widening circle that must include the essential top managers, whose suggestions and recommendations on how to accomplish objectives have to be a visible part of the final text.

The result of this approach is a proposal in which the needs identified and the solutions recommended reflect the basic underlying interests of top managers and key constituencies. The single text of this proposal has served as the vehicle for building the crucial agreement and commitment.

Does this approach work? A recent, well-known use of the single-text approach (that is, looking to interests instead of methods) allowed Israel and Egypt to reach a solution at Camp David in 1978. "The U.S. listened to both sides, prepared a draft to which no one was committed, asked for criticism, and kept improving the draft. Twenty-three drafts and thirteen days later, the U.S. had a text it could recommend. When Carter brought it to the table, Begin and Sadat accepted" (Fisher and Ury, 1981, p. 121). Because their underlying interests were clarified, both parties were satisfied, and the agreement allowed both Egyptian sovereignty and Israeli security.

The same approach was also used recently in a large technical organization: Line managers spent six weeks writing and rewriting a proposal for creating a group leader readiness program. Each draft was circulated to the top managers of the three main divisions involved. Interviews followed each circulation, and the new comments and ideas were included in the next draft. Senior management accepted the final proposal, and a long-term problem is now being seriously addressed.

Analyze the Competition. Some top managers are driven and motivated more by the need to better the competition than by the intrinsic values of career development activities. For example, these managers may perceive as a fad using career development to meet the problem of high turnover; they may say that the problem simply goes with the business and, more important, nobody else is dealing with it. To enlist the support of these managers, we need to document how other organizations are solving similar problems and why a career development program can be an opportunity, not a fad. Data need to be collected on such topics as

- Names and numbers of competitive organizations undertaking career development programs
- Focuses of their programs: functional area, target group, desired results
- Results of their programs: strategies, pre–post-program measures
- Duration of their programs

Competition-oriented top managers may be particularly impressed by data indicating that the competition has recognized a similar problem but has not yet developed a solution. The fact that the organization will derive a competitive edge by meeting the problem first is sure to generate support. (See also the "Point to Results Elsewhere" strategy in this section.)

Point to the Bottom-Line Possibilities. Because career development programs address specific needs and problems, they relate to long-term strategic plans and affect the organization's bottom line and business plans. Draw up several budgets, at least for the program's design and start-up. Estimate the cost of specific innovative and pertinent ideas. Also estimate the underlying, hidden costs, including those of not responding to documented needs and problems by, for example, explaining the costs related to specific needs and problems:

- If the problem is loss of promising employees, estimate the hiring and selection costs, training and education costs, and lessened productivity costs.
- If the problem is new employees leaving to join the competition, estimate the selection and hiring costs, costs of sending competitors trained people, and costs of losing trade secrets and ideas.
- If the problem is lack of promotion of women and minority people, estimate the costs of class-action suits, grievance costs, and legal fees.

An example of demonstrating hidden costs is the case of Bill Smith, a fifty-three-year-old senior executive, who was passed over for a major promotion and had no access to career counseling or other career development services to ease the transition. Table 15 shows how the hidden costs mounted

Table 15. Hidden Costs for an Unassisted Career Transition.

	Hourly Wage	Days/Hours Missed	Days at 50%	Actual Cost
Bill Smith	$54	40 days	70 days (30,240) / 2	$17,280
				15,120
Four corporate officers in conference, worrying	60	240 hours		14,400
Five support personnel	19		110 days (16,720) / 2	8,360
Above average expense account				4,000
Amount lost in sales, program implementation, research, and development				N/A
Total actual loss				$59,160

Source: Sprague, 1984.

over four or five months to almost $60,000. The actual cost of bringing in a consultant to help Bill Smith get through this career transition, get his professional life back together through optimum one-on-one counseling, would have been only $2,500.

The cost-benefit ratios of career development programs can also be demonstrated. For example, worker and middle management behavior changes can be estimated and expressed in dollars. The behavior changes cited in the following list emerged from a recent assessment following a four-month career development program in a major service industry:

Workers volunteered more, rather than sitting back and
waiting
More responsibility taken

More innovative ideas started

Projects started, developed, and finished on time or ahead
of schedule

Persistence in achieving goals

More productive work

Improved performance

Supervisors more aware of potential and worker competence

Enhanced employee self-confidence

Keep in mind that top managers listen more attentively to
quotes with dollar figures.

Build Networks from Top Manager to Top Manager. An
effective strategy, frequently used in noncompetitive organization, is to connect a top manager with a successful program to
another top manager who is exploring the possibilities of a similar program. For example, a human resources vice president was
looking for a systematic way to make career management opportunities readily available to more people. Someone had recommended offering a manager-as-career-coach workshop for
middle managers and designing a self-paced career resource center for use by all managers and workers. Although the workshop
finally was begun, little else happened until the vice president
toured another organization's outstanding career resource center. The top managers in that other organization were so enthusiastic about the changes they were seeing in their employees as
a result of the center that the vice president decided to set one
up in his organization. Now he is willing to let other dubious
top managers visit his organization's center. Top managers sold,
and will sell, other top managers.

Point to Results Elsewhere. Results speak for themselves.
Positive results in other situations engender courage, hope, and
enthusiasm. When statistics on successful career development
programs in other companies or industries are quoted, top managers pay attention. The kinds of facts that appeal to those ultimately accountable are exemplified by the following results of
one upward-mobility program:

- The upward-mobility rate produced was 47 percent; most transfers were achieved within eighteen months.
- Lateral mobility increased from 10 to 36 percent in twelve months.
- Ninety-seven people whose jobs were phased out are happily employed in six new career paths within the organization.
- Turnover decreased by 32 percent in eighteen months.

Such records of successes serve as valuable stepping stones in overcoming top manager resistance and building support.

Use Appropriate Language. Successful change agents use words, metaphors, slogans, and program names that are in concert with top management, and that build on to the organization's mission. When an organization's own words and concepts can be harnessed creatively, credit reverts to the top managers who previously selected those words and concepts and lends a positive, successful tone to the career development program. For example, graft a career development program onto an organization name, or part of a name, using it in a new way. One career management program at Holiday Inns, Inc., is named Career Directions (based on an organization product called a Directions Package), and another is named Career Crossroads. Both names are apt for a travel-related organization and relate to organization metaphors and slogans.

The kind of language top managers prefer and use gives clues to the most effective style for presenting a program or idea. If top managers typically engage in frequent, short conversations, make the presentations short and sweet; if top managers prefer communications in a Madison Avenue style, presentations must conform. It is also a good idea to assess top managers' learning styles (see Chapter Four) before picking the best way to pitch a presentation, as well as to remember Drucker's (1985) contention that the world can be divided into readers/writers and talkers/listeners.

Essentials for Top Manager Support and Endorsement

Top managers need not be involved directly in the day-to-day activities of a career development program, but they must be involved in the key steps (defining needs, determining new directions, deciding on first steps, maintaining change) and in the critical decisions, as well as be committed to the mission and direction of the program. Top managers must also offer those essential signs of endorsement and support that will help coalesce potential supporters into a strong constituency (Kanter, 1983); that is, they must be perceived by the rest of the organization as being strongly behind the career development program. The very presence of a top executive at a meeting related to the program, for example, makes it easier to get the resources, information, and support of others in the organization.

Career development projects, like other change projects, progress through five phases: need/problem definition, coalition building, vision building, implementation, and ongoing assessment and evaluation. (Note that these five phases are represented in the four parts of this book, although coalition building is an ongoing function that must be carried on throughout.) Top manager support and endorsement is essential in each phase, although the form of the necessary involvement varies. A prime concern throughout these phases is to secure the visible support of top management in order to assure that people in the organization recognize that the support is there.

During Need/Problem Definition (Phase One). Top managers need to be convinced of the real, specific need or problem (plateaued employees, rapid turnover, lack of bench strength in managerial ranks) and build their own understanding and commitment to rectifying the situation. Top managers do not have to be involved in collecting or analyzing data, but they must be directly involved in reviewing and discussing the data and defining the problem in order to gain an intellectual appreciation of its complexity. We need to spend time with top managers to make sure they go through this kind of intellectual process. Their intellectual appreciation of the complexity of a specific need or problem will also help top managers be more creative with and sensitive to those in the organization who resist, usually covertly, efforts at change. Responsibilities for top managers in the problem definition phase of a project (and the level of involvement required) follow:

- Reviewing climate survey and needs assessment data (high)
- Adding information about the need/problem and causes (low)
- Participating in an advisory group to review the data (high)
- Listening to formal presentation of needs/problems and recommendations (low)
- Selecting an advisory group to study the problem and make recommendations (low)

It is also important to weigh with top managers the importance of their level of involvement against the time and energy they have available, then select roles accordingly.

During Coalition Building (Phase Two). Until a majority of the people in an organization are behind the idea of a career development program, nothing of import will actually happen. This phase, identifying and developing a network of influential backers who will support and work towards a solution, is a strategic time for both human resource professionals and top management. Together, they need to do a thorough assessment of whose support and what support are required and plan ways to attract that support.

Subsequent responsibilities for top managers (and their levels of involvement) follow:

- Selecting an advisory group (low)
- Calling individuals and enlisting participation in advisory group (high)
- Talking on the importance of addressing the need (low)
- Feeding back information from climate survey or needs assessment (high)
- Visiting key people and encouraging involvement (high)

During Vision and Model Building (Phase Three). A key responsibility of top management, as already noted, is to create the visions and mission for the organization. In Phase 3, top managers must be involved closely in a career development program and be perceived as the forces and spokespersons behind it.

One of the four distinct characteristics of the ninety leaders interviewed by Bennis (1984, p. 17) was the ability to manage attention, usually through a "compelling vision that brings others to a place they have not been before." Because not all top managers—or national leaders—have this ability, human resource professionals must be ready to serve as facilitators in creating a vision and mission: making sure that the mission will stimulate new technology and ideas by challenging unresolved dilemmas; that the mission will bind together people from all parts of the organization in a common direction, while meeting individual needs and interests; that the mission will be seen as adventurous and challenging but possible—and worth its cost; that the mission will enliven, rejuvenate, energize, and accelerate people and call forth their perseverance and commitment over time. In helping develop a successful project mission statement, make sure the statement itself has one central theme, is brief and easily understood, and uses simple language.

Vision and model-building activities for top managers during this phase (and their levels of involvement) follow:

- Talking to employees on the mission of the program (low)
- Running a futures conference (high)
- Filming a video for employees on the mission (high)
- Discussing the program in a newsletter (low)
- Inviting people to participate in the program (low)
- Being interviewed for newspapers, TV, newsletters (low)
- Working with the advisory group to formulate the vision and mission of the program (high)
- Naming the program (low)
- Working to integrate succession planning with human resource planning (high)

During Implementation (Phase Four). For this phase, when the idea moves from the drawing board into reality, high levels of top management support are of greatest importance. Many visible, participatory activities are possible for top managers—and, all too often, unless human resource professionals are aware and skillful, top manager involvement is almost totally confined to this phase.

In orchestrating the participation of top managers during implementation, build on the trust, willingness to share, and confidentiality developed since the inception of the career development program. Political skills are vital. Examples (and levels of involvement) of implementation phase top manager activities follow:

- Presiding over kick-off programs (low)
- Filming a video to kick off the program (high)
- Presiding over openings and start-ups (low)
- Sitting on panels to answer questions on the corporate mission and objectives (low)
- Briefing people on the program (low)
- Writing and signing letters and memos (low)
- Participating in workshops and seminars (high)
- Acting as a formal mentor (high)
- Listening to presentations and recommendations (high)
- Sitting on an advisory committee to resolve difficulties with the program (high)

When top managers participate fully, when they look at issues in their own careers, when they want to become more skilled at coaching and counseling their own employees, career development programs are most successful. To facilitate this involvement and support, design a special seminar for top managers. The goals of the seminar would be to educate the managers to the main career issues of their employees, to give them structured assessment tools and techniques for assessing where they themselves are in their careers and what they want to make happen in the next four to ten years. The more top managers actively wrestle with career issues themselves, the more empathy, support, and legitimate concern they demonstrate to their employees. And, when top managers talk openly and candidly about their own career concerns, the tone is set for the whole organization's career development system.

Other ways to promote this high level of involvement, and help top managers work on their own careers, are to arrange for participation in coaching skills counseling sessions with outside consultants, participation in executive assessment and counseling programs, and participation in professional seminars at prestigious universities; to develop internal programs for top managers and minibriefings to elicit desire and support for more in-depth career workshops; to run manager-as-career-developer workshops, in which the focus is on how top managers can help their employees while helping themselves; and to work with top managers to ensure that the formal succession planning system accommodates organization cultures (see Chapter Three).

During Ongoing Assessment/Evaluation (Phase Five). Projects that lead to lasting change go beyond the implementation phase and involve ongoing evaluation. They demand creating mechanisms for pre–post-program assessment processes, which build in accountability and responsibility from the first phase, problem definition. To build top management support for this process from the very beginning, emphasize the importance of having both a picture of the way things were and a picture of the way things become. (Both pictures can use the needs assessment as a base; see Chapter One.) Top managers may have to work much harder at spelling out clearly the results desired from the project in phase one. However, such data are required for comparison, so that practical changes for the program can be suggested, appropriate assistance can be given to other organization units contemplating similar programs, and effective talk about final results can be possible.

Top manager evaluation and assessment activities (and the level of involvement required) follow:

- Demanding pre–post-program measures and reports (low)
- Redesigning rewards and procedures to reinforce the program goals (high)
- Regularly keeping track of results (low)
- Integrating into the data base existing organization statistics on, for example, turnover, hires from within, loss of promising employees, speed of replacing people (low)
- Tying development into key areas of responsibility (low)
- Talking to people who participated in the program (high)

For example, one organization's career management/mobility program aimed at increasing by 30 percent the number of employees who made a career move. The human resource professional coded the organization chart by length of time on the same job: red for over six years, blue for four to six years, yellow for eighteen months to four years, green for zero to seventeen months. The top marketing division manager then worked with his associate managers to assess the needs of each job and decide which employees were currently ready for change, or soon would be. The top manager also reinforced his commitment to increasing mobility by tying career development activities to the merit pay package. Two years later, results were clearly in evidence, and could be accurately assessed, on the organization chart, which now showed that the number of red and blue employees (four to over six years in place) had decreased by 46 percent—16 percent beyond the target amounts.

A Final Word

Top manager identification and involvement with career development programs are essential from beginning to end. Use every possible strategy, every bit of selling and political skill—as well as intellectual and conceptual skill—to build top manager support into career development programs in every phase: in defining the needs and present system, in setting the vision and determining new directions and possibilities, in developing the action plan and deciding on practical first steps, in maintaining the change.

Chapter Ten

Using Advisory Groups
to Build Broad Support
and Participation

"If key people are involved, you're halfway there."

Career development programs represent a potentially major change. They need to be presented to the organization only after garnering wide, active, positive support. One of the best ways to ensure the needed enthusiasm and participation is by forming an advisory group.

Advisory groups can play important roles in defining the present system and its needs (see Part One). Advisory groups are also useful in determining new directions and in setting the vision (see Part Two). But advisory groups play their most vital role in helping develop the action plan, in deciding on first practical steps, in getting a career development program off the drawing board.

Advisory groups are composed of individuals with a variety of perspectives, who can address critical career problems in thoughtful, creative ways. In short, advisory groups can form the bridge between the current state of career development in an organization to the future, ideal state, in part by providing stability and demonstrating some of the desired new management principles and results.

Advisory groups are usually made up of six to twelve key

people, representing different groups and levels within the organization. They are brought together not for their technical expertise but for their knowledge of diverse parts of the organization.
For this reason, an advisory group can be helpful in identifying
problems and assessing needs in the present system. This knowledge is also why advisory group members are equipped to offer
realistic advice on implementing a career development program.
They know what will work and provide an ongoing arena for
testing ideas. They provide sensitive insights on interoffice politics that would otherwise be difficult to learn. They also identify
line managers and key players with the career development
activities and keep human resource professionals as consultants
rather than advocates.

Members of the advisory group may clash at times because of their varying backgrounds. But, as Nadler (1979)
points out, from these clashes come better ideas, more realistic
solutions, and a greater sense of accomplishment and participation—all of which tend to reduce resistance to change and motivate more people to make the change effective.

Advisory groups do not have to be asked to undertake
the active role of traditional task forces, which often serve as
working committees and oversee whole projects from beginning
to end. Advisory groups respond, critique, and comment; they
have consultative power rather than line authority; and they
need not become involved in the labor-intensive, time-consuming tasks usually associated with task forces at the beginning of
projects.

In general, advisory groups become increasingly helpful
and involved as the career development program enters the design, strategic planning/public relations, and implementation
phases, as illustrated in Figure 19.

Benefits from Advisory Groups

Forming an advisory group allows top managers to demonstrate their support and commitment to the career development program by giving it importance and urgency. It also signals their belief in collaboration and teamwork, which may be

Figure 19. Level of Advisory Group Involvement.

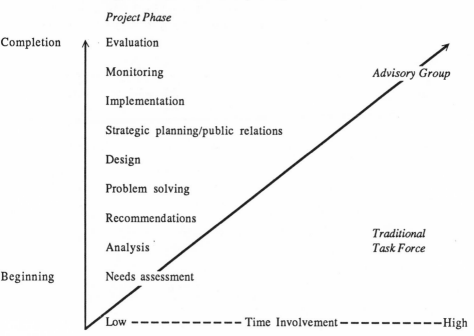

a new message in some organizations. Participation of people from various parts of the system in an advisory group increases the chances that the needs/problems they address will be effectively resolved. In return, advisory groups provide top managers with another means for giving rewards (assignments on advisory groups provide visibility and recognition). Advisory groups also give top managers the opportunity to observe the performance and capabilities of those people chosen. By gauging their abilities to handle increased diversity, complexity, and new pressures, top managers gain valuable information on their potential.

Among the benefits to middle managers and others in the groups are opportunities to enrich and enlarge their jobs, to develop an increased appreciation for the complexity of the organization and how to produce change and introduce new ideas. Membership in an advisory group enhances the development of employees by exposing them to other functional areas and people, by building stronger resource networks to help in their day-to-day jobs, and frequently by making them aware of new career opportunities through new networks, allies, and perceptions of competence.

These benefits, which are included in the list of sell/no-sell statements in Exhibit 6, are useful in considering how best to sell, or reemphasize the value of, advisory groups to top managers.

Exhibit 6. Selling the Benefits of Advisory Groups to Top Management.

Read through the following statements and assess which would "sell" in the organization and which would not. The sell statements can then be a central feature of strategies for building and assuring top management support.

Top managers in the organization will see advisory groups as

	Sell	No Sell
• Demonstrating that top management sees the career projects as a priority.	___	___
• Giving top managers another visible form of rewarding outstanding contributors.	___	___
• Giving top managers an opportunity to gauge capabilities and potential of group members.	___	___
• Assuring, through the use of a widely representative group, realistic solutions to career development needs.	___	___
• Ensuring that conflicts are aired and resolved prior to implementation of any strategy.	___	___
• Giving a chance for job enrichment to both the leader and members.	___	___
• Providing human resource professionals and line managers an arena in which to test other ideas concerning human resource planning.	___	___
• Keeping human resource professionals out of an advocacy/missionary role.	___	___
• Assuring that the pilot project will succeed.	___	___

Many Hats: The Roles of Advisory Groups

During its lifetime, the role or roles of an advisory group may change, and need to be renegotiated, several times. Throughout these changes, it is important that the scope and objectives of the role, or roles, are kept clearly defined.

In career development programs, advisory groups can serve as data collectors and problem solvers, design consultants, selection strategists, sales and public relations promoters, and providers of feedback and follow-up. Each advisory group will, of course, not necessarily play all these roles.

Data Collecter and Problem Solver. In this role, the advisory group can be used either to collect data from the organization through surveys, questionnaires, sensing sessions, or focus group interviews or to respond to data already collected by reporting on their potential implications. In either case, the group can provide grass-roots advice and can steer the effort accordingly; and the members feel useful, if not instrumental, in defining the present needs and system and in determining new directions.

For example, in a major service industry, an advisory group was formed after an organization-wide climate survey clearly indicated a need for career development within the organization's structure. The group was mandated to respond to the data and make recommendations for a comprehensive career development program.

The nine members of the group divided into three sections, to prepare lists of what would constitute success of the program to each of the affected constituencies: department heads, managers of department heads, and top managers. These indicators of success were turned into goals for the project: increased lateral mobility of department heads, speed in filling open positions, increased confidence of general managers in grooming and readying replacements, reduced turnover among department heads, and more utilization of cross-training options. The success indicators/goal statements served two purposes. They defined present needs for key target groups and provided a basis for pre–post-program evaluation. Based on the data collected before the program and at the end of the first year, results were dramatic.

Another organization, which faced a lack of mobility opportunities, had data from deep-sensing meetings conducted with all nonexempt personnel. The data were organized into number of moves by nonexempt workers in each department and racial, sexual, and educational background of those who moved from nonexempt to professional jobs in the past three years. The nearly twenty pages of raw data were given to an advisory group mandated to assess areas in which lack of mobility caused problems; ranking those areas by problem severity; suggesting plans, solutions, and tactics; receiving and assessing input from task forces working on parts of the problem; developing practical, affordable recommendations for senior management; testing recommendations with peers and employees before coming to a final agreement; and giving advice and feedback on strategies for implementation. Through these recommendations, the advisory group members function as problem solvers, a role subsequently supplemented by their advice and feedback during design and implementation phases.

Design Consultant. In this role, advisory group members work with internal and external consultants to evaluate proposed program components, develop objectives and criteria for assessing these components, and make recommendations. In the problem of the reservation agents at Holiday Inns, Inc., the application process was designed to foster self-assessment, network building, and discussions with managers about current skills and key performance areas. The advisory group prepared objectives and assessment criteria for this component, different approaches that fit the criteria, and recommended a final application process, which dealt expertly with the concern that too many people would apply for the program by making the process difficult enough to assure commitment. The process, which encouraged potential participants to expand their networks, was so successful that nearly a dozen of the first hundred applicants found new jobs even before the initial workshop, with some receiving on-the-spot offers during the required interviews (see Chapters Seven and Eight for discussions of this program). The special knowledge and expertise of the reservation agents and managers on the advisory group ensured the successful design of this component.

Because of their daily contact with employees and managers affected by the career development program, advisory groups can also give important advice about the design of schedules. For example, advisory group members can point out that "three days is too long to have those employees away from their jobs."

Selection Strategist. In addition to helping design application processes, advisory groups can also develop criteria for selecting participants from among those who apply to the program. Here again, the advisory group's "feel" for what will work is invaluable. Furthermore, the group members get to see close up the effectiveness of the application process.

In a program that was voluntary and open to all, for example, the advisory group developed a written form that took at least two hours to complete and was tough enough to eliminate participants who were not really committed to the program. The advisory group also published the selection criteria on the cover of the application, so applicants would know how they were to be rated. These criteria were

Effort and thoughtfulness
Completeness, answering all questions
Submission by application deadline
Length of service
Date of application

The initial response was so large, and the forms completed were of such high quality, that the advisory group had to break into subgroups to review and rank the applications. Three separate programs were scheduled over a six-month period to handle the volume.

Sales and Public Relations Promoters. Advisory groups assure that influential, affected constituencies are involved in the process of change. Members of the groups share their commitment and enthusiasm with others in the organization—and can sell the idea of a career development program, softly. Advisory groups also know how informal networks operate and can develop workable strategies for implementation. They know, for example, which is the most valued department in the division, so that selling the idea to that manager will sell it to everyone else.

In one organization, members of the advisory group distilled several program models into a single exciting, compact program and presented the final model to their peers and top management. Then, to sell the program, two members of the group went to each city in the region and presented an overview of the program, shared their excitement and the reasoning underlying the final program design, answered questions, assured others of their support, and gave out the application forms. As a result, the program was oversubscribed.

Another organization, after piloting a program with the strong backing of advisory groups in three divisions, offered a one-day awareness session on career development for key line managers and their human resource counterparts from other divisions. The day had four objectives: to help participants identify whether their division had any career development needs or problems; to share program models among the three divisions; to discuss results to date from each program; and to present an option to other divisions for consultation as they form their own advisory groups. Group members from the three divisions with pilot programs ran most of the sessions, describing what they learned and their successes and making recommendations. Based on these presentations, and the enthusiasm of each advisory group, four more divisions adapted the program to their own needs and began their own pilot projects.

Providers of Feedback and Follow-Up. Finally, the advisory groups assess the success of the career development program and the changes it brought about. For example, when Carolina Power and Light wanted to test a career resource center for its nonexempt employees before investing in it on a company-wide basis, the director of career development put together an advisory group made up of personnel representatives. After a briefing on the career resource center, the members of the group were to discuss employees' questions on such topics as career options, career paths, education, and skill requirements. Group members, therefore, became an extension of the training and development portions of the pilot program.

Once the target employees completed the program, the advisory group and the career development director evaluated the pilot program and made recommendations for improvements to the career resource center. Because of this united approach and the quality of feedback, the career director was able to sell top managers not only on the need for regional career resource centers but also on the need for middle managers to take a more proactive role in coaching and counseling their employees.

Issues in Setting Up Advisory Groups

Once a decision has been made to set up an advisory group, several other important decisions must be considered concerning, for example, membership, leadership, meeting schedules, time, and assuring participation. Creating a smoothly working, effective, temporary group takes forethought, planning, and constant nurturing. Success for advisory groups requires close attention to choosing the membership, selecting a competent leader or coleaders, clarifying the role of the leader, preparing for meetings, assuring participation and involvement of members, preparing for changing membership, and recognizing contributors.

Choosing the Membership. The important first decision is on who shall be members of the advisory group. Which individuals are most needed behind the idea because of their positions and expertise?

A political campaign model may provide insights on choosing members. According to Hirsch (1982), when organizations are presented with new ideas or solutions, the individuals within those organizations always fall into three categories: the "Fers," the "Gins," and the "Suadables." The Fers, who are for you, represent 15 percent of the entire organization. The Gins, who are against you and will resist or sabotage change, also represent approximately 15 percent of the organization. That leaves an important 70 percent, the Suadables, who can be turned into Fers if the plans are developed carefully.

Thus, once a specific need/problem and key target group have been identified, focus on potential advisory group members by asking three sequential questions: Who will be affected by taking on the problem? Will they be for, against, or persuadable concerning the career development effort? Whose support is essential for success?

One technique to answer these questions is to think of the need/problem and target group as the center of an open system, as in Figure 20. All the individuals and groups who will be affected by the problems of plateaued, isolated, nonexempt employees can be identified and placed in circles surrounding the need/problem and target group. This kind of a diagram organizes in a structured manner thought about groups and levels that need to be represented among the six to twelve members of the advisory group.

Which individuals and groups facing the need/problem can be determined as for, against, or persuadable to the idea of a career development program to meet the need? The plateaued employees themselves, for example, are undoubtedly for the effort, but what about their managers? Selecting those who know the organization best can be a definite asset because those key individuals know how to garner support in the organization: where it is and who needs to be persuaded.

People under consideration, Beckhard (1983) suggests, should have the following:

- *Sufficient clout and personal power in the organization to be able to give time to the group:* They must have some discretionary time in order to attend meetings and work effectively with the group.
- *The respect of their colleagues:* If this is so, individuals will be listened to because the people in question will be seen as a representative.
- *Sufficient interpersonal skills to work effectively in a group:* Leadership in this phase often requires persuasion, rather than formal power.

Figure 20. Open System for Selecting Members for an Advisory Group
on Plateaued, Isolated, Nonexempt Employees.

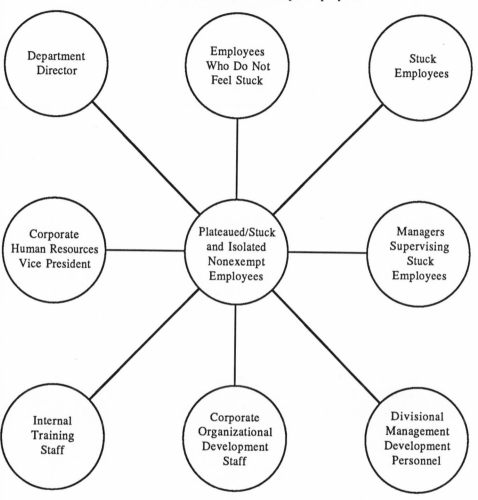

Most important, select people who want to be on the advisory group. No one should be coerced or pressured. A career development advisory group is no place for an unwilling participant or someone who thinks of it as just another job.

The checklist in Exhibit 7, which includes the important considerations described in this section, can be used to evaluate closely essential characteristics for effective group members.

Exhibit 7. Career Development Advisory Group Membership Checklist.

	Name	*Name*	*Name*	*Name*	*Name*
• Is the person interested in his or her own career?					
• Can the person manage the schedule and time to assure attendance?					
• Does the person want to be on the advisory group?					
• Is the person respected and listened to by peers?					
• Is the person respected and listened to by management?					
• Has the person a high degree of interpersonal skill?					
• Is the person an active participator, not just an observer?					

Selecting the Leader. Like most other groups, advisory groups need a leader or coleader to keep the ball rolling, schedule meetings, work out the agenda, conduct meetings, keep management informed, and interact with resource people and others. Particularly when the group is working outside the formal hierarchical structure, it is important that a formal leader be appointed.

Kanter (1983) suggests that a leader should be able to

• *Develop a clear vision of the future.* A leader must be able to articulate the benefits of the project, must be able to take a stand, and should be realistic yet flexible enough to take an occasional risk.

• *Build coalitions and political support for ideas.* Leaders need to know how to appeal to the real interests of their fellow employees and work easily with their peers.

• *Work successfully through groups.* A leader must be able to focus the group on the problem and conduct a meeting that enables the whole group to interact and at times disagree, so that new ideas surface. A leader must act as a coach or facilitator and keep the group moving, so that the concentration of the members is focused on the matters under discussion.

What happens when the advisory group leader is not the "right" person for the job? The career development program in one high-tech organization got off to a good start, in part due to the active sponsoring of an executive on the advisory group. When a coordinator took over as advisory group leader, during implementation of the action plan, problems arose. His mannerisms and formal style soon limited his ability to work within the group. He felt overly responsible for the group's work, took too much responsibility on himself, became unable to get the group to do its work. He ended up having fewer and fewer meetings and became more authoritarian and directive. Group members became demoralized, the advisory group slid into obsolescence, the program lost its vitality. Communication among advisory group members is critical; equally critical is selecting a leader whose personality blends reasonably well with the personalities of the other group members.

Clarifying the Role of the Leader. Once a leader is selected, his or her role, like that of the group as a whole, must be clearly delineated. If a human resource professional acts as coach and facilitator to the leader and the group, that role, too, needs to be clearly spelled out.

Having coleaders is often more efficient, enhances skill levels, and relieves some of the pressure. With coleaders, some roles can be shared (for example, keeping meetings on track), and others can clearly belong to one leader.

Among the myriad roles a leader plays are such typical administrative roles as developer of meeting agenda, scheduler of meetings, assigner and designer of premeeting work, and circulator of meeting minutes (Kruger, 1984). During meetings a leader also plays a critical role as facilitator, including keeping the meeting moving and on track, assuring participation of all members, clarifying roles and responsibilities, setting the standard for open and honest communication, and assuring results both during and after the meeting. In addition, the leader may be expected to provide regular communication or progress reports to key managers, present final recommendations to top management, and maintain the integrity of the mandate the group was given.

Last, the leader needs to help the group develop a set of ground rules or clear conditions for satisfying the mandate. These rules are usually simple but measurable and can be regularly assessed and discussed to monitor group processes. For example, a large association experimenting with an advisory group for the first time prepared the following ground rules:

Confidential information will stay with the group.
Members will do premeeting work and come prepared.
Regular attendance will be expected.
A written agenda will be circulated one week prior to meeting.
Open and honest communication will be reinforced.
Decisions and meetings will be documented in writing.
Organizational rather than personal issues will be the focus.
Meetings will begin and end on time.

These ground rules gradually came to apply to the way group members ran and participated in other meetings as well. This meant that a need/problem facing the organization (lack of commitment and the impersonal nature of the organization) was in some measure being addressed by the behavior of the group members. The advisory group became a practice session for a day-to-day management style.

Deciding the Logistics of Meetings. Advisory groups need to meet regularly at the beginning and at least monthly after initial work has been completed. Meetings work best when scheduled consistently (for example, every other Wednesday), with adequate advance notice given to all participants. It also helps to meet in varied locations, so the travel burden is shared. For those times when scheduling a meeting is impossible, the leader needs to check with members, on a one-to-one basis, or arrange a conference call. Such frequent, regular contact maintains the high priority of the project, assures ongoing feedback, and continually reminds members of the group that the project is a collaborative venture, not someone's pet project.

Creativity is required when basic logistics make frequent face-to-face meetings impossible. For example, an international organization whose advisory group members lived in several different countries used computer transmittals to facilitate collaboration and build consensus on an implementation plan. At another organization, also affected by international separation, the advisory group alternates meetings with phone interviews, which keeps down costs and assures collaboration at each step of the process.

Finally, short meetings, one to two hours long, are usually more productive. When meetings become too frequent or too long, members feel the project is infringing on their regular day-to-day responsibilities. It is the job of the chairperson or internal and external consultants to plan and prepare for the meeting. If these people do their jobs effectively, meetings can move at a fast, productive clip. In one organization, for example, because the three program models the advisory group received were dynamic and well prepared, subgroups needed less than three hours to assess each one and reach an enthusiastic consensus on a unique program model. Group members then worked quickly with the human resource staff to finalize the model and present it to the executive vice president, who became firmly committed to program success.

Assuring Participation and Involvement of Members. Meetings need to be designed so members share ideas and information, brainstorm, envision the future, and generate alternative solutions and innovations. The leader works to assure that all members participate frequently and receive a reasonable amount of time in which to present their ideas. Four easy-to-learn techniques help assure more equal participation: check-in, polling, subgroups, and the nominal group approach.

• *Check-In:* The beginning of each meeting is critical. The leader needs to set the climate at once. A structured check-in process assures strong starts. The leader needs to ask each person to share his or her progress on the project and encourage responding to successes in the development of the project since the last meeting. Such a check-in period lets people restore their cohesiveness; builds a more human, personal climate; and helps the leader discover any changes in thinking or purpose early in the meeting. The technique quickly builds the psychological inclusion of the total group, so that creative work can occur.

• *Subgroups:* During some phases of a career development program, discussions in greater depth or detailed assessments of information may be required. Subgroups fill the need for more depth in participation. At other times, there may be a need to assure quick generation of ideas and brainstorming. For situations like these, breaking into small groups allows much higher levels of participation and generates more information. At the same time, the decreased size changes group dynamics and allows more serious discussion of complex issues. A word of caution: The leader who plans to break the group into subgroups needs to give very specific directions, limit the time available, and monitor all groups to see that members are, indeed, keeping the discussion on track.

• *Polling:* Asking each person in the group his or her opinion on an issue sometimes causes discomfort, especially to those who would rather complain in private than disagree in public, but the leader must know where each person stands at each step of the way. Polling takes time, but it ensures consensus and ensures that group members support ideas and strategies. It is one of the primary tools for maintaining participation and involvement.

• *The nominal group approach:* Another way to assure full participation is to use the nominal group approach. Van de Ven and Delbecq (1971, p. 204) describe it this way: "Imagine a meeting room in which seven to ten individuals are sitting around a table in full view of each other. However, no one is speaking. Instead, each individual is writing ideas on a pad of paper, as the leader guides their thoughts. At the end of ten to twenty minutes, a structured sharing of ideas takes place. Each person, in round-robin fashion, provides one idea from his [or her] own list; this idea is then written on a flip chart by a recorder who is in full view of the group. There is *no discussion, only the recording of privately generated ideas.*"

According to Van de Ven, letting groups interact all the time can actually stifle creativity and produce uneven participation. This unique technique for assuring participation fosters the development of high-quality thinking by letting people really explore their own thoughts, resources, and experiences. At the same time, it avoids potential criticism and power plays by aggressive members of the group.

The nominal group approach works best when the advisory group is involved in finding facts, generating ideas, or making final decisions. In addition to assuring involvement of all members, this method is also a "time-saving process" (p. 210), since it can be activated and concluded with greater rapidity than interactive discussion groups.

Limiting the Group's Life and Changing Members. Advisory groups need to be short-term structures, lasting no longer than six to nine months. Busy people find it easier to commit themselves when they know their commitment is only for a limited period. After that time, if necessary, new members, who will bring in fresh ideas, can be added or substituted.

When a career development program reaches the implementation phase, adding new members is often critical. Because these new members represent the target group, they can provide more realistic feedback and highlight problems more quickly than those not involved as directly in the program. For example, in one financial organization, all members of the advisory groups for the four six-month career development programs each year are program participants. Overlapping hour-long meetings, led by the career development coordinator, foster increased learning, network building, and problem solving. The advisory group for the program starting in the year's first quarter meets for half an hour (1–1:30 P.M.) before the arrival of the advisory group for the program that starts in the second quarter and shares a meeting for half an hour (1:30–2 P.M.). Then the first-quarter advisory group leaves and the second-quarter advisory group continues to meet for a final half hour. This overlap gives the coordinator a chance to hear from each group member and have each member solve some problems and learn from others. In short, the newer members learn from the more experienced ones; networks expand and the coordinator is aided in the problem-solving process; and ideas are tested and decisions made to add or delete components of the program.

Recognizing Advisory Group Contributors. Although advisory group selection is in itself a form of recognition, public recognition of individual contributions is integral to successful programs. Such recognition can be given in a variety of ways; for example, by

> Preparing press releases for company newsletters
> Presenting token gifts upon the completion of a pilot program
> Hosting special luncheons for all those who have contributed to the success of a program
> Citing members of the advisory group for their hard work at the beginning of workshops
> Offering special, visible roles to participants when workshops are presented
> Asking advisory group members to participate in career-path interviews that can be placed in career resource centers for future use

A Final Word

Advisory groups are a smart, effective, critical strategy. They provide a temporary management structure that can move the organization from the current state to the envisioned future state. Good advisory groups contribute novel solutions to difficult problems and, in so doing, lay the groundwork for a smoother, more efficient career development system. Finally, what better way to develop a cadre of interested employees and managers than to give them the experience of working in a way that demands many of the same skills that top managers need?

Chapter Eleven

Implementing a Successful Pilot Program and Developing a Staff

> "You have to start small and plant many seeds along the way" (B. Krakau, personal communication, 1984).

The final task in implementing the vision with an action plan is to set up a pilot program and develop the career development unit. The key to success here is starting small, then reviewing each action and building slowly on past achievements. Successful programs repeatedly point to this strategy as the reason they are able to move from one accomplishment to another. Particularly because organizations and individuals are resistant to change, starting small is essential. As already emphasized in Part One, organizations and individuals seek to maintain their equilibrium; change threatens stability and creates anxiety.

Because a pilot program is small, it is not viewed as a threat and, therefore, those running the program face few challenges for control over the project, and its "test run" atmosphere allows further revision and experimentation. Pilot programs, like advisory groups, act as transition structures to the career development system of the future.

A Checklist for Setting Up a Pilot Program

This section lists the basic steps in formulating a successful pilot program. Many of these steps have already been addressed in preceding chapters.

211

Select an Appropriate Test Area Within the Organization.
The area, department, or division in which a pilot program can be successfully initiated meets the following criteria:

The specific need/problem is clearly in evidence.

The key target group can be found here.

Top managers are committed to the project.

Managers and employees are supportive, interested, and involved in career development.

Resources such as time, materials, and staff are available to support the pilot program.

Everyone involved (managers, employees, top managers) agrees to collect data and feedback.

Establish Clear Visions and Objectives. With a vision of an ideal future system firmly in mind and an appreciation of current conditions, determine what is to be accomplished. What would determine that the vision has been achieved? What would indicate success to employees? To managers? Chapter Fourteen contains sample lists of indicators that spell success to different groups in the organization.

Provide for Participation by Employees and Managers.
The pilot program needs to be planned in concert with key employees and managers of the area, department, or division in which it will take place. Participation in planning will build their commitment to the program and ensure their continued participation.

Establish Schedules, Roles, and Responsibilities. Clarify who will be responsible for what and when. Task matrices, PERT charts, timelines, and milestone charts are practical tools because they offer visible benchmarks by which all involved can measure progress.

Use Multiple Approaches. A combination of interventions is necessary to bring about lasting change, as has been repeatedly emphasized. Focusing on one intervention at a time may not produce sufficient momentum and may overlook the catalytic energy of natural combinations in effecting change. For example, we may need to help plateaued midlevel employees reconsider their skills and interests while at the same time we are working with their managers on redesigning jobs and possibly establishing a pilot job rotation program.

Anticipate Potential Obstacles. What might prevent the pilot program from being successful? How can those potential obstacles be neutralized, be prevented from affecting the pilot program? Anticipation is a better defensive strategy than reaction; fire prevention is more effective than fire fighting.

Establish an Evaluation Plan. What measures and indicators will be used to evaluate results of the pilot program? Will participants' reactions to activities be determined? Will behavior changes be assessed? Or will an attempt be made to evaluate what steps employees took as a result of their participation? (For a full discussion of establishing an evaluation plan, see Chapter Fourteen.)

Provide Time and Opportunity for Problem Solving. Because even the best plans rarely proceed as anticipated, adequate time needs to be set aside to monitor the pilot program, incorporate revisions, and make necessary changes.

Respond to Feedback from Participants. Unless the feedback and suggestions elicited from participants in the program are considered—and acted on—the pilot project will not be viewed as legitimate by those involved. To reiterate: If feedback is requested, it must be used.

Use the Success of a Pilot Program as Leverage to Take Further Steps. The small beginning pays off. Success of the pilot program builds support and enthusiasm. Other parts of the organization will be receptive and eager to participate in a program that works. Use the results of the pilot program to convince others to provide the resources needed to increase the scope of the program.

Organizing the Career Development Area

Starting small is important to success for new ideas. Career development is still a fledgling concept in most organizations. Few firms have answered such questions as these: Will the career development system be a separate unit or part of the human resources department? Whom will it report to? How will it be staffed?

In the few organizations that have established career development systems, several models are in use. (Two of these models are illustrated in Figure 21.) In one, career development is a unit under the human resources area that is equal to the traditional human resource development, human resource man-

Figure 21. Two Models for Organizing the Career Development System.

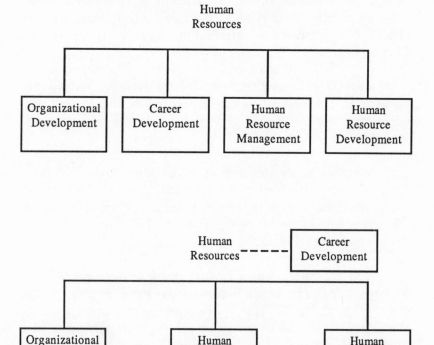

agement, and organization development units, as was described in the Introduction.

This model encourages teamwork among career development, work-force planning data, and training, education, and resource development. In another model, the career development unit reports directly to a vice president of human resources. This model is used particularly in organizations where a major issue, such as a consent decree or shortages and attrition of important employee groups, is deemed critical. A final model, now receiving increasing support, builds the responsibility for career development into the role of a decentralized human resource area. For example, at Corning Glass Works, fifteen human resource specialists train, develop, educate, and provide career development expertise in the line divisions, reporting back to a corporate human resource director and staff, who give them support and technical assistance.

Although these models can be an ideal for the future, currently few who undertake career development responsibilities have the luxury of diversified staffs committed to support the effort. More typically, a single individual in the human resource management or human resource development area is designated to handle the career development program. This person initiates, oversees, administers, monitors, and even conducts many of the organization's career development activities. Support may be garnered from various areas, ranging from the word processing center to the training staff, but the individual with major responsibility generally finds it necessary to personally undertake dozens of separate tasks. No wonder that person so often voices the lament heard throughout the investigations of career development programs for this book: "There's only me—and I have to be skilled at everything!"

Skills Needed in a Career Development Staff

The skills needed by those responsible for career development projects span the full range of program elements, from building commitment at the start, to designing initial programs through follow-up and program revision. These skills include not only techniques and knowledge but also ways of understanding and thinking about career development in the context of a specific organization.

The career development literature most frequently mentions management abilities in order to plan and administer the career development program, and training abilities, in order to design and conduct appropriate interventions for the employees involved. These areas of competency encompass leadership skills, administrative skills, technical skills, and interpersonal skills. One way to describe these myriad skills is to organize them into six major roles: systems thinker, program administrator, counselor, trainer, evaluator, and risk taker.

Systems Thinker. Career development programs require organizers and participants to think in terms of both the formal and informal systems of the organization and its environment. Such systems thinking influences design and administration of a career development program as well as approaches used with individual participants. For example, for a career development program to be firmly grounded in reality requires understanding the organization's level of commitment to human resources. Similarly, knowledge of the organization's work force and strategic planning allows realistic assessment of the potential of career development activities.

Systems thinkers need to comprehend and act on much more than is evident in organization charts and reports. They must work with variables in the internal environment (organization norms, politics, and culture) that substantially influence individual careers and career development activities. Systems thinking must also extend to the external environment in which the organization operates and to variables that affect both the organization and individual careers: other organizations, customers, and trends within that sector of the economy. For example, the professional environment of engineers and computer programmers is very different from the professional environment of accountants. Only by keeping abreast of such environmental variables can we design and conduct programs based on reality rather than best guesses and good intentions.

Another important aspect of systems thinking is understanding how organizations evolve. Organization development can be viewed as a process of planned change that moves the organization toward the examination of its processes (such as decision making, planning, and communications) and the adaptation of those processes to needed changes day to day (Burke and Hornstein, 1972). In this framework, career development is a process drawing from and affecting all areas of the organization. Thus, the career development program is installed as a process that interacts vitally with the entire organization rather than as simply an experiment that helps a few participants for a short time. In this way, systems thinking helps build commitment throughout the organization, establish appropriate opportunities for supportive learning by participants, and develop organization-wide processes for motivating and rewarding career development activities.

Program Administrator. This is the role of a "doer," with responsibility for much of the implementation and administration of the career development program. The role requires no less than the initiation and achievement of a program that may in some manner involve, or at least affect, every employee of the organization.

The program administrator starts by initiating ideas and generating organizational commitment and support, then continues with planning program elements and organizing activities. The role includes a range of management skills (planning for career development, organizing activities, communicating about career development with employees and managers) and a range of specialized career development skills (developing and designing such resource materials as job banks, in-house training programs, resource centers, talent banks). Some of the most valuable skills required to carry out this role are negotiation, budget formulation, communication (written or verbal), program planning, program design, organization, time management, research, quality control, and delegation.

Because these competencies are so many and varied, a personal assessment of talent in this area is useful. Some questions to ask include: What necessary skills do I now have? What skills do I need to acquire? How can I quickly acquire those I lack? What skills do others have that they might to commit to the program?

Another ongoing skill required of administrators is provision of program continuity; and this is largely a function of communication and information. Program directors are in the position of continually prodding top management to lend commitment and resources and to link career development to varied human resource elements. They also continually prod and encourage all employees and managers involved to consider career development an ongoing part of organizational and individual effectiveness. These functions require acting as an information channel, gathering and disseminating information on the organization and its environment, the need for career development, program successes, and future plans.

Counselor. One of the first roles those responsible for career development programs may be asked to play is that of counselor. Often an employment or benefits specialist with some counseling responsibility is dubbed the career development person. This role requires a complex set of skills. Counselors must understand the career development process (the steps and four critical questions employees must consider) and have the skill to support employees through the process. In particular, counselors need good interviewing skills. They need to listen actively, ask open-ended questions, and understand and apply a decision-making model. Of critical importance is appreciating the distinction between giving advice and counseling; that is, the difference between telling individuals what to do in contrast to helping them talk through and uncover a direction for themselves. (See Chapter Six for discussion of a career counseling model.)

Good communication skills are essential, and so is familiarity with the sources of information in the organization; for counselor effectiveness is enhanced by the network of people to whom counselors can refer clients for further information.

Trainer. Few career development endeavors are designed without training programs. These may range from short introductory workshops to seminars and follow-up sessions that take participants through all steps in the career development process. Managers may also need training in career counseling and coaching techniques and in developing on-the-job experiences that further career goals; personnel officers may need training in addressing career development during recruitment and evaluation.

In all, or at least some, of these sessions, the trainer is likely to be the person responsible for the career development program. Inside training staff and outside training professionals also can be used, but financial and political considerations often dictate that the individual with major program responsibility actually design and present the training.

Among the specific training skills particularly relevant to career development are structuring exercises (design), giving presentations, creating learning climates, facilitating group discussions, and giving constructive feedback.

Because career development is a very personal experience, differing somewhat with each individual, any training program must take into account adult learning theory (see Chapter Four). A dynamic, enthusiastic, and entertaining presentation of the material is not enough. Although such qualities add to the training program, they are most effective when combined with appropriate training designs and the skill to enable individuals to learn and act through self-examination and exchange with others. In career development, full understanding and achievement rarely come from the passive acceptance of information, although this may be all that is available from an introductory presentation. People actually participating in the process also need the benefit of self-discovery and individual feedback.

Thus, designs for career development training need to incorporate opportunities for individual work, small group interaction, and personal feedback. Exercises that contribute to such designs must be clearly directed toward enhancing these opportunities, while moving participants through various stages of the career development process. A trainer who is competent in this area can design or select highly relevant exercises and facilitate group work that minimizes confusion and frustration while it maximizes learning and achievement.

Because, in career development, much of the learning happens within a given group, creating a learning climate is particularly important. The trainer skilled in creating a learning climate approaches the situation in an adult-to-adult manner, encourages full participation, reinforces personal sharing and acquisition of skills, and makes personal contact with each individual.

The goal of the trainer is to create an environment for addressing each participant's needs, rather than addressing only those items shared by the full group. In order to reach this goal, the trainer must be adept in generating discussions within the full group and smaller groups—really free exchanges that may seem to wander away from the subject—because they allow learning through shared experience. When the trainer combines the skill to promote general discussion with that of giving individual feedback, participant learning and growth in career development is assured.

Evaluator. Among the numerous reasons for a career development program to need a competent evaluator is to prove to top management that the program is indeed working. Another important reason is that career development is not a static process. Employees, organizations, and environments change continually, and career development programs must be ready to change and adjust appropriately. Further, career development involves a large degree of discovery, though it is not a continual experiment; and, if the process is to incorporate its own evolution and findings, activities and events must be monitored and assessed as they occur, in order to make necessary changes and adjustments.

The evaluator will find knowledge and skill in several types of formal evaluation methodology to be useful, since different people want evaluation for different purposes (see Chapter Fourteen for evaluation strategies). Among useful types are process evaluation (a study of various parts of the system and how they are linked through ongoing monitoring, documentation, record keeping, and analysis) and impact evaluation (a determination and analysis of relationships of outcomes to stated goals, generally measured by comparisons—that is, comparing before and after, comparing results of experimental and control groups; see Little, 1978).

Both formal evaluation and informal monitoring require collecting a great deal of information: on program participants and their activities; on system-wide events, decisions, changes, and plans that can affect employee career futures. Both also require adeptness at developing information tracking and management systems, including computerized storage and retrieval.

Because evaluation generally means communicating analyses and conclusions, the evaluator also must be competent in organizing and writing reports. In addition, a certain amount of creativity may be needed to demonstrate results, because accurate evaluation can be elusive. Indeed, according to Nadler (1974), career development is a high-risk learning activity, with one element of the risk being the near impossibility of evaluating development experiences, unlike training and education experiences.

Risk Taker. Those who accept career development responsibilities are also innovators and agents of change; thus, much that they do is new and untried. The career development program could fail, fall on its face, be cut from next year's budget, or even succeed but at too great a cost. Then again, the career development program could succeed in a cost-effective way and provide kudos and visibility. Innovators of such a program must be willing to assume this role of risk taker.

One element of risk relates to the expectations created in the managers constantly prodded to assume responsibility and in the program participants constantly encouraged to expend time and energy—expectations that might not be fulfilled.

Risk takers must also understand their own careers well in order to put so much on the line in an area steeped in change and risk. Important here is to understand change theory—and remember to start small—to anticipate the reactions of individuals and institutions to change and to respond in a thoughtful manner without undue panic. Knowledge and understanding, as well as tolerance for ambiguity, are perhaps the best preparation for the risk taker role in career development.

A Final Word

This chapter addressed the last critical tasks in deciding on practical first steps: setting up a pilot program to provide the transition between the current state and the ideal future and developing a career development unit, including the skills career development people need for success and effectiveness. One of the most important things to remember is to start small and build slowly, in order to lessen resistance to change and increase chances for lasting success.

PART FOUR

Ensuring Results and Maintaining the Change

Too often ignored or short-changed in many career development plans is how to maintain the changes created, how to ensure that the career development program continues beyond the limited pilot program period. Among the strategies to assure results considered in Part Four are creating long-term approaches, evaluating the effectiveness of the program, publicizing its results, and staying abreast of new trends and opportunities for career development.

Questions to be answered in order to achieve this step include

- How can a career development system become a reality? How can change be institutionalized?
- What strategies can be used for evaluation?
- What techniques can be used to let people know about career development successes?
- What are future trends and opportunities for career development?

The first chapter in Part Four presents a variety of long-term strategies that can be used to sustain the change. Techniques for assessing the effectiveness of the program are covered in Chapter Thirteen, and Chapter Fourteen presents techniques for publicizing the career development program. The Conclusion discusses future trends and new directions for career development.

223

Chapter Twelve

Institutionalizing the Career Development System

"An effective career development system should take on a life of its own."

Despite the vogue for high-speed computers to make quick business decisions, stores with one-stop shopping, and careers in the fast track, real, lasting change is never achieved in a speedy, one-step manner. One-shot career development programs generate immediate, positive feedback and promote quick participant involvement. They make people feel good—for a short period of time—and can be an important step in the right direction. But what about next month? Next year? Five years from now?

The goal must be to make career development part of the organization's ongoing developmental strategy, a vital part of the organization's culture. This is the reason for starting small and building slowly. This is the reason for involving top managers and other key individuals from the very beginning. The goal is to fan the spark of commitment in order to institutionalize an innovative career development program; in order to expand the organization's ability to help employees define, develop, and utilize their skills and interests; in order to grow into a career development system.

A career development system (as defined in the Introduction) is an organized, formalized, planned effort that achieves a balance between individual career needs and organizational

225

work-force requirements. It integrates a series of components and activities that involve the employee, management, and the policies and procedures of the organization. It is an ongoing program rather than a one-time event.

Vital Differences

The Career Development System. The characteristics of a career development system are that it

- Utilizes multiple activities and events
- Features activities that focus on all groups in the organization whose support and involvement are desired; it does not single out groups or departments for inclusion in any one activity
- Works within the current organizational structure, while seeking to bring about significant change within that structure
- Emphasizes long-term goals and progress
- Encourages individual responsibility for continuing progress; it encourages employees to follow-up specific activities with some kind of concrete action
- Utilizes theories of change as a conceptual framework from which activities arise
- Seeks links to ongoing organizational strategies and activities
- Brings new, ongoing formal structures into the organization

When employees within a system undertake a career development project, which will not disappear with the next campaign to trim the budget, they tend to be more motivated, take more seriously their responsibilities for participation and follow-up, and see their own efforts as more meaningful and productive. Commitment from all levels and areas of the organization grows as managers and employees witness the progress, the visible change, that occurs as career development becomes part of the fiber of the organization. In addition, as the system expands, so do its benefits.

A Career Development Event. The characteristics of a career development event are that it

- Occurs in a short time period: days or weeks
- Focuses on a single activity
- Does not develop links to organizational strategies and activities already in place
- Seeks short-term payoffs rather than long-term change
- Is often isolated to one area of the organization and does not spread to other areas
- Targets a specific audience and does not require support or involvement beyond that group
- Emphasizes the completion of an activity, rather than ongoing progress

One-time events, particularly well-timed events with positive, visible results, have their place within career development systems. Such an event can act as a pilot program, giving the organization, its managers, and its employees tangible indications of what can happen to help specific groups and problems; it can build commitment for the idea of a career development system. The goal-setting workshop or the mentor program starts people thinking about career development and helps bring recognition of the need for an ongoing system.

Events that are repeated over time and in various parts of the organization (for example, a one-day seminar) also can serve as an incentive. After several successful events take place, top managers may decide to capitalize on these successes and structure them into a fully operational system.

When scheduled and used wisely, one-time or repeated events can make a real contribution to establishing and maintaining a career development system. Table 16 sums up the benefits and drawbacks of one-time events.

Creating the Shift to a System

Extending a career development pilot program over a long period will not make it grow into a career development sys-

Table 16. What Is Right and Wrong with Events.

What's Right with Events	What's Wrong with Events
Can be a quick success	Low potential for meaningful par-
Manageable by a small staff	ticipant change and development
Affordable	Difficult to keep up momentum
Immediate cheers and applause	Difficulty in showing results that
for the developer	demonstrate program utility
Unlikely to "rock the boat"	Appetites are whetted, not satisfied
Easier for managers and top man-	Impossible to link to ongoing hu-
agement to support	man resource development activ-
Likely to "quiet the troops" for	ities
a while	Dependence on participants to ini-
Little advance planning and diag-	tiate their own follow-through
nosis is necessary	Time for only a simple focus, which
Can serve as a pilot program, with	may not fit all employees
time to evaluate and work out	Difficult to track results
kinks later	Little commitment is built
Less resistance	Likely to be cut from tight budgets
Less pressure to deliver on promises	Use of one design is unlikely to
Less stress and strain on all in-	take environment/context
volved	changes into account
Less pressure to show results	Little chance for demonstrating re-
Less responsibility for accom-	turn on investment
plishment of participants	

tem. Instead, it is necessary to design the program in such a way that its basic structure requires an extended approach and that it remains viable over the long term. Cyclical momentum is needed; that is, program components that cause employees and managers to see career development as cyclic, with no particular beginning or end.

A current program has a good chance to maintain its momentum, to reach its full potential and impact when

- Most participants in the program agree that they are not sure when to expect their career development activities to end.
- The career development program includes a variety of different activities, some of which may overlap and some that participants may undertake differently.
- Career development activities are integrated with and supported by other ongoing human resource development activities.

- The career development process is likely to become self-perpetuating, continued by employees and managers after their participation in formal events.
- As much emphasis is placed on assisting and monitoring participant implementation of career development as on their initial self-assessment, goal setting, and planning.
- Plans are formulated to evaluate, revise, and improve career development activities each time they occur.
- Top management sees a connection between the career development program and long-term company goals.

In addition to the strategies mentioned throughout the book (for example, the discussion in the Introduction of the career development system or the description in Chapter Eleven of setting up a pilot program), other strategies can move a pilot program toward an operational system: utilizing preprogram preparations, integrating acquisition of special skills, assigning project work, building support groups and networks, and promoting mentor relationships.

Utilize Preprogram Preparation. Because participants often come to career development, or training, events as a reaction, without any specific purpose or knowing what to expect, they may be reluctant to make any significant commitment and simply sit back, passively waiting for information and instructions. Participants must be moved as quickly as possible toward independence and individual responsibility, in order to promote interaction, information sharing, and individual initiative.

Requiring that participants undertake some activity before they attend the first formal career development component is an effective way to build commitment. As part of the selection process, a preparatory assignment can involve, for example, background reading, collecting information about the organization, developing self-assessment data. The application form called *The Starting Line* in the Holiday Inn program for reservation agents (see Chapters Seven and Eight) was such a preparatory assignment. In it, employees who wanted access to the career development program had to interview two people outside their division. Nearly a dozen of the applicants got new jobs as a result of these informational interviews and never entered the program. For another program, the advisory group helped develop an application form that took at least two hours to complete and was tough enough to eliminate those who did not really want to work (see Chapter Ten).

Integrate Acquisition of Special Skills. Employees participating in career development programs often have similar needs for learning or improving skills that will assist them in their future development. Such skills, which are useful in a variety of jobs and levels in the organization, include written communication, oral presentation, interpersonal communication, assertiveness and influence, time management, motivation, and effective negotiation.

Human resource development activities for acquiring these skills can be directly integrated into a career development program, contributing to the momentum of the program by giving participants a head start on their career goals. Note, however, that setting up a skills acquisition activity requires a thorough assessment of the needs of both employees and the organization.

Assign Project Work. Another innovative, although time-consuming, way to build momentum and help participants acquire other important skills is through assigning projects. These projects need to focus on developing individual skills (creativity, assertiveness, presentation skills) as well as career development skills (building networks, finding opportunities for visibility, teamwork).

Project groups incorporated into the Holiday Inn program for reservation agents are an example of the effective use of this strategy to develop and polish skills in leadership, research, networking, presentation, creativity, and organization and to provide visibility and empowerment.

Build Support Groups and Networks. Support groups and networks provide valuable assistance to employees participating in career development by helping them define skills, understand organizational realities, and plan career directions. As participants learn about and join existing networks and support groups or develop appropriate new ones, they enhance their motivation to follow through on initial efforts and maintain career development momentum.

Within an organization, support groups and networks may be informal or formal entities. They may be continuing groups that meet and grow over time or they may be short-term groups formed to help one another, and the organization, accomplish specific substantive tasks.

Most people find they need to give and receive support for different purposes at different times. An employee trying to determine career options may need support from others who have successfully completed the process. An employee who wants to build skills in finance or risk management, for example, may need support from professionals already working in those areas. Other employees may need the inspiration and motivation of people with similar goals and needs—support that can come through involvement in a career development program, a women's or young professionals' network. For example, professional football players faced with early retirement, many lacking college degrees and support, were helped by a resource network of retired players who had made the transition successfully. The network, categorized by geographical area and career field, encouraged formal and supportive interaction through workshops and directories. Thus, networks and support groups can offer career development participants information on the organization, motivation by example, visibility for accomplishments and goals, increased contacts with people who can assist with career moves, information about skill requirements in specific professional areas and relevant skill-building opportunities, and realistic evaluation of self-assessment and goals.

Promote Mentor Relationships. Like a support group or network, a mentor can provide a career development participant with valuable feedback, information, guidance, and motivation. The employee lucky enough to establish an appropriate mentor relationship during the career development process will learn the ropes from someone in a position to advise and pave the way.

In many instances, a mentor can take a more direct role on behalf of his or her protégé than can a support group. For example, the mentor can offer individual counseling and guidance, can introduce the protégé to useful contacts, can act as a role model for career direction and day-to-day behavior, and can sponsor the protégé for skill-building and advancement opportunities. This continuous, personal contact can also motivate the employee to work toward a goal, since anything less than achievement would "let down" the mentor who reached out a helping hand. Career directions and accomplishments are as likely to be based on personal relationships as on skills and experience; and a mentor can help a protégé achieve those relationships.

The payoffs from the relationship extend beyond the giving and receiving of the mentors and protégés themselves. The organization benefits substantially through the informal, no-cost learning and development of employees, circumstances that can only enhance their productivity and loyalty.

The mentor relationships, which further the momentum of a career development system, can be formalized by assigning participants to mentors (see Chapter Five for a detailed description of this employee intervention). These relationships can also be promoted in a less formal manner, through activities designed to increase understanding of the value of mentoring and help identify possible mentors.

A System in Action

A good example of a program with the elements essential for ensuring the momentum to move to a career development system is the Management Readiness Program (MRP), begun at Merrill Lynch in 1980. The program was set up to respond to Merrill Lynch's need to identify talented employees, particularly women and minority employees, and prepare them for promotion to management.

MRP helps targeted employees expand their knowledge of the career choices available to them and build networks with peers, managers, and mentors; provides specific managerial and professional training; and encourages ongoing efforts to maximize individual potential and facilitate entry into managerial positions. Strategies used include counseling, participant skill inventories, management development courses, skills training, and a mentor program. Managerial involvement is built in. Managers help select participants and serve as mentors and guest speakers to groups.

The program takes place over a six-month period for a group of twenty-four to thirty-two employees. It began as a pilot program: The division chosen contained the largest number of first-line supervisors who were potential management candidates, as well as the largest number of women and minority employees. Before the pilot program, top management, including the president, received overviews of the program and reviewed the basic design. The executive vice president in charge of the targeted division briefed all his high-level managers. During the pilot program, top managers were kept informed of progress.

After a successful pilot program, the MRP was offered to other divisions and departments. Now, as one group graduates, another begins. The program remains under the organization's management resources staff, but external consultants continue to work with two internal staff members to plan, review, and evaluate the program and to solve problems as they occur. This external-internal team allows a productive mix of experience and knowledge in both career development and organizational behavior. The MRP has five distinct phases: selection, start-up, planning, implementation, and completion (Figure 22 provides an overview).

Selection. MRP candidates, as well as possible mentors for those candidates, need to be identified in the first phase. Department managers receive packets of applications and program descriptions, discuss the MRP with potential candidates, and complete recommendations for each candidate. Ultimate selection to the program, however, depends on the recommendations of a selection review committee.

Managers serve as mentors in the program and are kept

Figure 22. Structure of the Management Readiness Program.

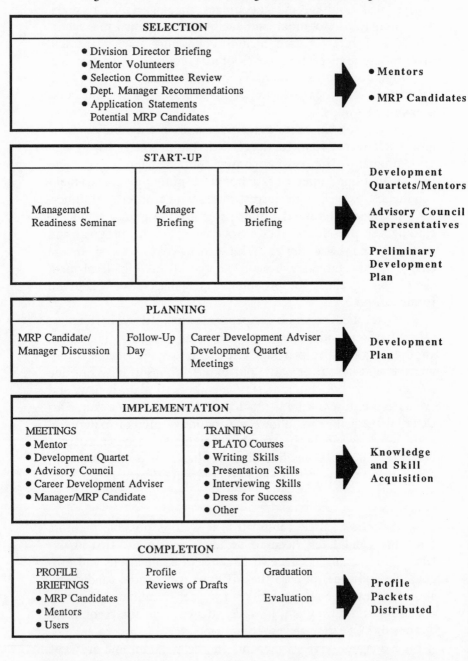

SELECTION

- Division Director Briefing
- Mentor Volunteers
- Selection Committee Review
- Dept. Manager Recommendations
- Application Statements
  Potential MRP Candidates

- Mentors
- MRP Candidates

START-UP

| Management Readiness Seminar | Manager Briefing | Mentor Briefing |

Development Quartets/Mentors

Advisory Council Representatives

Preliminary Development Plan

PLANNING

| MRP Candidate/ Manager Discussion | Follow-Up Day | Career Development Adviser Development Quartet Meetings |

Development Plan

IMPLEMENTATION

MEETINGS	TRAINING
- Mentor	- PLATO Courses
- Development Quartet	- Writing Skills
- Advisory Council	- Presentation Skills
- Career Development Adviser	- Interviewing Skills
- Manager/MRP Candidate	- Dress for Success
	- Other

Knowledge and Skill Acquisition

COMPLETION

PROFILE BRIEFINGS	Profile Reviews of Drafts	Graduation
- MRP Candidates		Evaluation
- Mentors		
- Users		

Profile Packets Distributed

fully informed of the important role they can play as a consulting force for their protégés and for the program itself. A manager who decides to participate is assigned as mentor to four participants, each representing a different department. The mentor is also one organizational level above each protégé's own manager. Mentor managers are given tools and techniques to help them be effective career coaches, as described in Chapter Six.

Start-Up. A three-day, highly interactive seminar for participants, which includes a session for managers and mentors, is the focus of this phase. In one session, participants increase individual self-awareness by reviewing their career histories, identifying their values and skills, starting to answer the question Who am I? and delving into what is truly important to them, on the job and personally. In another session, a panel of top managers answers questions about organization-related issues, giving participants an opportunity to probe organization norms, discuss their concerns, and hear about future trends. In a final session, participants go through a goal-setting process in order to establish a specific career goal to work for during the next six months of the program. They are also assigned to mentors, and each mentor's quartet elects a representative to the program's advisory council, which meets monthly to serve as a sounding board and offer suggestions for program improvement to the career development staff.

The seminar includes an intensive half-day session during which managers receive tools and techniques to help them become career coaches (see Chapter Six), so that they can assist their employees in defining goals and planning developmental activities. Mentor managers also receive coaching tools and techniques, plus a manual that details the kinds of exercises their quartets of employees will be participating in. Mentors from previous programs are on hand to share their experiences and answer questions for new mentors.

Planning. Participants develop a formal, written, development plan in this phase. They first identify the skills and knowledge needed to achieve the specific career goal they established, then state the level of proficiency they want to reach, the specific activities they plan to undertake to achieve that level, the deadlines they set for themselves, and the people and resources they plan to use while working toward their goal.

A follow-up session supports work by the participants on their development plans. During this day, participants discuss ideas for meeting their goals, meet with a panel of previous MRP participants, and have their final plans reviewed by career development staff, who are prepared to provide written feedback on each plan.

Implementation. Participants begin to acquire actual skills and knowledge in this phase. The organization provides classroom and computer-based courses focusing on business writing, effective presentation, selection interviewing, supervisory success, managerial success, resource management, and time management. Other courses, which also use the organization's training and education capabilities, help participants understand financial statements, equal employment opportunity/ affirmative action programs, issues and perspectives in management (including personnel management), and compensation.

Mentors are particularly important during this phase. Mentors can discuss planning, budgeting, networking, organizational structure, and other topics with their protégés. Mentors can offer practical advice on the ways to move up the career ladder at Merrill Lynch. Mentors enhance their protégés' visibility and network opportunities by introducing them to others within the organization, during visits to regional operations centers, computer service centers, sales offices, and even the New York Stock Exchange.

Completion. In-depth participant profiles are the key product of this phase. The profiles are prepared on preprinted forms, divided into major sections that give participants an opportunity to display their backgrounds and goals and describe major accomplishments on the job, satisfactions in current work, and plans for acquiring the skills necessary to reach career goals. To ensure that the profiles are polished and concise, participants meet with a business-writing instructor, in groups and individually. Once completed, the profiles are distributed to division heads throughout the organization. Nearly all the division heads report that the profiles are a valuable resource when searching for management candidates.

A formal end of the program is also part of this phase. This "graduation," attended by senior management executives, represents the end of formal activities and the beginning of self-perpetuating individual development through continuing the mentor relationship, using the networks, acquiring further new skills and knowledge.

The program/system has provided more career movement than originally anticipated. Within six months of program completion, well over half of the participants in each group go through job changes: promotions, lateral transfers, upgrades, and special assignments.

Incorporating Principles of Change

Benne and Birnbaum (1969) identified several change principles particularly relevant to effective career development. Using these principles is important in institutionalizing any career development effort. The Merrill Lynch system is used to demonstrate these principles.

Assure Complementary and Reinforcing Changes. "To change behavior on any one level of a hierarchical organization, it is necessary to achieve complementary and reinforcing changes in organization levels above and below that level" (Benne and Birnbaum, 1969, p. 331).

In the Merrill Lynch program, particular attention is given to those above the level of program participants. Managers are asked to recommend candidates from among their employees, by completing a thorough recommendation form that includes the reasons for the recommendation, descriptions of the employee's major strengths and developmental needs, and a rating of the employee's current performance and potential for advancement. These same managers receive tools and training as career coaches so that they can effectively help develop and review participant plans and implementation strategies. Many managers volunteer as mentors to participant groups. The manager mentors of each group have to be one level higher than the participants' managers and in different departments.

Begin Change at Stress Points. "The place to begin change is at those points in the system where some stress and strain exist. Stress may give rise to dissatisfaction with the status quo and thus become a motivating factor for change in the system" (Benne and Birnbaum, 1969, p. 331).

At Merrill Lynch, two areas of stress helped to prompt the decision for a career development program. First, the organization needed a "pipeline" of managerial talent to continue effective operations and progress, but not enough managers wanted to be involved in the process of selection and training. Second, the organization needed to improve progress toward affirmative action by identifying and developing talented women and minority employees. Both areas of stress generated pressure and paved the way for a willingness to change.

Consider the Organization Culture. "Both the formal and the informal organization of an institution must be considered in planning any process of change" (Benne and Birnbaum, 1969, p. 333).

The design of the Merrill Lynch program took into consideration the formal structure of the organization (divisions, departments, levels), as well as organization culture. Through a detailed assessment of previous attempts at management development, by discussing components of activities that had worked and analyzing those that were not successful, the consultants were able to better understand the values inherent in the informal system (adherence to chain of command, high professionalism, and strong feedback) and to create a program that took those values into account. (See also the discussion in Chapter Three of investigating organization culture.)

Start with Top Management. "If thoroughgoing changes in a hierarchical structure are desirable or necessary, change should ordinarily start with the policy-making body" (Benne and Birnbaum, 1969, p. 333).

As soon as the basic design of the MRP program was established, top management received an overview to assure their support. It is essential in any such program that commitment from top policymakers be sought as early as possible and that they be kept informed of progress as the program gets under way. This not only influences decisions that can affect the program's continuation but also informs participants, and potential participants, that the organization has a stake in their involvement.

Keep Change Gradual. Change theory addresses issues that concern the speed of change. There is ample evidence that real change can only happen over a longer period of time than most people would like.

A society or organization seldom changes spontaneously or abruptly. Changing directions, values, and methods is extremely difficult. The contrast between the changes from the graduated income tax and prohibition provide a good case in point. Both were enacted about the same time in response to growing social needs. Both called for radical change. But one was imposed gradually; the other, immediately. One evolved slowly in response to the times; the other sought a quick, simple solution to a complicated problem. One continues to be the most successful social legislation of its kind in history. The other was a complete failure and had to be withdrawn.

Even when change responds to seemingly widely shared needs and desires, it will succeed only if it is deliberate and gradual enough to assure understanding and support rather than distress and defensiveness. For career development programs, this means that, as in the Merrill Lynch program, adequate time must be spent in planning, analyzing the environment, garnering support, achieving understanding, and testing the program before it is offered throughout the organization.

A Final Word

To be successful and have a lasting, positive impact on participants and their organizations, career development must be fully integrated into the way an organization does business. Anything short of this is a single event, which may make some people feel good but only for a short while.

To build a successful system, like the one at Merrill Lynch, requires a thorough understanding of the principles of change. In this way, the principles can be related to the structures already part of the organization in question. Give careful thought to who is to be included in the change process, how change will affect both the informal and formal systems of the organization, where change can appropriately begin, and how rapidly change can be introduced, in order to successfully institutionalize change.

Chapter Thirteen

Keeping the Organization Informed

"Do you think publicity doesn't pay? We understand there are twenty-five mountains in Colorado higher than Pike's Peak. Can you name one?"

When a career development program and its achievements are well publicized, employees and managers are more likely to take interest in their own career development and to interest the organization in establishing career development as an essential, ongoing system. Every effort needs to be made to publicize the program from its very inception because

- Even if initial efforts are small (for example, a pilot program, a few introductory workshops), they are more likely to expand and continue if they become known.
- Activities that begin as pilot programs in only one part of the organization are more likely to be adopted by other areas when they are well publicized.
- Successes create a bandwagon effect; the more people hear about them, the more they want to participate.
- Commitment to the program, from people at all levels, is enhanced when they hear more about what is taking place.

The challenge is to select and develop effective publicity vehicles and techniques, those that will best advance the goals of the career development program, that will inform and educate the most people. As in all good public relations, letting people know about career development is a continuing process; it means sending out the message over and over again, in as many ways and places as possible.

This chapter looks at the rewards of good publicity; suggests some specific resources and techniques for designing publicity campaigns, both inside and outside the organization; and provides tips, reminders, and examples of effective publicity approaches.

Publicity Payoffs

Publicity is a strategy for creating a positive environment for a career development program from the beginning. Good publicity enhances the program by providing information, encouraging commitment, building momentum, developing responsibility, and increasing employee and organization visibility.

Providing Information. Many managers and employees, at all levels in the work force, know little about career development: the activities it involves and how it can benefit the organization and themselves. One way to inform them about career development is through true stories of activities and accomplishments. For example, the career development program for employees of the city of Dallas published a lengthy article in the employee newsletter. The article explained that "many people are concerned with getting the most out of the job, [but] few realize that developing one's career does not necessarily mean striving for one promotion after another" (*Cityside Dallas,* February 17, 1983). It went on to describe the program, how and why it had been initiated, and what it hoped to deliver to managers and employees.

Encouraging Commitment. Top managers, managers, and employees become more committed to a project when they view it as a serious activity with positive results. But they cannot establish the view of career development that sparks their commitment to participate or, at least, assist in assuring the program's success unless they are informed about it. Newsletters that describe the successful moves and changes of program participants are excellent tools to build this commitment. Such newsletters can report enrichment activities completed by employees on their current jobs as well as promotions.

Building Momentum. Career development, as already emphasized, is more likely to succeed if it gains momentum over time, if interest increases among growing numbers of employees in a wide variety of activities that influence their career futures. Momentum in career development means that success breeds success; and, for that to happen, success needs widespread publicity. The bandwagon effect is initiated by good information about the program. Time and time again, when one division or department of an organization sponsors a successful career development activity, the word spreads and other departments are quick to follow suit.

Developing Responsibility. When participants see publicity about a program they are involved in, they begin to take more seriously their participation in it. The realization that the program is one the organization supports and that other people know about gives participants a sense of involvement in something special and positive. When participants in a high-tech organization successfully completed their "employee-driven" program, they volunteered to recruit other employees. The program's success encouraged them to maintain their own interest in career development and to encourage others.

Increasing Employee Visibility. Specific publicity gives visibility to the individuals named and generally rubs off on all those involved in the program. All are viewed as doing something positive for the organization and as taking an interest in learning and growth. Such publicity also serves to further other employees' careers. For example, when one organization's paper featured the success story of a career development workshop participant, it encouraged departmental pride and motivated many more employees to sign up for the program.

Increasing Organization Visibility. Appropriate publicity gives good internal and external visibility. Parts of an organization often have little mutual contact and less knowledge of the work accomplished in different areas. Internal publicity gives employees more information about one another and about work and responsibilities in different areas.

Publicity that travels outside the organization, through articles in professional journals or local newspapers and presentations given at industry-wide conferences, signals others that the organization is concerned and creative about utilizing its human resources. Such visibility can also enhance other organization endeavors, such as recruitment and retention.

Publicity Resources and Techniques

The dozens of ways to tackle the task of advertising accomplishments in career development begin at one extreme, with word of mouth inside the organization, and expand to the other extreme, with nationwide print and electronic media, as Figure 23 illustrates. Adequate publicity campaigns for career development programs fall somewhere between the extremes. They may take advantage of existing internal publications (magazines, newsletters, reports), create publicity materials (flyers, brochures, video programs), and utilize external media (professional journals, local newspapers or television shows). An important first step in planning is to determine all possible means of publicity, then find the ones that match the program's goals, timing, and budget.

Inside the Organization. The communication vehicles already available in the organization are usually easily accessible and, as a result, are the easiest and most expedient ways to begin an internal publicity drive. Among these are word of mouth (from participants to their colleagues), video presentations, newsletters, magazines, printed material, annual reports, memos from top management, and oral presentations. Three of the most useful—newsletters, oral presentations, and printed material—are described in this section:

• *Newsletters:* Organization or special career development newsletters are a quick, capable way of delivering infor-

Figure 23. Publicity Technique Options.

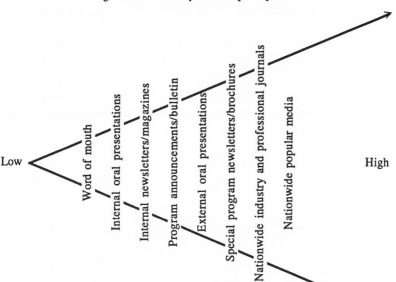

Low   High

Word of mouth

Internal oral presentations

Internal newsletters/magazines

Program announcements/bulletin

External oral presentations

Special program newsletters/brochures

Nationwide industry and professional journals

Nationwide popular media

LEVEL OF EFFORT

mation throughout the organization—the more appealing and interesting the approach, the better. They are a good place for timely news stories (announcements of upcoming workshops, the opening of a career resource center) and feature stories (longer articles explaining the career development process, profiles of participants who have made the program work for them). Also, newsletters can often accommodate regular submissions, such as monthly items in a column on what is happening in career development. Meet early with the editor of the publication to determine what is needed for stories and regular submissions.

For example, when General Electric's Nuclear Energy Business group opened its career resource center, the organization newsletter featured an article that began by asking,

Would you rather be an engineering assistant
than a secretary? Would you rather be a computer

operator than a warehouseman? It may be possible, provided you acquire basic skills and your goals are realistic.

The center provides written guides to help employees work through this program at their own pace. It can conceivably take several weeks, and is accomplished with only occasional visits to the center to pick up more material or literature [*Nuclear Energy News,* August 12, 1983].

At Security Pacific Bank, the newsletter publicized its new career development program for managers in an article that began this way:

You suspect that your staff may be looking to you for more career guidance than you're currently providing. Perhaps you're ready for more responsibility and feel you're not moving along fast enough. You catch yourself fantasizing about the perfect job—challenging, exciting, gratifying. Or perhaps you went to a class reunion and listened with envy to classmates' tales of careers and lifestyles.

Whatever the cause, you know you want more or something else from your career [*Managing Security Pacific Resources,* February 1983].

• *Oral Presentations:* Another way to successfully broadcast the news about career development is in oral presentations to specific departments or to interdepartmental groups, such as personnel directors or department heads. These presentations can supplement the mass appeal of newsletter publicity by aiming at a target population and by adding the capacity to generate discussion and answer questions. Oral presentations are most often made by human resource professionals. These presentations are particularly useful in the initial planning and start-up stages of the program. Later on, participants or line managers can give realistic views of their experiences.

At Gillette, for example, presentations were made to personnel directors in other divisions, organization training managers, and division heads on the initial career development project in one division, which generated visibility for the pilot program and promoted interest in its expansion. At the same time, participants themselves added to the program's visibility through informal word of mouth. At Holiday Inns, Inc., where the reservations division was the site of the pilot program, the division director made a presentation to the hotel division about the success of the program.

For the city of Dallas program, employee rap sessions provided word-of-mouth publicity. Employees who participated in a career development program discussed what they had done with others, and past participants were trained to lead future rap sessions.

• *Printed materials:* Printed materials can be excellent publicity vehicles and can range from the announcements of workshops posted on a bulletin board to widely distributed flyers presenting program overviews. Some programs have designed their own flyers and brochures, which include articles about career development program events and success stories, as well as educational information about the career development process.

At Goddard Space Flight Center, for example, the *Career Development Center Bulletin* includes announcements of upcoming seminars (with registration forms), feature articles about career development ideas and concepts, articles on the progress of individual participants, book reviews, and other informative material.

At Northrop Aircraft Company in Los Angeles, publicity materials were generated specially for the career resource center, including a brochure about career development that employees received with their paychecks. The 1984 brochure, based on a Pilot Your Career theme, began by reminding readers, "Just as a pilot must have a flight plan to arrive at his or her destination, you also need to plan to give your career direction." Employees were directed to answer ten questions, negative answers to any of which indicated the employee needed to think more about his or her career—and should come to the career resource center to turn the negative answers to positive ones.

At Kaiser Permanente, Southern California, the entire conceptual approach of the career development effort is designed to be presented in the form of a Walking-Talking White Paper to the top two reporting levels of the organization. High-level managers will be asked to respond to the philosophy, content, and programmatic ideas by ranking, underlining, editing, and commenting right on the position paper itself. Comments will later be collated and used to gain commitment and to formulate the actual career development effort. A further objective of this unique approach is to stimulate the curiosity of top administrators so that the program in its earliest stages will be widely publicized.

Outside the Organization. External publicity is often more difficult to generate than internal publicity because the means are further removed from the career development program. Nevertheless, many programs have become known outside the organization because someone took the time to write an article for a professional journal or make a presentation at a meeting of colleagues from other organizations. Such external publicity enhances both the organization's public relations department and internal morale, particularly when correlated with internal publicity mentioning that the program was featured in a particular journal article, external newsletter, or other media. Some sources for external publicity are professional journals (published by professional human resources associations, such as the International Personnel Management Association, American Society for Training and Development, and American Society for Public Administration); industry publications (published by professional industry associations, such as the American Banking Association and American Manufacturing Association); career development publications (published by groups specifically interested in career development); local newspapers, local radio and television; and presentations at meetings of local, regional, or national professional groups.

Research may be needed to pinpoint the most likely vehicles for external publicity. The best place to start is where contacts already exist. For example, someone who is involved in the career development program and is also an officer in the local chapter of a professional organization may be able to schedule a panel on career development at a conference. The organization's public relations department may have useful contacts with local newspapers. Or someone in the organization may already have written for an industry journal and be able to contact the editor.

Research on external publicity resources is likely to uncover more possibilities than imagined, including publications specifically on career development. For example, *The Career Development Bulletin,* published by the Center for Research in Career Development at Columbia University, carries articles about recent career development activities in various organizations, editorial articles on issues in career development, research findings, and other related information. The *Newsletter About Life/Work Planning,* published by the National Career Development Project of United Ministries in Higher Education and edited by Richard Bolles, includes success stories, workshop announcements, and advice to human resource professionals.

A Matrix of Rationales. Since different publicity techniques are used for different reasons, it may be useful to outline what is expected from them. The matrix in Figure 24 provides a format for readily viewing what the publicity seeks to achieve and which technique might produce that result. It can be expanded and filled in to fit the realities of the organization involved.

Designing a Publicity Plan

Before a publicity campaign can be tailored to the needs of the organization, the following key questions need answers:

- What are the goals for career development publicity? Do they make sense in terms of the career development program's goals?

Figure 24. Matrix of Publicity Techniques and Rationales.

Techniques

Rationales	Organization Newsletter	Special Flyer	Presentations to Department Heads	Employee Rap Groups	Journal Articles	Professional Association Meeting Presentations
Inform about Career Development Concepts	X	X	X	X	X	
Drum up Initial Curiosity	X	X		X		
Reach a Target Group			X	X	X	X
Announce a Workshop	X	X				
Gain Visibility to Participants	X	?	?	X		?
Reach an External Audience					X	X

- What are the budget and time constraints?
- What media resources does the organization already have in place that could be used for publicity?
- What external media can realistically be utilized?
- What new publicity vehicles for the career development program are worth developing?
- How can both formal and informal word-of-mouth publicity be encouraged?
- Who should be assigned responsibility for publicity?
- What is the timetable? What are the deadlines?
- How will the publicity be followed up and evaluated?

Although each career development program and each organization will develop its own publicity guidelines as it evolves, the suggestions in the sections that follow have general applicability.

Start Early. Publicity can, and should, begin even before the first introductory activity, as soon as the career development effort (large or small) is initiated. In this way, people who might become involved later start to learn about career development and begin to think that it may have something for them. For example, advance publicity for Georgia Power's (1984) *Career Planning Guide,* prepared for the organization's 2,700 executives and managers but available only on request, was so successful that 1,400 requests (representing 10 percent of total employees) came in before the guide went to press.

Publicize Both the Concept and the Activities. Since many people have very little idea what career development really means, it is important to introduce them to the concept. Generate publicity that includes both announcements of program activities and background on what career development is all about. For example, the Goddard Space Flight Center's *Career Development Center Bulletin,* in announcing a seminar in career perspectives, also noted that "Because both people and jobs change, periodic reassessment and review of career achievements, objectives, and options is a necessary part of the career development process. Career planning which takes into account individual and organizational change allows an employee maximum control over his or her career."

Formalize the Process. The publicity process should be seen as a formal, rather than casual, process. Financial and human resources need to be committed to it from the beginning. Waiting until newsworthy opportunity strikes may be too late.

Get Participant Participation. Employees who have participated in career development program activities demonstrate the saying that satisfied clients are great salespersons. Participants should be encouraged to talk about career development in their informal discussions with colleagues, make presentations about the program, write articles about their experiences for newsletters, and generally continue to lend their support whenever possible. Such activities contribute to developing pride by sharing responsibility for future program success.

Name the Program. A career development program needs a distinct, readily identifiable, catchy acronym or descriptive title. And the title should be used often in publicity. Merrill Lynch chose the descriptive name Management Readiness Program for its career development program. At General Electric's Nuclear Energy Business Group, a career development coaching program for managers was called MC2 (Managerial Career Coaching). At Holiday Inns, Inc., one program was called Career Crossroads, to signify that it could be a crossroad in an employee's life and to suggest the idea of an inn at a crossroad.

Name the People. People like to know specifically who is doing what, and people like to see their names in print. On every possible occasion, the names of those who have made noteworthy strides should be used in written publicity about the career development program. Use people to tell about career development, too. For example, instead of an editorial for a newsletter, get a quote from an interview, as did an article in the newsletter for employees of the city of Dallas. In it, the director of the city's personnel department said, "Although many people are concerned with getting the most out of their jobs, few realize that developing one's career does not necessarily mean striving for one promotion after another. Some employees are happy with their current positions and are looking for more of a job enrichment kind of thing. Other employees may want to step back and see what they really want. It is our job to help them get there" (*Cityside Dallas,* February 17, 1983).

Sell Success. Successes will seem small at first. Not all of those who attend a workshop make sudden changes that affect the rest of their lives. Look for small successes, one person doing one thing differently now, and publicize them as examples of the kind of success anyone can make happen. Remember that success breeds success.

Target the Audience. Gaps and redundancies in publicity can be avoided when the audience is accurately identified at every step of the way. At some points in the career development program, the appropriate audience for publicity might be the entire organization; at other points, it may be top management, a single department, or all employees at a certain level. Different publicity strategies may be required for different audiences; and targeting the exact audience enables the development of publicity that is specific, direct, and personal. For example, in a career development effort at Lawrence Livermore Laboratories, an illustrated presentation on the program was offered to line managers as a part of a management practice briefing series. Presentations were also made to intact work groups and to organization groups (Hanson, 1981).

Consult the Experts. Build on the groundwork of others whenever possible. One way to do this in publicity is to check with those already involved in the organization's public relations, employee communications, or related areas. They are likely to have useful contacts and ideas that can help get the publicity campaign under way.

A Final Word

This chapter emphasizes that publicity about career development is most appropriately seen as a continual process, not just an event. An article or flyer may do an excellent job of announcing the initiation of the program, but the idea will not necessarily attract most people right away. Publicity needs to broadcast the concept and activities of the career development program again and again, so that it becomes common knowledge. Even then, if people stop hearing about it, they may forget it.

The continuing and cyclical nature of publicity can create a snowball effect, attracting more people and developing greater commitment as the program's successes become well known. As this happens, the program is strengthened, creating still more opportunities for good publicity. Publicity is not just a matter of making the program look good. It is a matter of gaining the kind of acceptance necessary to assure that employees, and the organization, benefit from the most effective career development program possible. That first notice tacked on a bulletin board was just the beginning.

Chapter Fourteen

Assessing the Effectiveness of the Career Development Effort

"If the language of business is dollars, then the alphabet is numbers" (Fitz-enz, 1984, p. xiii).

Describing the effectiveness of a career development program in the language of business is essential in order to convince the organization of the program's benefits. As already emphasized, top managers pay attention when they hear about dollars and end products.

In the past, evaluation of human resource programs has often been neglected or poorly done. Fitz-enz (1984) suggests that this occurs because most human resource professionals are not familiar, or comfortable, with quantitative techniques; because of a myth of subjectivity, which says that results in the human resource area cannot be quantified; and because human resource professionals often see themselves as too busy designing and running programs to take the time to evaluate them.

In reality, however, human resource functions must be measured in the same terms as the rest of an organization. If the rest of the organization is held accountable through numbers and results, so must career development. If other measures are used throughout the organization, those same measures must also apply to career development. Human resource professionals must be held accountable for their results and efforts.

Creating an Evaluation Plan

A degree in statistics or the support of a full-time data analyst is not necessary for effective evaluation. However, evaluation must be conceptualized as an ongoing process, integral to career development efforts, not as something tacked on to the end of a program.

In fact, evaluation can be viewed as the nucleus of a career development program, because it must interact with other components: with the needs assessment, with goals (or vision) and objectives, with program planning and implementation. Needs assessment provides vision and objectives; program activities respond to objectives; results are produced. As Figure 25 illustrates, evaluation serves as the hub of this cyclic process, and for effective evaluation constant interaction and feedback among these components is mandatory.

Figure 25. Evaluation as the Nucleus of a Career Development Program.

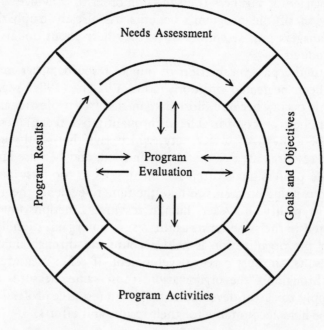

Source: California State Department of Education, 1977.

Creating an evaluation plan in the beginning of a career development program, therefore, is of great importance; it provides other benefits as well. According to Fitz-enz (1984), implementing a system for measuring results also helps

- *Focus on important issues:* Setting measurement objectives helps clarify what aspects of the program have high priorities and need attention.
- *Clarify expectations:* A measurement system is directive and clarifying. Establishing clear measures prevents having to rely on results after the fact.
- *Involve, motivate, and foster creativity:* Making evaluation explicit encourages people to identify new and important issues that can be measured and ingenious ways of measuring.
- *Bring human resources closer to line departments:* By being able to report results in a business fashion, human resources will be viewed more as a mainline function than as a pleasant activity.

In creating an evaluation plan, one needs to consider a number of key questions: Who needs what data for what purpose? How does the evaluation plan relate to the program's vision and objectives? What data will be collected and how? How will findings be reported? Each question is explored in the following sections.

Who Needs What Data for What Purpose? Which key people need what kind of information to indicate what sort of success for what intent? What indicates success for one group may not for another; different groups have different intents. Top management may consider the career development program a success if savings are reported because, for example, external searches to replace key managers are no longer necessary. Managers may consider the program successful if it provides them with the tools and resources to better manage and develop their people. Employees may consider the program a success if it helps them revitalize their current jobs.

Determining the indicators of success for each group affected by the career development program is critical to answer the question "Who needs what data for what purpose?" The most direct way to find these indicators is to ask each group; and determining indicators of success can be a valuable beginning activity for an advisory group. Remember that any analysis of success must be tied closely to the program's vision and objectives.

At one large telecommunications organization, for example, success indicators were developed for a program to help employees make the transition from a technical to a marketing environment; indicators of success were identified for employees, managers, the organization, and the human resource department. The specific objectives of the program were to identify a profile of skills needed by successful marketing representatives and to design a process for employees to assess themselves on those skills; a method for managers and employees to hold development discussions; and a set of organizational tools, such as an employee exchange program, that would allow employees who did not fit their current job to move to another functional area.

The following list of indicators of success makes it clear that, although success for one group may not mean success for others, there is a core set of indicators that relates to the basic vision and objectives of the program.

Employees find that these factors indicate success to them:

- A process to plan and manage their career interests
- An opportunity for involvement in career decisions with their managers
- A way to define realistic career targets that match organization needs
- A specific, concrete plan for their own development, identifying developmental activities and schedules
- Enhanced communication with their managers about careers and career development

Managers find that these factors indicate success to them:

- A process to plan and manage employee careers
- A process and the tools to enable them to establish developmental plans with employees
- Ability to share career management responsibilities with employees and the organization and to have those roles defined and supported with the necessary tools and programs
- Resource planning information to help them assess whether employee goals are appropriate within the context of the organization's needs and requirements
- Ability to develop pools of qualified employees to meet forecasted job openings
- Staffing flexibility

Organizations find these factors indicate success to them:

- Increase in career development discussions between account managers and their employees
- Planned rather than haphazard career choices
- Employees matched to jobs for which they are best suited, resulting in increased motivation and increased productivity
- A process to exchange employees into best-fit career areas
- Enhanced data-base capability for future staffing decisions
- Increased attractiveness of the organization to potential employees
- Good sales people staying in the sales area
- Satisfaction of representatives and account managers with the program

The human resource staff finds that these factors indicate success to it:

- Program credibility
- Enhanced reputation of their area in responding to line problems

- Opportunity to increase the program beyond the scope of the pilot program

Some of the indicators in this list may need to be ranked according to their relevance to the program's objectives, and some are much more easily measured than others. The challenge, of course, is to create observable, measurable benchmarks that correspond to the needs of key players. Considering the purpose, the intent, will help. Evaluation can, for example, be used for any of the following:

To get additional resources or personnel
To convince other parts of the organization to implement the program
To provide the organization with a recruiting or public relations tool
To demonstrate savings by improving factors such as attrition, replacement, and productivity
To improve the quality of the program components, such as workshop materials or design
To gain visibility for the human resource department

Evaluation results can also be used to make important decisions on the future direction of a program. The evaluation can be used to determine whether

To continue the program
To bring the program in-house, if previously dependent on external resources
To expand, modify, or extend the program
To change staffing patterns for the project

How Does the Evaluation Plan Relate to the Program's Vision and Objectives? The needs assessment data were collected to identify specific needs/problems and key target groups, so that this information could form the basis for a vision and objectives—the vision and objectives need to be the points of reference in creating an evaluation design. The specific problem, for example, may be high turnover among computer specialists, and the vision may be to reduce attrition by 15 percent. The very specific objective might be to reduce attrition in the first two years of employment from 25 percent to the industry average of 20 percent through broadening the orientation program and training supervisors to provide ongoing feedback. Reexamining the vision and objectives clarifies which results need evaluating.

Relating the evaluation to the program's vision and objectives also helps define what is to be ignored. In the case of high turnover of computer specialists, the evaluation will focus on how orientation program features and supervisor feedback affect attrition rates, not how they affect performance appraisal ratings. Clearly, communicating the factors within the program's purview produces a match between expectations and outcomes.

What Data Will Be Collected and How? First determining what data are important to measure eases the task of considering how to measure the data. Myriad evaluation models are available. Some researchers make a distinction between process and outcome data; others, between direct and indirect measures. Process data focus on the events and activities of a program; outcome data, on the results. Direct measures, according to Fitz-enz (1984), deal with costs; indirect measures, with time, quantity, and quality. Most clearly understood and most easily translated to career development activities, however, is a model for evaluating training programs developed by Kirkpatrick (1975). In this model, four kinds of data are collected: reaction, learning, behavior, and results. Table 17 compares these kinds of data on what each measures and when and how to collect each. This section includes definitions of these kinds of data with examples appropriate to career development programs.

• *Reaction data* measure attitudes, feelings, and impressions. They are useful in determining whether participants enjoyed the program's activities and believed they were worthwhile. Reaction data are gathered by questionnaires, sometimes

Table 17. Collecting and Measuring Four Kinds of Data.

	Measures What	When to Collect	How to Collect
Reaction	Attitudes, feelings, impressions	Immediately after a program	Questionnaires, interviews
Learning	Acquisition of concepts, principles, facts, techniques	Immediately after a program	Pre–post-program questionnaires, simulations, interviews
Behavior	Demonstrated changes in behaviors and actions	Three to six months after program	Pre–post-program questionnaires to both employees and supervisors, interviews
Results	Reduction in turnover, absenteeism, attrition, increase in productivity, cost savings, return on investment	Six months to one year after program	Current records, data, savings/cost-benefit analyses

Source: Adapted from Kirkpatrick, 1975.

supplemented by short interviews with a sample group of participants, and should be collected immediately after participation in the activity. Reaction data can be helpful in determining program modifications when the questionnaire asks, for example, Which of the following did you find useful? How would you change the component on skill identification? Exhibit 8 is an example of a questionnaire for gathering reaction data to evaluate a career development workshop.

• *Learning data* are used to measure the extent to which career development participants have acquired key concepts, principles, facts, and techniques. Measurement is made, for example, by ascertaining whether, as the result of a career development workshop, participants can list ten key skills, describe three environments they would like to work in, and list five work-related values. Learning data are useful in assessing the effectiveness of particular learning activities; that is, finding how effective a particular skill identification technique was in helping

Exhibit 8. Questionnaire for Evaluating
a Career Development Workshop.

Directions: React to the following statements by circling the appropriate scale numbers. Please feel free to make specific comments where indicated.

		LOW				HIGH
1.	To what extent were the objectives of this program made clear at the outset?	1	2	3	4	5
2.	How effective was the format chosen to present this program?	1	2	3	4	5
3.	The presenters of this program					
	a. Were knowledgeable.	1	2	3	4	5
	b. Gave clear instructions on what was to be done on the exercises.	1	2	3	4	5
	c. Clearly presented the theoretical assumptions underlying the program topic.	1	2	3	4	5
	d. Were open to questions and flexible in their approach.	1	2	3	4	5
4.	The exercises					
	a. Were clearly relevant to the program's objectives.	1	2	3	4	5
	b. Were as realistic as possible.	1	2	3	4	5
	c. Facilitated group interaction.	1	2	3	4	5
5.	The program held my interest.	1	2	3	4	5
6.	I would recommend this program to a colleague.	1	2	3	4	5
7.	The program was relevant to my job responsibilities.	1	2	3	4	5
8.	What were the program's strong points?					

9. What were the program's weak points?

10. What suggestions for improvement do you make for future programs on this topic?

participants list the ten key skills. This type of data is also useful in comparing the effectiveness of several interventions; that is, finding whether a workshop, a workbook, or a career resource center is more effective in helping participants identify three potential career moves. Learning data, which should be collected immediately after participation in a particular activity, can be gathered through such techniques as pre–post-program questionnaires and simulations, both of which can be created specifically to measure particular areas, and interviews.

For example, Holiday Inns, Inc., used a pre–post-program assessment questionnaire to gather data on whether participants had specific career goals; were able to identify personal skills, strengths, needs, and areas for improvement; and had action plans for improving current job performance. A key finding was the change in employees' perceptions of themselves as having realistic career goals and a plan for reaching those goals. These perceptions changed from weak to strong as a result of participating in the program.

Following a career/life planning workshop, Massachusetts Mutual Life Insurance designed a career development scale specifically keyed to fifteen objectives, which included increased understanding of the career development process, increased knowledge of career direction, and increased understanding of specific steps that must be taken to move toward career objectives. When compared to a control group, workshop participants showed a statistically significant gain in their mean career development scale scores.

• *Behavior data* measure demonstrated changes in behaviors and actions, focusing on what participants do after they take part in a career development activity. Behavior data are invaluable in determining whether the participants actually behave differently after the program. For example, if one objective of the program is to increase the number of employee-manager career discussions, behavior data reveal whether, and how often, such discussions take place.

Behavior data are usually collected after three to six months or through several samples collected, for example, after three months and then again six or nine months later. Behavior data are best collected by combining such approaches as follow-up questionnaires, which can be directed to both participants and their managers (or co-workers), and individual and group interviews.

For example, at Lawrence Livermore Laboratories (Moseley, 1982) behavior data were gathered by conducting an extensive follow-up study of 336 participants (64 percent) who attended career/life workshops between January 1976 and June 1980 and 290 of their managers (55 percent). More than half of the participants (53 percent) reported that they had made significant changes in their jobs, their careers, and their lives since the career/life planning workshop. Some of the significant changes appeared to be increased quality of work, increased morale, and increased communication with managers. Managers reported that they believed that the organization would recover the cost of sending employees to the program. Finally, 92 percent of the participants stayed at the laboratories, while only 8 percent left.

The follow-up questionnaire included such questions as the following:

- Since participating in the workshop, to what extent do you think you have changed in the following areas:
     The quality of your work
     Communication with supervisors
     The quantity of your work
- Since participating in the career planning workshop have you
     Changed departments
     Taken courses to upgrade current skills
     Changed job tasks (duties)

Super and Thompson's (1981) sixty-item Career Concerns Inventory can be used to assess pre–post-program learning by employees as evidenced by a shift in concerns (see Chapter Four). The inventory measures employee concerns related to four of the life stages identified by Super: exploration, establishment, maintenance, and disengagement. Employee responses reveal the stage and developmental tasks that concern them. For example, a concern related to the maintenance stage is "reading the new literature and publications in my field; getting to know new equipment and procedures."

The Career Adjustment Inventory (Crites, 1978) is another instrument that could assess pre–post-program changes in behaviors and actions. This inventory, designed to measure employee attempts to master career developmental tasks related to career maturity, is based on the premise that six career developmental tasks (organizational adaptability, position performance, work habits and attitudes, co-worker relationships, advancement, and career choice and plans) must be mastered to achieve career adjustment during the establishment stage, which lasts from entry to midcareer. An example of an item designed to measure organizational adaptability is "I know whom to go to for something I want at work." The inventory could also measure change on key learnings and concepts.

• *Results data* measure the return on investment; reductions in turnover, absenteeism, and grievances; increases in quality and quantity of production; and cost savings. Results data are gathered six months to a year after the career development program, from current records and data and from savings and cost-benefit analyses. Results data translate into dollars and cents the answers to such questions as Do participants in the program receive a greater number of promotions than those who do not participate? Do they leave the organization in fewer numbers? Do their illness rates decrease? Do they make a greater number of lateral moves that require less time and money in training? Be aware, however, that there is seldom a cause-and-effect relationship between a career development program and an outcome measure of, for example, attrition. Many other intervening variables can affect an employee's decision to leave an organization. Further, using the attrition rate as the outcome measure for evaluation may indicate no change or even a potential increase, while other indicators, such as number of career discussions with managers, may indicate very positive results.

To obtain results data, relate pre–post-program comparisons to the objectives of the program, using, for example, data on attrition, replacement costs, time lost on the job. Examine existing organization records, which are usually easy to acquire, to establish relevant figures, both baseline and outcome, on attrition, employee promotions, movement, absenteeism rates, performance ratings. In this way, establish what changes have occurred, what the difference is, between the time the program began and six months to a year after the program.

Calculate the costs of the career development program itself: salaries, space, materials. In addition, establish the costs to the organization of, for example, replacing a manager by outside hiring and inside replacement. Exhibit 9 contains a turnover cost model (Fitz-enz, 1984) that illustrates the calculations for obtaining figures on potential savings in such cases.

To get the results data, subtract program costs from the calculated savings. The answer provides the exact amount the career development program has saved the organization.

Or divide the calculated savings by the program costs; the answer is the cost-benefit ratio. If the ratio is greater than 1:0, the organization received a return on its investment (Stump and Leibowitz, 1983).

At Corning Glass Works (McGarrell, 1983), for example, an 8:1 benefit-to-cost ratio was calculated for the first year, and a 14:1 ratio annually, for an orientation program the organization runs for new employees and their managers. The ratios were calculated as follows:

- A 17 percent decrease in the number of voluntary separations among those with three years or less of service $847,000
  A decrease in the time required to learn the job: from six months to five months $494,000
  Total $1,341,000

- *Cost estimates:* Materials and salaries of developers, instructors, administrators
  First year only $171,000
  Ongoing annual $95,000

- *Benefit/cost ratio:*
  First year: $1,341,000:171,000 = 8:1
  Ongoing annual: $1,341,000:95,000 = 14:1

Exhibit 9. How to Measure the Cost of Hiring or Replacing Personnel.

FOR NEW HIRES:
  Direct Hiring Costs
  1. Advertising $_____
  2. Agency and search fees   _____
  3. Internal referral bonuses   _____
  4. Applicant expenses   _____
  5. Relocation expenses   _____
  6. Salary and benefits of staff   _____
  7. Employment office overhead   _____
  8. Recruiter's expenses   _____
  9. Total direct hiring costs   _____
  10. Divide line 9 by number hires
      Cost per hire   _____

  Indirect Hiring Costs
  11. Management time per hire   _____
  12. Supervisor/lead time per hire   _____
  13. Orientation and training per hire   _____
  14. Learning curve productivity loss or opportunity loss
      per hire
  15. Total indirect hiring costs per hire   _____
  16. Total hiring costs per hire   _____
  17. Multiply line 16 by number hired
      Total hiring costs   _____

FOR REPLACEMENTS:
  Direct Internal Replacement Costs
  18. Applicant expenses   _____
  19. Relocation expenses   _____
  20. Salaries and benefits of staff   _____
  21. Employment office overhead   _____
  22. Total direct replacement costs   _____
  23. Divide line 22 by number placed
      Direct costs per placement   _____

  Indirect Internal Replacement Costs
  24. Management time per hire   _____
  25. Supervisor/lead interview time per hire   _____
  26. Training time per hire   _____
  27. Learning curve productivity loss or opportunity loss
      per hire
  28. Total indirect replacement costs per placement   _____
  29. Add lines 23 and 28. Total cost per placement   _____
  30. Multiply line 29 by number placed   _____
  31. Total turnover costs   _____
  32. Target percentage reduction   _____%
  33. Potential savings $_____

The following formulas were used to estimate Corning Glass Works' productivity gains:

- For improved retention rate:

| Number of employees quitting with three or fewer years service, 1980 | X | Expected 17 percent decrease with orientation | X | $30,000 investment in new hire | = | Annual productivity gain |

- For shortened learning curve, from six months to five months:

| One month average base salary X 65 percent | X | Number of new hires per year | = | Annual productivity gain |

At Lawrence Livermore Laboratories, the cost effectiveness of the 1980 career/life planning workshops was determined by analyzing the annual cost data (Moir and Moseley, 1981). On the basis of 108 participants enrolled for a total of 3,672 training hours (34 hours per workshop), the cost of each workshop was computed as follows:

Wages of training staff (salary plus benefits, including preparation and classroom time, for 1.25 trainers and 0.25 clerical support staff)	$60,000
Cost of materials	2,250
Wages for participants' time in class (salary plus benefits)	80,000
Total annual cost of training	$142,250
Course cost per participant	$1,317.00
Course per participant training hour	$38.74

If the base dollar value of an average Lawrence Livermore Laboratories employee for one year is $40,000 (salary plus benefits) and if only one-third of the employees who attended the workshop in one year were, conservatively speaking, 10 percent more effective, then the program would pay for itself, as shown in the following table:

Cost effectiveness:

33 percent of 108 participants	=	36
Base dollar value of one employee	=	$40,000
10 percent of $40,000	=	$4,000
36 X $4,000	=	$144,000
Cost of 1980 program	=	$142,250

Another way of making the necessary pre–post-program comparisons is to use a three-part experimental research model, referred to as a *pre-post control group design,* that compares employees who participate in career development programs with employees who do not participate. A first assessment, which focuses on potential learning and behavior change, is administered before the program begins to two groups: one consists of the employees who are going to be in the program; and the other (or control) group consists of employees who are not going to participate but are in other respects as similar as possible to the participants. This first component establishes baseline measures. Immediately following the program, the second measure, focusing on the learning that took place in the program, is administered to both groups. Finally, after an appropriate amount of time (for example, three months), a third measure, focusing on behavior since the program, is administered to both groups. This third component establishes outcome measures to allow comparing, for example, attrition and promotion rates and to establish clear conclusions about program effects.

How Will Findings Be Reported? The best way to communicate the evaluation data for a career development program often depends on the learning style of those who will receive the report (see Chapter Four). In addition, as has repeatedly been emphasized, for most top managers, money talks; but hard data are even more effective when supplemented with anecdotes or case studies. In fact, top managers are often quite impressed with the richness and quality of information that these approaches offer, which moves them more than the formats they ordinarily see. In some organizations, arrangements have been made for top managers to meet with participants of career development programs to share first hand the results. Hearing such comments as the following (from participants in the Holiday Inns, Inc., Crossroads program) often has a powerful effect:

> "An eye-opening experience in which I stopped being stagnant and indecisive about my career goals."
> "It is the beginning journey on my voyage to new career paths, and it helps equip me for the trip."

This and other kinds of sharing of successes and accomplishments are effective selling or public relations tools (see Chapter Thirteen). But whatever approaches are used, in all cases, a written report must be prepared, describing the program: its vision and objectives, costs, evaluation plan, results, unanticipated side effects, and possible changes for improved effectiveness.

A Final Word

An essential component of a career development system is a well-thought-out evaluation plan that considers what kinds of data are needed to make what decisions and how the data will be collected and reported. The key is not to wait until results need to be demonstrated but to think about evaluation from the very beginning.

Conclusion

Considering Future Trends

"I have seen the future and it works."

The first step is often the hardest to achieve, whatever the project. All too often it is hard to convince top management in an organization of the value of an idea. This chapter summarizes the key issues that need to be considered to assure that the organization takes the first step and continues the next steps to implement a career development system. The model introduced in this book is a vital framework that can be used to build support: Each step emphasizes involving and gaining the commitment of all who will be affected to work to achieve a career development system.

Table 18 summarizes the major steps. The first three steps—defining the present system, determining new directions and possibilities, deciding on practical first steps—aim at putting into place the elements essential for change: needs, vision, and action plans, as outlined in the Introduction. The fourth step focuses on results and maintaining the change. The framework for this book requires that these steps be taken one after the other; but the reality is that they may need to be addressed concurrently, particularly the tasks within each step. For example, one of the first tasks should be to establish an advisory group that can assist in data collection and program design, although the subject of advisory groups is not addressed until Chapter Ten. Further information on resources and materials that can be useful in starting and continuing a program is located in Resource C.

Table 18. Steps and Tasks in Establishing a Career Development System.

Step 1. Needs: Defining the Present System
Establish roles and responsibilities of employees, managers, and the organization.
Identify needs; establish target groups.
Establish cultural parameters; determine organizational receptivity, support, and commitment to career development.
Assess human resource structures; consider possible links.
Determine prior attempts at solving the problem or need.
Establish mission/philosophy of program.
Design and implement needs assessment to confirm/collect more data.
Establish indicators of success.

Step 2. Vision: Determining New Directions and Possibilities
Create a long-term philosophy.
Establish vision/objectives of the program.
Design interventions for employees, managers, and the organization.
Organize and make available career information needed to support the program.

Step 3. Action Plan: Deciding on Practical First Steps
Assess and obtain support from top management.
Create a pilot program.
Assess resources and competencies.
Establish an advisory group.
Involve advisory group in data gathering, program design, implementation, evaluation, and monitoring.

Step 4. Results: Maintaining the Change
Create long-term formalized approaches.
Publicize the program.
Evaluate and redesign the program and its components.
Consider future trends and directions for the program.

Potential obstacles also need to be anticipated, as suggested in the checklist for the pilot program (Chapter Eleven). Some obstacles that might need to be overcome during a planning process could be a change in top management, a change in funding, or a new strategic direction for the organization. Other obstacles might include our own lack of a particular skill or expertise or blockage from such key groups as unions. A well-considered plan needs to be flexible enough to respond to such obstacles.

A set of broader questions also should be considered: What might stop the organization from implementing the program? What will happen if the organization decides to do nothing? What are the potential disadvantages or risks of implementing the program? Anticipating these questions will help ensure an effective, flexible system plan.

Finally, building a career development system takes time, just as any other organizational change does. Reasonable and visible markers need to be built into the process that will provide a sense of accomplishment. Also, colleagues in other organizations who have achieved success may be able to offer both ideas and support.

Looking Ahead

What does the future hold for career development? A look ahead may give us useful insights on how to better position current programs. It seems certain that career development, as an area of expertise, will grow in importance, and a career development systems model with a workable, flexible approach can play a pivotal role in future organization issues, concerns, and directions.

Among the changes in the near future, according to Harris and Harris (1983), will be a shift from industrial to metaindustrial organizations. Employees in these metaindustrial organizations will be knowledge workers: better educated, more technically oriented, with stronger demands for self-development and control over their work and working conditions. Human resource professionals in the future, who must respond to the needs of these workers and the metaindustrial work culture, will be strongly affected by the following trends and shifts in emphasis:

- *Strategic planning:* Human resource professionals will utilize the tools and techniques of strategic planning in order to contribute to the organization's efforts to identify mission, priorities, goals, and programs.
- *Systems orientation:* Systems concepts and technologies will be applied to the design and delivery of human resource functions and will integrate all related activities and programs.

- *Futuristic management:* Human resource professionals will be involved in studies of future possibilities and employ such tools as trend monitoring, long-range projections, impact evaluations, imagineering, scenario building, and change strategies.
- *Transformational management:* Human resource managers will facilitate the use of transformational management skills by helping employees and managers move from traditional, formal structures to the less structured approaches of matrix management and temporary work relations; by educating employees to cope with life crises, role transitions, and other types of change; and by designing programs to, for example, overcome obsolescence and help employees enrich their current jobs.
- *Decentralized human resource management:* This shift will go beyond simply involving line managers and supervisors in human resource activities to include such approaches as delegating personnel responsibility to management, auditing line management performance in personnel activities, and creating strategies for senior management planning and forecasting.
- *Executive involvement:* Human resource professionals will work to gain the attention of top management through knowledge of societal trends and through such approaches as developing a counseling service for the particular needs of top managers.
- *Research orientation:* Human resource professionals will be more involved in research, developing skills in such areas as human factor analysis, employee-machine interface, and the characteristics of high-performing organizations.
- *Human capital emphasis:* Human resource accounting models demonstrating productivity payoffs will receive increasing attention.
- *Creative approaches to work patterns:* Human resource professionals will creatively support such technological changes as work stations and innovative management and supervisory programs. A key emphasis will be on helping managers deal with the exchange of information.

- *Organization cultures:* "A primary focus of human resource and organization development endeavors will be the transforming of organizational cultures so that they conform to new realities" (Harris and Harris, 1983, p. 67). Key questions in this transformation will include: Where do we work? When should we work? Why do we work?
- *Synergy and networking:* Human resource professionals will play a major role in furthering information exchange and networking in order to promote knowledge worker currency and development.
- *International human resources:* Multinational managers will need to be prepared and international relocation programs created.

According to Naisbitt (1985), further considerations also will shape the organizations of the future: human resources will provide the competitive edge in an information society; competition for employees will increase little and that for middle managers will decrease; roles will shift from manager as order giver to manager as facilitator, from specialists to generalists, from hired labor to contract labor; management will shift from a top-down style to a networking style. Naisbitt also predicts an increase in nontraditional work patterns, such as flextime, and in entrepreneurship within large corporations. Greater emphasis will be placed on comparable worth, on quality and productivity, on employee education and health, on intuitive approaches as opposed to quantitative models, and on the relationship between new human values and productivity.

These views into the future hold strong implications for career development. Many of the trends emphasize the utilization of employees, others emphasize shifts in traditional work patterns and styles. Skills required of human resource professionals in the future are consistent with those required for systems models: process skills, influencing sales skills, relationship building skills, proactivity, emphasis on action, change agent skills, and creative planning skills. Human resource professionals looking to their own futures should consider acquiring managerial experience, influencing skills, computer knowledge, and the expertise to begin to shift the human resource function to a profit center.

Mergers and Acquisitions: The Future Is Now

A trend toward mergers and acquisitions characterizes the 1980s and is predicted to continue into the future. That most of these mergers (nearly 75 percent) do not work out is frequently due to human resource factors (Frantzreb, 1983). This means that a potential merger or acquisition in an organization signals a good opportunity for the human resource system to gain visibility and acceptance. Many of the human resource objectives of a merger dovetail with the objectives of a career development system; for example, utilizing present employees in the available jobs. To help facilitate a merger or acquisition, human resource professionals can assess the available human resources of the merging organizations, create interventions to avoid clashes and optimize blending, monitor absenteeism and attrition rates, and appraise the success of the human resource aspects of the merger through attitude surveys.

For example, a large telecommunications organization in the Southwest recently used a merger as the impetus to establish a career development system. A computer-assisted program allowed employees to consider their key strengths and skills. These profiles were then shared, through career discussions, with the employees' managers, who were trained in coaching skills. The program anticipated producing data for best fit of people to jobs, reducing redundancy and strengthening the working relationship between employees and their new managers.

A Final Word

This book provides an organization change model of career development, detailing the four steps to achieving a career development system: defining the specific needs and present system, determining new directions and possibilities, deciding on practical first steps, and maintaining the change. This chapter provided a brief summary of those steps and a quick look at future trends and issues of significance to career development.

Resource A

Needs Assessment Examples

These specific examples of items and methods, some of which focus on particular problems, are provided to assist in designing practical needs assessments.

Items to Assess Attitudes

A needs assessment focusing on attitudes can include such items as the following (from Burack and Mathys, 1980, pp. 20-21). For each item, employees respond on a five-point scale from Agree to Disagree.

- I believe the company has an obligation to provide a lifetime career plan for every employee.
- It is the company's responsibility to apprise each of its employees about organization career paths and requirements.

Items to Assess Career Goals

A needs assessment focusing on career goals that employees would be interested in can include such items as the following, which were used by the Hartford Insurance Company. For each item, employees were asked to respond on a five-point scale ranging from No Need to Very Strong Need.

- Assistance in clarifying my career goals
- Matching my skills and abilities with other jobs at the Hartford
- Providing information on job options

Items to Assess How Well Needs Are Met

NASA's Goddard Space Flight Center designed a needs assessment that considers needs as well as the degree to which they are currently being met. Exhibit 10 illustrates part of this form of assessment.

A Survey to Assess Multiple Factors

This standardized needs assessment survey (Farren, Kaye, and Leibowitz, 1983) focuses on several key elements needed to determine the scope of a career development system. The survey can be scored by computer and provides multiple data sources to help an organization identify its needs and plan the next steps to take. The following items are examples of those used to assess the key elements: current behavior, program outcomes, manager skills, job characteristics, and human resource development systems.

Current Behaviors. Employees and managers rate, on a low-to-high scale, the degree to which employees exhibit behaviors. Sample behaviors include

- Have career discussions with manager and colleagues
- Demonstrate sufficient skills to perform job at satisfactory level

Program Outcomes. Employees and managers rate possible outcomes of a career development program on a ten-point scale from most important to them to least important. Sample outcomes include

- Career discussions held more frequently with manager and colleagues
- Specific written plan for reaching career goals

Manager Skills. Managers assess their current level of skill in certain key career development behaviors. Employees also

Exhibit 10. Goddard Space Flight Center's Needs Assessment.

Directions: Listed below are possible needs of employees like yourself. In the column on the *left*, mark an X in the box that best describes how important the need is to you.

In the column on the *right*, mark an X in the box which best describes how well that need is being met. [The sample answer X's included for the first need demonstrate a strong need, which is being met.]

Strong Need	Moderate Need	Weak Need	No Need	I Need:	Need Being Met	Need Partially Being Met	Need Not Being Met
X				To learn about Civil Service Job opportunities.	X		
				A better understanding of my abilities and work-related interests and values			
				To know about training opportunities available at GSFC.			
				To know about career opportunities available within GSFC.			

rate their managers. A one-to-five scale, from low to high, is used. Sample behaviors include

- Know a variety of ways to do on-the-job development with employees and colleagues
- Help employees write realistic development plans

Job Characteristics. Employees consider such job characteristics as increase in pay and increase in status and pick three that would be most likely to motivate them to change jobs.

Human Resource Development Systems. Employees assess a variety of human resource systems, such as management development and assessment centers, as to whether they exist in the organization and the usefulness of each to their career.

The survey also includes a set of final questions asking employees about such factors as the support they receive from their managers and the organization in developing their careers. This gives them an opportunity to answer some open-ended questions.

A Multiphased Approach to Needs Assessment

In a multiphased approach used by AT&T General Departments, an initial survey is followed by a more focused in-depth survey and discussion groups.

To Assess Employee Attitudes. A general attitude survey identifies employee issues and concerns related to their careers. Findings may show, for example, that seven out of ten employees see themselves as uninformed about job openings, that only one out of ten employees agrees that the best-qualified people are usually chosen for promotion, and that seven out of ten employees rate the job being done to prepare people for advancement as fair to very poor.

To Assess Attitudes in Greater Depth. A more focused survey includes such sample items as the following. (The answer that seems most appropriate is circled by the employee.)

- Within the past twelve months, how many career discussions were held between you and your manager?
  None   One or two   Three or four   More than four
- Were the discussions usually initiated by
  You   Your manager   Both
- Overall, what would you say was the quality of these discussions?
  Low   Moderate   High
- As an employee, do you believe you should participate in decisions made about your next assignment?
  Yes   No

To Probe In-Depth Assessment. Small discussion groups with managers delve into findings from the more focused survey through such questions as the following:

- What does career development mean to you?
- What do you view as your responsibility for employee development?
- What would help or reinforce managers to spend more time coaching employees on career issues?

Resource B

Program Models

Succession Planning—A Developmental Approach

See Figure 26.

Vision: To build and develop a replacement pool of management candidates.

Target Group: Employees with high potential as managers.

Objectives:

- To identify managerial competencies tied to future directions in the organization
- To provide promising candidates an opportunity to assess these competencies
- To structure a manager-employee discussion around performance and development
- To create a profile of the skills and readiness of potential management candidates to be used by a management committee

Master Middle Manager Program

See Figure 27.

Vision: To teach managers and group leaders career coaching skills, how to manage their own careers, and organizational career development issues and strategies.

Figure 26. Model for a Developmental Approach to Succession Planning.

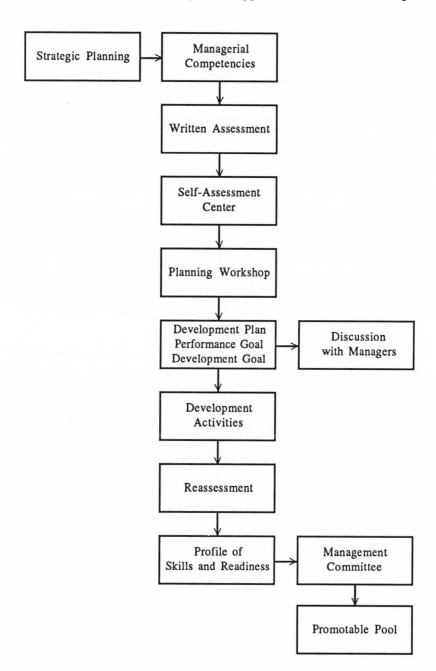

Figure 27. Model for a Master Middle Manager Program.

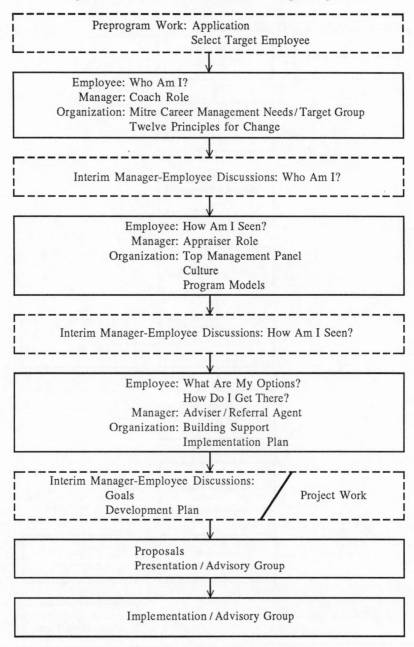

Target Group: Group leaders and middle managers.

Objectives:

- To manage their own careers
- To coach employees regarding career management
- To formalize career management in their divisions

A Manager-as-Career-Developer Program

See Figure 28.

Vision: To greatly enhance the managers' skill and confidence in supporting employee development and provide a forum for rewarding excellence in this domain.

Target Group: Middle managers with plateaued employees.

Objectives:

- Increase skill of managers in assessment, feedback, goal setting, and development planning for employee development
- Provide an opportunity for managers to assess their own careers and plan their next steps
- Provide tools, techniques, and coaching to support managers working closely with two plateaued employees, in order to help the employees enrich their jobs or take lateral transfers
- Create a forum for monitoring and acknowledging excellence in development of employees

Length of the Program: Four to six months.

An Employee Enrichment and Exploration Program

See Figure 29.

Vision: To help employees discover their skills, interests, values, and work styles, in order to enrich their current jobs and prepare them for other options.

Figure 28. Model for Manager-as-Career-Developer Program.

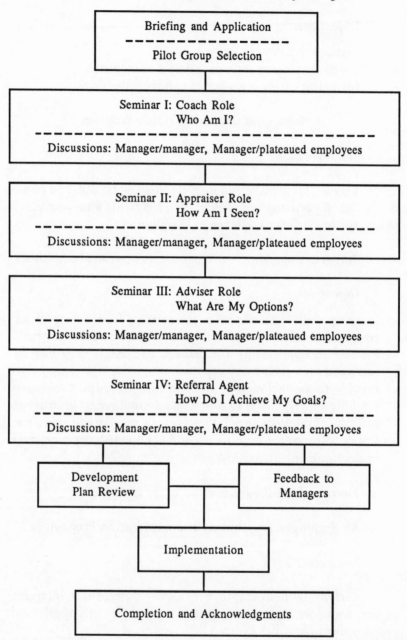

Figure 29. Model for an Employee Enrichment and Exploration Program.

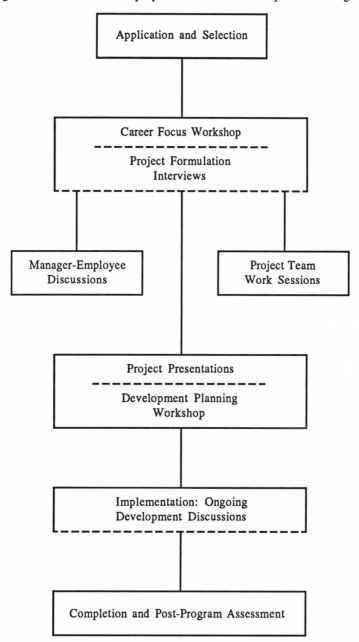

Target Group: Nonmanagement employees with minimum of two years experience in the organization.

Objectives:

- To have employees assess their own skills, values, interests, and work styles
- To give employees feedback on how they are seen
- To teach employees about job enrichment and encourage them to explore options and commit to a specific job enrichment project
- To help employees contribute to the knowledge of other employees through sharing projects
- To establish and implement a development plan

Length of Program: Two to three months.

Time: Three days in workshops.

Bridging Positions: Employee Outreach

See Figure 30.

Vision: To identify entry-level exempt positions that could provide bridges from nonexempt jobs and test promising outreach candidate programs.

Target Group: Promising nonexempt employees with minimum of two years of service in the organization.

Objectives:

- To uncover exempt positions requiring no technical background that could form bridges for nonexempt employees
- To design a process for identifying promising nonexempt employees who could move into exempt positions
- To establish a method for matching promising nonexempt employees with exempt positions for which they qualify

Figure 30. Model for Employee Outreach Program.

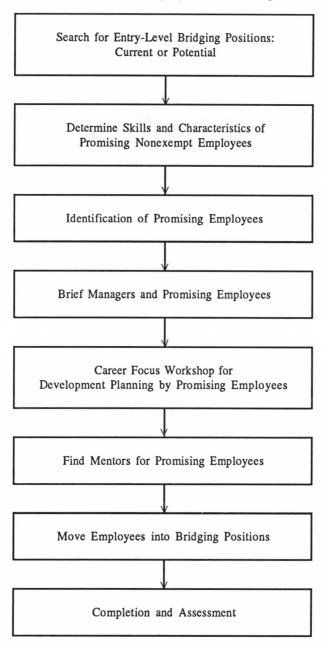

- To help establish a development plan for promising employees that prepares them for exempt positions
- To establish a mentor system to help promising employees achieve success in new positions

Length of Program: Twelve months.

A Job Trade Program: Exploring the Organization

See Figure 31.

Vision: To provide more job mobility for employees and reduce the number of plateaued employees.

Objectives:

- To increase the chances for career mobility by creating temporary job trades
- To increase the productivity and responsibility of employees in managing their own careers
- To familiarize employees with other departments and divisions of the organization
- To reward managers for developing employees' careers

Length of the Program: Six months.

Figure 31. Model for Job Trade Program.

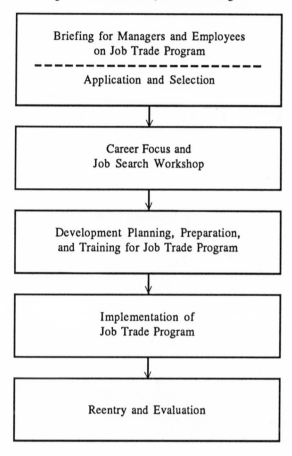

Resource C

Resources for Career Development Professionals

Professional Organizations

1. American Society for Training and Development, Inc. (ASTD)
   1630 Duke Street, Box 1443
   Alexandria, Virginia 22313
   (703) 683-8100
   Professional Practice Area: Career development

2. American Association for Counseling and Development (AACD)
   5999 Stevenson Avenue
   Alexandria, Virginia 22304
   (703) 823-9800
   Division: National Career Development Association

3. Academy of Management
   P.O. Drawer KZ
   Mississippi State University
   Mississippi State, Mississippi 39762
   (601) 325-3928

4. Human Resource Planning Society
   P.O. Box 2553
   Grand Central Station
   New York, New York 10020
   (212) 490-6387

5. American Psychological Association
    1200 17th Street, N.W.
    Washington, D.C. 20036
    (202) 955-7600
    Division: Organization and Industrial Psychology

6. American Management Association
    135 W. 50th Street
    New York, New York 10020
    (212) 386-8100

Journals

1. *Harvard Business Review*
    Boston, Massachusetts 02163

2. *Human Resource Management*
    John Wiley and Sons, for the Graduate School of Business
    and Administration of the University of Michigan
    605 Third Avenue
    New York, New York 10158

3. *Organizational Dynamics*
    American Management Association
    135 West 50th Street
    New York, New York 10020

4. *Personnel*
    A. C. Croft, Inc.
    245 Fischer Avenue, B-2
    Costa Mesa, California 92626

5. *Training and Development Journal*
    American Society for Training and Development
    1630 Duke Street
    Box 1443
    Alexandria, Virginia 22313

6. *Vocational Guidance Quarterly*
    American Association for Counseling and Development
    5999 Stevenson Avenue
    Alexandria, Virginia 22304

7. *Training*
    50 South Ninth Street
    Minneapolis, Minnesota 55402

8. *Personnel Administrator*
    606 N. Washington Street
    Alexandria, Virginia 22314

9. *Journal of Applied Psychology*
    Journal of Counseling Psychology
    American Psychological Association
    1200 17th Street, N.W.
    Washington, D.C. 20036

10. *Journal of Vocational Behavior*
    Academic Press
    111 Fifth Avenue
    New York, New York 10003

11. *Academy of Management Review*
    P.O. Drawer KZ
    Mississippi State University
    Mississippi State, Mississippi 39762

Newsletters

1. National Career Development Association. A division of
    American Association for Counseling and Development.
    Publishes a quarterly journal and newsletter. Members of
    the division receive both publications.
    5999 Stevenson Avenue
    Alexandria, Virginia 22304

2. *The Career Center Bulletin*
    Columbia University
    314 Uris Hall
    New York, New York 10027
    (212) 280-2830

3. *Training News*
    38 Chauncy Street
    Boston, Massachusetts 02111
    (617) 542-0146

4. *Newsletter About Life/Work Planning*
   The National Career Development Project
   P.O. Box 379
   Walnut Creek, California 94597
   Richard N. Bolles, Editor
   (415) 935-1865

5. Career Planning and Adult Development Network
   1190 Smith Bascom Avenue
   Suite 211
   San Jose, California 95128
   (408) 295-5461

6. *The HR Planning Newsletter*
   Wargo & Company
   1658 Cole Boulevard
   Suite 160
   Golden, Colorado 80401
   (414) 785-2688

Assessment Instruments

Instrument	Measures	Source
1. Strong-Campbell Interest Inventory	Career interests	Consulting Psychologists Press 577 College Avenue Palo Alto, California 94306
2. Myers-Briggs Type Indicator	Personality	Consulting Psychologists Press
3. Self-Directed Search by John Holland	Career interests	P.A.R. Box 98 Odessa, Florida 35556
4. Quick Job-Hunting Map	Skills	Ten Speed Press Box 7123 Berkeley, California 94707
5. Study of Values	Values	Houghton Mifflin Co. Wayside Rd. Burlington, Massachusetts 01803
6. Work Motivation Inventory by J. Hall and M. Williams	Work motivators: Basic needs; Safety needs; Needs for Belongingness; Ego-status needs; Self-actualization needs	Teleometrics International P.O. Drawer 1850 Conroe, Texas 77301

#	Instrument	Description	Publisher
7.	Organization Health Survey by P. T. Kehoe and W. J. Reddin	Productivity; Leadership; Organization structure; Communication; Conflict management; Human resource management; Participation; Creativity	Organizational Tests, Ltd. P.O. Box 324 Frederieton, N.B. Canada
8.	Organizational Climate by R. Likert	Authoritarianism; Paternalism; Consultation; Participation	McGraw-Hill Book Co. 1221 Avenue of Americas New York, New York 10020
9.	Organizational Climate by G. Stern and C. Steinhoff	Thirty scales for measuring aspects of managerial climate	Test Scoring and Evaluation Services Syracuse University Syracuse, New York
10.	Work Environment by R. H. Moos and P. M. Insel	Ten scores on characteristics of climate	Consulting Psychologists Press 577 College Avenue Palo Alto, California 94306
11.	Decision-Style Inventory	Potential effectiveness of a decision	University Associates 7596 Eads Avenue La Jolla, California 92037
12.	Career Anchors by E. Schein	Assesses patterns of self-perceived talents, abilities, motives, values, and needs	University Associates
13.	Management Effectiveness Profile System	Management skills (three areas: task, people, personal)	Human Synergistics 39819 Plymouth Road Plymouth, Michigan 48170

Instrument	Measures	Source
14. Management Skills Profile	Management skills (eight key dimensions)	Personnel Decisions, Inc. Foshay Tower Suite 2300 521 Marquette Avenue Minneapolis, Minnesota 55402
15. Performax	Interpersonal style, behaviors (four dimensions)	Performax 12255 State Highway 55 Minneapolis, Minnesota 55441
16. LIFO	Interpersonal style, behaviors under stress (four dimensions)	Stuart Atkins, Inc. 9301 Wilshire Blvd. Suite 306 Los Angeles, California 90210
17. Career Leverage Inventory	Assess strength of multiple career goals	Career Systems, Inc. 7361 McWhorter Place Annandale, Virginia 22003
18. CAREERSPEAK Survey for Managers	Assesses managers' skills in coaching/counseling	Career Systems, Inc.
19. Minnesota Importance Questionnaire by J. B. Round, Jr.	Assessment of job-related needs	Manual for the Minnesota Importance Questionnaire: A Measure of Vocational Needs and Values, Vocational Psychology Research Work Adjustment Project Department of Psychology University of Minnesota

20. Minnesota Satisfaction Questionnaire	Assessment of job satisfaction	
21. Job Description Index by P. Smith, L. Kendall, and C. Hulin	Index of job satisfactions	The Measurement of Satisfaction in Work and Retirement Bowling Green State University Bowling Green, Ohio
22. Career Maturity Inventory by J. Crites	Consistency and realism of career choices	California Test Bureau McGraw-Hill Monterey, California
23. Career Development Inventory by D. Super, A. Thompson, R. Lindeman, J. Jordon, and R. Myers		Career Development Inventory Consulting Psychologists Press Palo Alto, California
24. Measures of Occupational Stress, Coping and Strain by S. Osipow and A. Spokane	Measures stress factors and coping strategies	Marathon Consulting and Press Columbus, Ohio

Other Career Development Tools and Resources

CAREERSPEAK Materials Kit for Managers Kit for Employees	Career Discussion materials for employees and managers	Career Systems, Inc. 7361 McWhorter Place Annandale, Virginia 22003

Films

Career Development—A Plan for all Seasons, from CRM/ McGraw-Hill, 110 15th Street, Del Mar, California 92104.

Where Do I Go From Here? from EFM Films, 85 Main Street, Watertown, Massachusetts 02172.

Books

Brown, D., Brooks, L., and Associates. *Career Choice and Development: Applying Contemporary Theories to Practice.* San Francisco: Jossey-Bass, 1984.

Burack, E., and Mathys, N. *Career Management in Organizations: A Practical Human Resource Planning Approach.* Lake Forest, Ill.: Brace-Park Press, 1980.

Dalton, G., and Thompson, P. *Novations: Strategies for Career Management.* Glenview, Ill.: Scott, Foresman, 1985.

Derr, B. *Work, Career, and Family.* New York: Praeger, 1980.

Egan, G. *The Skilled Helper: A Model for Systematic Helping and Interpersonal Relating.* Belmont, Calif.: Wadsworth, 1975.

Gutteridge, T., and Otte, F. *Organizational Career Development: State of the Practice.* Washington, D.C.: ASTD Press, 1983.

Gysbers, N., and Associates (eds.). *Designing Careers: Counseling to Enhance Education, Work, and Leisure.* San Francisco: Jossey-Bass, 1984.

Hall, D. *Careers in Organizations.* Pacific Palisades, Calif.: Goodyear, 1976.

Hall, D. *Career Development in Organizations.* San Francisco: Jossey-Bass, 1986.

Hill, N. *Counseling at the Workplace.* New York: McGraw-Hill, 1981.

Jellinek, M. *Career Management for the Individual and the Organization.* Chicago: St. Clair Press, 1979.

Kaye, B. *Up Is Not the Only Way.* San Diego: University Associates, 1985.

Leibowitz, Z., and Hirsh, S. (eds.). *Career Development: Current Perspectives.* Washington, D.C.: ASTD Press, 1984.

Leibowitz, Z., and Lea, D. *Adult Career Development: Concepts, Issues, and Practices.* Arlington, Va.: National Association of Career Development, 1986.

London, M. *Developing Managers: A Guide to Motivating and Preparing People for Successful Managerial Careers.* San Francisco: Jossey-Bass, 1985.

London, M., and Stumpf, S. *Managing Careers.* Reading, Mass.: Addison-Wesley, 1982.

Mancuso, J. *Occupational Clinical Psychology.* New York: Praeger, 1983.

Miller, D. *Careers 80/81: A Human Resource Consultant's Views of Career Management and Development and a Guide to 600 Current Books and Articles.* Saratoga, Calif.: Vitality Associates, 1980.

Montross, D., and Shinkman, C. (eds.). *Career Development in the 1980's: Theory and Practice.* Springfield, Ill.: Thomas, 1978.

Nadler, L. (ed.). *The Handbook of Human Resource Development.* New York: Wiley, 1984.

Pfeiffer, J., Heslin, R., and Jones, J. *Instrumentation in Human Relations Training.* (2nd ed.) San Diego: University Associates, 1976.

Pfeiffer, J., and Jones, J. (eds.). *A Handbook of Structured Experiences for Human Relations Training.* (7 vols.) San Diego: University Associates, 1979.

Pfeiffer, J., and Goodstein, L. *The Annuals: Developing Human Resources.* San Diego: University Associates, published yearly.

Raelin, J. *The Salaried Professional: How to Make the Most of Your Career.* New York: Praeger, 1984.

Schein, E. *Career Dynamics: Matching Individual and Organizational Needs.* Reading, Mass.: Addison-Wesley, 1978.

Schein, E. *Organizational Culture and Leadership: A Dynamic View.* San Francisco: Jossey-Bass, 1985.

Schmidt, T. *Managing Your Career Success.* Belmont, Calif.: Lifetime Learning Publications, Wadsworth, 1982.

Sonnenfeld, J. *Managing Career Systems, Channeling the Flow of Executive Careers.* Homewood, Ill.: Irwin, 1984.

Souerwine, A. *Career Strategies: Planning for Personal Achievement.* New York: American Management Association, 1978.

Walker, J. *Human Resource Planning.* New York: McGraw-Hill, 1980.

Warrick, D. (ed.). *Contemporary Organization Development: Current Thinking and Applications.* Glenview, Ill.: Scott, Foresman, 1985.

West, J. *Career Planning, Development, and Management: An Annotated Bibliography.* New York: Garland, 1983.

Whiteley, J., and Resnikoff, A. *Career Counseling.* Monterey, Calif.: Brooks/Cole, 1978.

References

Abdelnour, B., and Hall, D. T. "Career Development of Established Employees." *Career Development Bulletin,* 1980, *2* (1), 5-8.

Ackerman, L. "Model Building." Paper presented at meeting of the Organization Development Network, Oct. 1985.

Aetna Life and Casualty. *Develop Yourself. A Career Path Handbook.* Hartford, Conn.: Aetna Life and Casualty, 1979.

Bailyn, L. *Living with Technology: Issues at Mid-Career.* Cambridge, Mass.: MIT Press, 1980.

Baird, L., and Kram, K. "Career Dynamics: Managing the Superior/Subordinate Relationship." *Organizational Dynamics,* Spring 1983, 46-63.

Bayton, J. A., and Chapman, T. M. "Professional Development: Making Managers of Scientists and Engineers." *The Bureaucrat,* 1977, *1* (4), 408-425.

Beckhard, R. "The Change Process." Unpublished paper, Sloan School of Management, MIT, 1983.

Beckhard, R., and Harris, R. *Organizational Transitions: Managing Complex Change.* Reading, Mass.: Addison-Wesley, 1977.

Benne, K., and Birnbaum, M. "Principles of Changing." In W. Bennis, K. Benne, and R. Chin (eds.), *The Planning of Change.* (2nd ed.) New York: Holt, Rinehart & Winston, 1969.

Bennis, W. "The Four Competencies of Leadership." *Training and Development Journal,* Aug. 1984, pp. 14-19.

Botten, D., and Hansen, J. *Management Continuity Program, Kaiser Permanente.* Los Angeles: Kaiser Permanente, Southern California Region, 1984.

Bowen, D., and Hall, D. T. "Career Planning for Employee Development: A Primer for Managers." *California Management Review,* 1977, *20* (2), 23–35.

Bradford, D. L., and Choen, A. R. *Managing for Excellence: The Guide to High Performance in Contemporary Organizations.* New York: Wiley, 1984.

Breyer, D. *Work Salience Among Managers: A Life Cycle Study.* Suffolk, England: Suffolk University, 1983.

Buckles, R. J., Siebert, J. W., and Hosek, R. J. "How Atlantic Richfield Advances Scientists and Researchers." *AMA Forum,* May 1984, *73* (5), 29–33.

Burack, E. H., and Mathys, N. J. *Career Management in Organizations: A Practical Human Resource Planning Approach.* Lake Forest, Ill.: Brace-Park Press, 1980.

Burke, W. W., and Hornstein, H. A. (eds.). *The Social Technology of Organization Development.* Fairfax, Va.: NTL Learning Resources Corporation, 1972.

Butler, D. W. "Forecasting the '80's' and Beyond—Parts I and II." *Training and Development Journal,* Nov. 1982, pp. 64–70.

Byham, W. C. "Changing Supervisory and Managerial Behavior, Part II." *Training and Development Journal,* 1977, pp. 10–16.

California State Department of Education. *Program Evaluators Guide.* Sacramento: California State Department of Education, 1977.

Carnazza, J. T., and others. "Plateaued and Non-Plateaued Managers: Factors in Job Performance." *Journal of Management,* 1981, *7* (2), 7–25.

Crites, J. O. *Theory and Research Handbook, Career Maturity Inventory.* Monterey, Calif.: California Test Bureau, McGraw-Hill, 1973.

Crites, J. O. *Career Adjustment Inventory.* Monterey, Calif.: California Test Bureau, McGraw-Hill, 1978.

Dahl, D. R., and Pinto, P. R. "Job Posting: An Industry Survey." *Personnel Journal,* Jan. 1977, p. 40.

Dalton, G. W., Thompson, P. H., and Price, R. L. "The Four Stages of Professional Careers." *Organizational Dynamics,* Summer 1977, pp. 19-42.

Doerflin, S. "Directions for Career Planning." *Personnel Administrator,* Oct. 1985, pp. 93-107.

Doyle, M., and Strauss, D. *Manage Your Meetings.* San Francisco: Interaction Associates, 1980.

Drucker, P. *Innovations and Entrepreneurship: Practice and Principles.* New York: Harper & Row, 1985.

Farr, J. L., and others. *Behavior Anchored Scales: A Method for Identifying Continuing Education Needs for Engineers.* University Park: Pennsylvania State University, 1980.

Farren, C., Kaye, B., and Leibowitz, Z. *CDQ Cards.* Annandale, Va.: Career Systems, 1980.

Farren, C., Kaye, B., and Leibowitz, Z. *Career Development Needs Assessment.* Annandale, Va.: Career Systems, 1983.

Fisher, R., and Ury, W. *Getting to Yes.* Boston: Houghton Mifflin, 1981.

Fitz-enz, J. *How to Measure Human Resource Management.* New York: McGraw-Hill, 1984.

Frantzreb, R. B. (ed.). "The HRPlanning Newsletter." 1983, *5* (1), 1-11.

French, W. *The Personnel Management Process.* Boston: Houghton Mifflin, 1974.

Gabarro, J. "When a New Manager Takes Charge." *Harvard Business Review,* May–June 1985, pp. 110-123.

Geddie, C., and Strickland, B. "From Plateaus to Progress: A Model for Career Development." *Training,* June 1984, pp. 56-61.

"Getting Your Best Ideas Accepted." Unpublished paper, Farren-Smith Associates, Montreal, 1979.

Georgia Power. *Career Planning Guide.* Atlanta: Georgia Power, 1984.

Gilligan, C. *In a Different Voice.* Cambridge, Mass.: Harvard University Press, 1982.

Gutteridge, T. G., and Otte, F. L. *Organizational Career Development.* Washington, D.C.: ASTD Press, 1983.

Hackman, J. R., and Oldham, G. R. *Work Redesign.* Reading, Mass.: Addison-Wesley, 1980.

Hagberg, J., and Leider, R. *The Inventurers.* Reading, Mass.: Addison-Wesley, 1978.

Hall, D. *Careers in Organizations.* Pacific Palisades, Calif.: Goodyear, 1976.

Hanson, M. C. "Implementing A Career Development Program." *Training and Development Journal,* July 1981, p. 89.

Harris, P. R., and Harris, D. L. "Twelve Trends You and Your CEO Should Be Monitoring." *Training and Development Journal,* Oct. 1983, pp. 62–69.

Harris-Bowlsbey, J., Leibowitz, Z., and Forrer, S. *DISCOVER: A Computerized Career Development System for Organizations.* Iowa City, Iowa: American College Testing and Counseling System, 1982.

Hersey, P., and Blanchard, K. *The Management of Organization Behavior: Utilizing Human Resources.* Englewood Cliffs, N.J.: Prentice-Hall, 1977.

Hickman, C. R., and Silva, M. A. *Creating Excellence: Managing Corporate Culture, Strategy and Change in the New Age.* New York: New American Library, 1984.

Hirsch, L. Talk given to Organization Development Network, 1982.

Holiday Inns, Inc. *Career Directions—Exempt Positions.* Memphis, Tenn.: Holiday Inns, Inc., 1983.

Holland, J. L. *Making Vocational Choices: A Theory of Careers.* Englewood Cliffs, N.J.: Prentice-Hall, 1977.

Holland, J. L. *Making Vocational Choices: A Theory of Vocational Personality and Work Environments.* (2nd ed.) Englewood Cliffs, N.J.: Prentice-Hall, 1985.

Hotelling, K., and Forrest, L. "Gilligan's Theory of Sex Role Development: A Perspective for Counseling." *Journal of Counseling and Development,* Nov. 1985, *64,* 183–186.

Howard, A., and Bray, S. W. "Career Motivation in Mid-Life Managers." Paper presented at meeting of the American Psychological Association, Montreal, Sept. 1–5, 1980.

Kanter, R. M. *The Change Masters: Innovation for Productivity in the American Corporation.* New York: Simon & Schuster, 1983.

Kaplan, A. G. "Androgyny as a Model of Mental Health for Women: From Theory to Therapy." In A. G. Kaplan and

J. P. Bean (eds.), *Beyond Sex Role Stereotypes.* Boston: Little, Brown, 1976.

Kaumeyer, R. A. *Planning and Using Skills Inventory Systems.* New York: Van Nostrand Reinhold, 1979.

Kaye, B., and others. "Whose Career Is It Anyway?" *Training and Development Journal,* May 1984, pp. 112–116.

Kirkpatrick, D. L. *Evaluating Training Programs.* Washington, D.C.: ASTD Press, 1975.

Kolb, D. A., and Plovnick, M. S. "The Experiential Learning Theory of Career Development." In J. Van Maanen (ed.), *Organizational Careers: Some New Perspectives.* New York: Wiley, 1977.

Kruger, M. M. "How to Make a Management Advisory Committee Work for You." *Training and Development Journal,* June 1984, pp. 86–90.

Leibowitz, Z., Farren, C., and Kaye, B. "Will Your Organization Be Doing Career Development in the Year 2000?" *Training and Development Journal,* 1983, pp. 14–20.

Leibowitz, Z., and Schlossberg, N. "Training Managers for Their Role in a Career Development System." *Training and Development Journal,* July 1981, pp. 72–79.

Leibowitz, Z., and Schlossberg, N. "Critical Career Transitions: A Model for Designing Career Services." *Training and Development Journal,* Feb. 1982, pp. 13–19.

Levinson, D. J. *The Seasons of a Man's Life.* New York: Knopf, 1978.

Levinson, D. J. "A Conception of Adult Development." *American Psychologist,* Jan. 1986, pp. 3–13.

Levinson, P. L. "Face-Off or Face to Face?" *Management,* Summer 1981, p. 12.

Lewis, M. L. "Managing Career Transitions." *Organizational Dynamics,* Spring 1982, pp. 68–77.

Little, A. D. *Evaluation Issues.* Washington, D.C.: Law Enforcement Assistance Administration, 1978.

McGarrell, E. "An Orientation System That Builds Productivity." *Personnel Journal,* 1983, *60,* 32–41.

Meckel, N. T. "The Manager as Counselor." *Training and Development Journal,* July 1981, pp. 65–69.

Miller, D. B. "Training Managers to Stimulate Employee Development." *Training and Development Journal,* Feb. 1981, pp. 47-53.

Moir, B., and Moseley, K. E. "Career/Life Planning for Employees at the Lawrence Livermore Laboratories." Paper presented at Institute of Electrical and Electronics Engineers' Careers Conference, Denver, Oct. 22-24, 1981.

Moore, L. "From Manpower Planning to Human Resources Planning Through Career Development." *Personnel,* May-June 1979, pp. 14-18.

Morgan, M., Hall, D. T., and Martier, A. "Career Development Strategies in Industry: Where Are We and Where Should We Be?" *Personnel,* March-April 1979, pp. 13-50.

Moseley, K. *Evaluation Report: Career Life Planning at Lawrence Livermore Laboratories.* Livermore, Calif.: Lawrence Livermore Laboratories, 1982.

Nadler, D. A. *Concepts for the Management of Organizational Change.* New York: Graduate School of Business, Columbia University, 1979.

Nadler, L. "Implications of the HRD Concept." *Training and Development Journal,* May 1974, pp. 3-13.

Nadler, L. *Corporate Human Resources Development: A Management Tool.* New York: Van Nostrand/American Society for Training and Development, 1980.

Naisbitt, J. *Megatrends: Ten New Directions Transforming Our Lives.* New York: Warner Books, 1982.

Naisbitt, J. *Reinventing the Corporation.* New York: Warner Books, 1985.

Neugarten, B. L. "Adaptation and the Life Cycle." *Counseling Psychologist,* 1976, *6* (1), 16-20.

Opinion Research Corporation. *Strategic Planning for Human Resources: 1980 and Beyond.* New York: Opinion Research Corporation, 1980.

Oshry, B., and Oshry, P. *Power and Position.* Boston: Power and Systems Training, 1977.

Ouchi, W. G. *Theory Z.* Reading, Mass.: Addison-Wesley, 1981.

Pascale, R. "Fitting New Employees into the Company Culture." *Fortune,* May 1984, pp. 28-34.

Pearson, J. M. "The Transition into a New Job: Tasks, Problems, and Outcomes." *Personnel Journal,* April 1982, pp. 286-290.

Pinto, P. "Career Development." In H. Meltzer and W. Nord (eds.), *Making Organizations Humane and Productive.* New York: Wiley, 1981.

Raelin, J. A. "Career-Stage Profiles of Engineers." Paper presented at Institute of Electrical and Electronics Engineers Careers Conference, Boston, Mass., Oct. 2-4, 1985.

Sacco, G., and Knopka, W. "Restructuring the Dual Ladder at Goodyear." *Research Management,* July-Aug. 1983, *26* (4), 36-40.

Sathe, V. "Some Action Implications of Corporate Culture: A Manager's Guide to Action." *Organizational Dynamics,* Autumn 1983, pp. 4-23.

Schein, E. H. "The Individual, the Organization, and the Career: A Conceptual Scheme." *Journal of Applied Behavioral Science,* 1971, 7, 401-426.

Schein, E. H. *Career Dynamics: Matching Individual and Organizational Needs.* Reading, Mass.: Addison-Wesley, 1978.

Schein, E. H. "The Role of the Founder in Creating Organizational Culture." *Organizational Dynamics,* Summer 1983, pp. 13-28.

Security Pacific National Bank. *Officer and Staff Development Resource and Services Packet.* Los Angeles: Security Pacific, 1984.

Selin, G. T. *Strategic Management System: The Practitioner's Guide.* Clarkston, Ga.: Selin Company, 1984.

Sheppick, M. A., and Taylor, C. "Up the Career Path." *Training and Development Journal,* Aug. 1985, pp. 46-48.

Souerwine, A. H. "The Manager as Career Counselor: Some Issues and Approaches." In D. Montross and C. Shinkman (eds.), *Career Development in the 1980's.* Springfield, Ill.: Thomas, 1981.

Sprague, L. "The High Costs of Personal Transitions." *Training and Development Journal,* Oct. 1984, 60-62.

Steadham, S. V. "Learning to Select a Needs Assessment Strategy." *Training and Development Journal,* Jan. 1980, pp. 56-61.

Stoner, J. A., and others. *Managerial Career Plateaus.* New York: Center for Research in Career Development, Columbia University, 1980.

Stump, B., and Leibowitz, Z. "Career Development Evaluation Handbook." Unpublished manuscript, 1983.

Super, D. E. *Career Education and the Meanings of Work.* New York: Teachers College, Columbia University, 1975.

Super, D. E., and Thompson, A. E. *Career Concerns Inventory.* New York: Teachers College, Columbia University, 1981.

Suzzman, Y. M. "Learning from the Japanese: Management in a Resource-Scarce World." *Organizational Dynamics,* Winter 1983, pp. 68–80.

Thompson, J. "In Search of Excellence: A Conversation with Tom Peters." *Training and Development Journal,* Aug. 1983, pp. 16–22.

Tichy, N. M. "Managing Change Strategically: The Technical, Political, and Cultural Keys." *Organizational Dynamics,* Autumn 1982, pp. 59–64.

Uttal, B. "The Corporate Culture Vultures." *Fortune,* Oct. 1983, pp. 66–72.

Van de Ven, A., and Delbecq, A. L. "Nominal Versus Interacting Group Processes for Committee Decision Making Effectiveness." *Academy of Management Journal,* June 1971, pp. 3–5.

Walker, J. W. "Individual Career Planning." *Business Horizons,* Feb. 1973, p. 69.

Walker, J. W. *Human Resource Planning.* New York: McGraw-Hill, 1980.

Ward, L. "Warm Fuzzies Versus Hard Facts: Four Styles of Adult Learning." *Training,* Nov. 1983, pp. 31–33.

Waterman, J. *The MATCH Self-Assessment Program.* Palo Alto, Calif.: Judith Waterman Associates, 1985.

Watzlawick, P., Weakland, J., and Fisch, R. *Change Principles of Problem Formation and Problem Resolution.* New York: Norton, 1974.

Yankelovich, D. *New Rules: Searching for Self-Fulfillment in a World Turned Upside Down.* New York: Random House, 1981.

Index